THE LEGAL SINGULARITY

How Artificial Intelligence Can
Make Law Radically Better

The Legal Singularity

*How Artificial Intelligence Can
Make Law Radically Better*

ABDI AIDID AND BENJAMIN ALARIE

UNIVERSITY OF TORONTO PRESS
Toronto Buffalo London

© University of Toronto Press 2023
Toronto Buffalo London
utorontopress.com
Printed in the USA

ISBN 978-1-4875-2941-3 (cloth)   ISBN 978-1-4875-2943-7 (EPUB)
ISBN 978-1-4875-2942-0 (PDF)

Library and Archives Canada Cataloguing in Publication

Title: The legal singularity : how artificial intelligence can make law radically
 better / Abdi Aidid and Benjamin Alarie.
Names: Aidid, Abdi, author. | Alarie, Benjamin, author.
Description: Includes bibliographical references and index.
Identifiers: Canadiana (print) 20230192467 | Canadiana (ebook) 2023019253X |
 ISBN 9781487529413 (cloth) | ISBN 9781487529437 (EPUB) |
 ISBN 9781487529420 (PDF)
Subjects: LCSH: Law – Data processing. | LCSH: Artificial intelligence – Law
 and legislation. | LCSH: Technology and law.
Classification: LCC K564.C6 A33 2023 | DDC 340.0285/63 – dc23

Cover design: jbgraphics

We wish to acknowledge the land on which the University of Toronto
Press operates. This land is the traditional territory of the Wendat, the
Anishnaabeg, the Haudenosaunee, the Métis, and the Mississaugas of the
Credit First Nation.

University of Toronto Press acknowledges the financial support of the
Government of Canada, the Canada Council for the Arts, and the Ontario
Arts Council, an agency of the Government of Ontario, for its publishing
activities.

Canada Council
for the Arts

Conseil des Arts
du Canada

ONTARIO ARTS COUNCIL
CONSEIL DES ARTS DE L'ONTARIO
an Ontario government agency
un organisme du gouvernement de l'Ontario

Funded by the   Financé par le
Government   gouvernement
of Canada   du Canada

Contents

THE LEGAL SINGULARITY

Chapter One

Introducing the Legal Singularity

I. Introduction

We are on the path to the legal singularity. Advances in technology, especially the improvement and widespread proliferation of artificial intelligence (AI), are driving us relentlessly down this path. By legal singularity, we mean a stable and complete legal order, capable of addressing and resolving practically all types of legal uncertainty in real time and on demand. Over the coming decades, the emergence of this legal singularity will fundamentally transform our existing legal systems and, with them, our societies.[1]

The stakes are high. Navigating the path to the legal singularity safely is necessary for humanity to flourish during the rest of the twenty-first century and beyond. For society to evolve and leverage these new technologies effectively, we will need to develop an ever deeper and more responsive legal infrastructure.

Today's tools – our institutions and legal processes – are not up to the task. Courts are inaccessible.[2] Laws are complicated.[3] Legal procedures

---

1 There is increasing awareness among members of law's epistemic community of the idea of the legal singularity, as evidenced by the sheer amount of attention – including criticism – that the idea has generated in the past few years. A recent book by Simon Deakin & Christopher Markou collects some of these responses and critiques. See Simon Deakin & Christopher Markou, *Is Law Computable? Critical Perspectives on Law and Artificial Intelligence* (Oxford: Hart Publishing, 2022).

2 Omri Ben Shahar, "The Paradox of Access Justice, and Its Application to Mandatory Arbitration" (2016) 83:4 U Chi L Rev 1755.

3 Scholars have been writing about legal complexity for generations. Examples include Peter H Schuck, "Legal Complexity: Some Causes, Consequences, and Cures" (1992) 42:1 Duke LJ 1 and Daniel Katz Martin & JB Ruhl, "Measuring, Monitoring and Managing Legal Complexity" (2015) 101:191 Iowa LR 191.

are baffling to the uninitiated.[4] Lawyers are expensive. Incentives are misaligned. Legal doctrine can be outdated and outmoded. Most importantly, legal outcomes are too frequently unfair and unjust.[5]

The good news is that the very technologies that are upending our existing practices will also enable us to construct the deeper and more responsive legal infrastructure that is sorely needed. The stability and resilience of the legal singularity will require more adaptability in our legal systems than they exhibit today. Fortunately, if we can get things right, the technology for a profoundly beneficial legal singularity will be in place just as we need it most.

This book is the first step towards articulating a vision of a legal singularity and motivating a discussion about its pathways and consequences. In these pages, we explore the implications of the transition towards a legal singularity and offer an analysis of the most significant open questions surrounding it. These questions include the following:

- *What is the legal singularity?*
- *Is the legal singularity desirable?*
- *How can we make the legal singularity as normatively attractive as possible?*
- *What should we be concerned about in relation to the legal singularity?*
- *How long will it take the legal singularity to arrive?*
- *What can we do now to ensure that the legal singularity does not exacerbate harm?*
- *What does the legal singularity mean for the future of lawyers, judges, and government?*

We describe these as open questions because we do not have authoritative answers to offer. Fundamentally, the story that this book tells is one about the continued and deepening confluence of technology with law,

---

4 AAS Zuckerman, "A Reform of Civil Procedure: Rationing Procedure Rather Than Access to Justice" (1995) 22:2 J of L and Society 155.

5 The most frequently discussed examples of unjust legal outcomes come from the world of criminal justice, particularly in the United States, where scholars have long noted the presence of racial biases in conviction and sentencing. An excellent metastudy by Ojmarrh Mitchell canvasses the relevant research and shows, among other things, that African Americans "generally are sentenced more harshly than whites." Ojmarrh Mitchell, "A Meta-Analysis of Race and Sentencing Research: Explaining the Inconsistencies" (2005) 21:4 J of Quantitative Criminology 439 at 442. See also Jens Ludwig & Sendhil Mullainathan, "Fragile Algorithms and Fallible Decision-Makers: Lessons from the Justice System" (2021) 35:4 J Econ Perspectives 71.

institutions, and social and economic development. Like many new stories, it is vaguely familiar, as versions of it have played out before. Legal development in civil and common law systems has been the backstory to much of the world's economic and social development over the past several centuries (and reaching further back, we would argue, throughout recorded human history).[6] What is new about the story at this point are the rapid developments we are currently witnessing in artificial intelligence (AI) research and the portent of even more significant developments in the future.

Indeed, as readers are doubtless aware, significant progress is being made in numerous areas of AI research, from breakthroughs in computer vision[7] and speech generation and recognition,[8] to natural language processing,[9] robotics,[10] and deep learning.[11] Yet sometimes, talk of an AI future obscures precisely how much AI has *already* permeated institutions and households. As we write this paragraph, our word-processing software uses AI algorithms to identify spelling and grammar mistakes and propose corrections.[12] Some of our readers may have found this book through similarly predictive technology, like a "recommended"

---

6 For a helpful discussion of the academic debates about the relationship between law and development, see Kevin E Davis & Michael J Trebilcock, "The Relationship between Law and Development: Optimists versus Skeptics" (2008) 56:4 Am J Comp L 895.

7 One particularly interesting example of an advance in computer vision dates back to 2016, when researchers from the University of Saskatchewan and the Canadian Food Inspection Agency examined whether computer vision could succeed in "identifying plant species from seed morphological features." The "work showed that texture-based seed species classification could achieve correct classification rates of over 95%." Xin Yi et al, "Seed Identification Using Computer Vision: A Proof of Concept Study" (2016) 37:1 Seed Technology 93 at 93, 99.

8 Bahar Gholipour, "New AI Tech Can Mimic Any Voice," Scientific American (2 May 2017), online: <https://www.scientificamerican.com/article/new-ai-tech-can-mimic-any-voice/>.

9 Bonan Min et al, "Recent Advances in Natural Language Processing via Large Pre-Trained Language Models: A Survey" (2021) ArXiv abs/2111.01243.

10 "What Are the Most Important Advances in AI?" in Michael L. Littman et al, *Gathering Strength, Gathering Storms: The One Hundred Year Study on Artificial Intelligence (AI100) 2021 Study Panel Report* (Stanford University, September 2021).

11 Jeffrey Dean, "A Golden Decade of Deep Learning: Computing Systems and Applications" (2022) 151:2 Daedalus 58.

12 Brett Graham & Alessandra Marguerat, "Using Natural Language Processing to Search for Textual References" in David Hamidović, Claire Clivaz & Sarah Bowen Savant, eds, *Ancient Manuscripts in Digital Culture: Visualisation, Data Mining, Communication* (Leiden: Brill, 2019).

section of a bookstore website or results from a search engine.[13] Many new offices have smart assistants and smart climate control; homes are being retrofitted with smart technology of all kinds, including sensors monitoring air quality for radon gases and home-automation tools to control lighting, blinds, garage doors, and on and on. Many of us ask AI agents connected to speakers in our kitchens to play a podcast of our choice as our morning coffee brews. Some new vehicles are equipped with adaptive cruise control and even autonomous parking capabilities. Just as often, professional tasks are sped up by leveraging data science techniques to achieve better performance. A growing number of these applications are permeating our most important domains: for instance, a team of researchers led by professors Carol Y Cheung and Tien Yin Wong have developed AI models to detect Alzheimer's disease – with a high degree of accuracy – simply from retinal photographs.[14]

A quick glance at some of the leading publications suggests popular interest in AI's impact and growth: the *New York Times*, for instance, recently featured headlines such as "How Artificial Intelligence Is Edging Its Way into Our Lives,"[15] "The Great AI Awakening,"[16] and "AI Is Everywhere and Evolving."[17] But excitement about AI's potential is just as often tempered by concerns about its risks. Opinion headlines like "If You Don't Trust A.I. Yet, You're Not Wrong" might capture the public mood just as well.[18] To a great extent, these fears are understandable. As Cynthia Dwork and Martha Minow explain, the observable

---

13 There is indeed some academic research about predictive technology in online shopping. For example, see Neil Chabane et al, "Intelligent Personalized Shopping Recommendation Using Clustering and Supervised Machine Learning Algorithms," (2022) 17:12 PLOS ONE 1; and Anand V Bodapati, "Recommendation Systems with Purchase Data" (2008) 45:1 J Marketing Research 77.

14 CY Cheung et al, "A Deep Learning Model for Detection of Alzheimer's Disease Based on Retinal Photographs: A Retrospective, Multicentre Case-Control Study" (2022) 4:11 The Lancet Digital Health 806.

15 "How Artificial Intelligence Is Edging Its Way into Our Lives," *New York Times*, (14 February 2018), online: <https://www.nytimes.com/2018/02/12/technology /artificial-intelligence-new-work-summit.html>.

16 Gideon Lewis-Kraus, "The Great A.I. Awakening," *New York Times* (22 December 2016), online: <https://www.nytimes.com/2016/12/14/magazine/the-great-ai -awakening.html>.

17 Craig Smith, "A.I. Is Everywhere and Evolving," *New York Times* (9 March 2021), online: <https://www.nytimes.com/2021/02/23/technology/ai-innovation -privacy-seniors-education.html>.

18 Frank Pasquale & Gianclaudio Malgieri, "Opinion: If You Don't Trust A.I., Yet, You're Not Wrong," *New York Times* (30 July 2021), online: <https://www.nytimes .com/2021/07/30/opinion/artificial-intelligence-european-union.html>.

lack of "social trust" in AI is attributable to, among other reasons, some of AI's high profile failures and growing public awareness of private technology firms' privacy intrusions.[19] Some of the distrust in AI is also attributable to a more deeply human reason: people tend to dislike uncertainty. Much of the public dialogue about AI has focused on the effects it will have on the labour market writ large, and so it is natural for observers to be concerned about their own place amidst the change. The AI-permeated future we can anticipate looks to many people like a dense fog concealing a frightening unknown.

This book represents our best attempt to peer into the fog and outline the potential promise and perils for humanity on the path towards the legal singularity. We contend that for the beneficial promise of the legal singularity to be realized, we will have to overcome foreseeable dangers. Some of these foreseeable dangers have already been well-identified. Scholars such as Ruha Benjamin and Safiya Umoja Noble, for instance, have explained that uncritical development and adoption of algorithmic technologies can reproduce – and indeed deepen – racial inequities.[20] Our optimism about AI is not one that ignores these challenges. In fact, we are optimistic about AI precisely because we believe it makes us more capable of addressing these very issues than our current methods allow.

Of course, there will also be dangers and hazards that – because of the limitations of our perspective – we cannot foresee. While we have striven to approach our task with humility and have done our level best to exercise our imaginations, we must necessarily leave the identification of the remaining dangers to others.

Still, even the most critical observers understate just how dramatic advances in AI are likely to be. Much of what we typically associate with technological advances amount to, in the grand scheme, incremental improvements. Self-driving cars might improve fuel efficiency,[21] brake and accelerate more smoothly than human drivers,[22] and, in the best

---

19 Cynthia Dwork & Martha Minow, "Distrust of Artificial Intelligence: Sources and Responses from Computer Science and Law" (2022) 151:2 Daedalus 309.

20 See generally Ruha Benjamin, *Race After Technology: Abolitionist Tools for the New Jim Code* (Cambridge, UK: Polity, 2019); Safiya Umoja Noble, *Algorithms of Oppression: How Search Engines Reinforce Racism*, (New York: NYU Press, 2018).

21 Center for Sustainable Systems, "Autonomous Vehicles Factsheet," Pub. No. CSS16-18, University of Michigan, 2022.

22 Varshit Dubey, Ruhshad Kasad & Karan Agrawal, "Autonomous Braking and Throttle System: A Deep Reinforcement Learning Approach for Naturalistic Driving" (Paper delivered at 13th International Conference on Agents and Artificial Intelligence, Vienna, February 2021) [unpublished].

cases, improve vehicle safety.[23] But the vehicles are still just driving. AI-assisted medical imaging might help radiologists identify problematic lesions. But they are still just performing medical diagnostics. Indeed, virtually all the public-facing technologies that have become emblematic of our technologized future – autonomous vehicles, facial recognition, and so on – are scaled applications of long-existing technologies. Most of us are not even considering the yet undiscovered applications that are being or will soon be developed by scientists and technologists around the world. Like the frog in the well-known apologue, people and institutions are comfortable soaking – at least for a while – in tepid waters. But, without preparation, our AI future is likely to feel like a sudden boil.

Keen readers might wonder if our projections about the future of the law are conjectural. The answer is yes, and perhaps to some extent inescapably so. But it is well-informed conjecture. We write this book as participants and keen observers on the front lines of developments that show that we are already on a path towards the legal singularity. As legal technologists, we have spent the last several years co-founding and working at Blue J, a fast-growing North American legal technology company, to directly develop systems that will allow the law to be less uncertain. As legal academics, we have a bird's-eye view of legal research, legal education, and the legal profession that allows for a robust diagnosis of the law's shortcomings and a vision of its future. As engaged members of our communities and of wider society, we have a shared interest with our readers in ensuring that these developments augur a better future. In our view, the transition to a significantly superior legal system is in progress, and the time to participate in shaping it is now.

II. What Is the Legal Singularity?

The legal singularity is the idea that law will reach functional completeness, in the sense that practically any legal question will have an instantaneous and just resolution. In the legal singularity, the law will be knowable with a high degree of certainty – perhaps not perfect certainty, but practical certainty – for much of human activity. But how?

---

23 Here, we only say that self-driving vehicles have the *potential* for improved safety, but, at the time of writing, this is a highly contested claim. Marjory S Blumenthal & Laura Fraade-Blanar, "Can Automated Vehicles Prove Themselves to be Safe?" (2020) 36:4 Issues in Science & Technology 71.

As we explain in these pages, the first serious step towards this technologized future is the widespread availability of legal prediction. Currently, many legal questions are not answerable with anything approaching certainty. Short of going to court and getting a definitive ruling from a judge, legal questions are answered through laborious research and learned intermediaries performing analysis that is, among other things, *expensive*.[24] Today, new tools are emerging that allow much of this work to be computed. The legal material that lawyers and judges work with (cases, contracts, regulations, statutes, treaties) can be treated as training data for prediction algorithms. These prediction algorithms can effectively synthesize this information to produce accurate predictions of how the law would apply to a novel set of circumstances. In the hands of lawyers, this means the ability to provide legal advice instantaneously at low cost with high accuracy. For judges, this means an improved ability to render decisions consistent with the law. For everyone else, this means the chance to have a real-time sense of one's legal rights and obligations.

Here, we do not mean to conjure images of robots that exercise superhuman foresight or otherworldly planning and judgment skills. While we certainly accept those outcomes as theoretically possible in the long run, our concerns begin more immediately. Even today, AI-informed technologies can process certain kinds of information at a speed that far exceeds human capacity.[25] As we demonstrate in this book, commercially available AI-enabled legal tools can already predict with a high degree of statistical accuracy how future courts are likely to rule on some legal questions, an outcome made possible by machine learning's ability to synthesize voluminous case law. Outside of the legal field, algorithmic prediction is being deployed in areas ranging from financial services[26] to government decision-making.[27] In a world that

---

24 Olufunmilayo B Arewa "Open Access in a Closed Universe: Lexis, Westlaw, Law Schools, and the Legal Information Market" (2006) 10:4 Lewis & Clark L Rev 797.
25 As one example, consider a recent study in *Science* with the following finding: "Our all-optical deep learning framework can perform, *at the speed of light*, various complex functions that computer-based neural networks can execute" (emphasis added). Xing Lin et al, "All-Optical Machine Learning Using Diffractive Deep Neural Networks," (2018) 361:6406 Science 1004 at 1004.
26 Saikat Chatterjee, "How to Train Your Machine: JPMorgan FX Algos Learn to Trade Better," *Reuters* (30 April 2019), online: <https://www.reuters.com/article/us-jpm-trading-machines-idUSKCN1S61JG>.
27 Anusha Dhasarathy, Sahil Jain, &Naufal Khan, "When Governments Turn to AI: Algorithms, Trade-Offs, and Trust," McKinsey & Company (3 September 2022), online: <https://www.mckinsey.com/industries/public-and-social-sector/our-insights/when-governments-turn-to-ai-algorithms-trade-offs-and-trust>.

relentlessly seeks better solutions to old problems, it is only a matter of time before these technologies have widespread application.

The legal singularity will evolve and be able to absorb and accommodate changes to our social, economic, and technological contexts. If it is successful, it will not be dogmatic (though it is perhaps this threat of dogmatism that springs to many commentators' minds when they contemplate the legal singularity). Indeed, the nature of the legal singularity will be to provide quiet confidence that justice will prevail. Disputes will be resolved justly and in the best interests of society. Powerful actors will be held accountable to a greater extent than they are even in today's most advanced legal systems. Weaker parties will have their positions bolstered.

To avoid potential misunderstandings before turning to describe in detail what we envision for the coming legal singularity, it behooves us first to contextualize the idea of the legal singularity by distinguishing it from the related ideas of the technological singularity and the economic singularity.

a. The Technological Singularity

The prospect of the continued increase in scientific and technological progress led Irving J. Good in 1965 to predict that we could witness an "intelligence explosion" in the future.[28] This has sometimes been referred to as a "technological singularity."[29] In Good's own words,

> Let an ultraintelligent machine be defined as a machine that can far surpass all the intellectual activities of any man, however clever. Since the design of machines is one of these intellectual activities, an ultraintelligent machine could design even better machines; there would then unquestionably be an "intelligence explosion," and the intelligence of man would be left far behind ... Thus the first ultraintelligent machine is the last invention that man need ever make, provided that the machine is docile enough to tell us how to keep it under control. It is curious that this point is made so seldom outside of science fiction. It is sometimes worthwhile to take science fiction seriously.[30]

---

28 Irving John Good, "Speculations Concerning the First Ultraintelligent Machine" (1966) 6 *Advances in Computers* 31.
29 *Ibid.*
30 *Ibid* at 33.

Thus, at some point, following Good's logic, there will emerge a *technological singularity* – an artificial general intelligence that is capable of "recursive self-improvement" without any direct human involvement.[31] At such a point, assuming that it is possible, it is posited that there will sometime thereafter be the emergence of a superintelligence and that this technological singularity will lead to radical upheaval in human civilization.

Not everyone believes that this is plausible. The idea of a technological singularity has been derided as "the rapture for nerds." And the possibility of a technological singularity emerging at any point, let alone within the next several decades, is hotly debated among technologists and academics.[32] Many argue that it will never happen. Well-known inventor, futurist, and Google engineer Ray Kurzweil argues that there will be human-level artificial general intelligence by the middle of this century and that, by 2045, "the pace of change will be so astonishingly quick that we won't be able to keep up, unless we enhance our own intelligence by merging with the intelligent machines we are creating."[33] Others, such as the cognitive scientist Douglas Hofstadter, have been critical of the idea of the technological singularity, deriding the works of Kurzweil and others as "an intimate mixture of rubbish and good ideas."[34] Even without a consensus about whether it will actually occur, the very notion of a technological singularity has been hugely influential. As Wendell Wallach explains, the concept has long influenced "popular culture and public policy through a collection of insights, theories and debates."[35] Today, the spectre of a technological singularity evokes political responses, too: in a report prepared for a May 2022 resolution, the European Parliament's Special Committee on

---

31 The term "recursive self-improvement" is helpfully explained by Wenyi Wang: "Recursive self-improving systems create new software iteratively. The newly created software should be better at creating future software." Wenyi Wang, "A Formulation of Recursive Self-Improvement and Its Possible Efficiency" (2018) at 2 [unpublished], online: <https://arxiv.org/pdf/1805.06610.pdf>.

32 *Ibid.*

33 Scott Amyx, "Wearing Your Intelligence: How to Apply Artificial Intelligence in Wearables and IoT," *Wired* (7 August 2015), online: <https://www.wired.com/insights/2014/12/wearing-your-intelligence/>.

34 See Frank Bentayou, "Ray Kurzweil Predicts the Rise of Cyber-Humans in 'How to Create a Mind,'" *Cleveland* (9 December 2012), online <https://www.cleveland.com/books/2012/12/ray_kurzweil_predicts_the_rise.html>.

35 Wendell Wallach, Book Review of *The Singularity: We Will Survive Our Technology* by Doug Wolens (2016) 56:3 Jurimetrics 297 at 297.

Artificial Intelligence in a Digital Age (AIDA) assuaged some fears by reassuring parliamentarians that there were "doubts" as to whether a singularity can occur, but still counselled in favour of taking the risks of AI seriously enough to develop responsive policy.[36]

The legal singularity and the technological singularity share some of the same prerequisites, namely the widespread proliferation of artificial intelligence and rapidly improving computing power. But the ideas are conceptually distinct in at least two important regards. First, the technological singularity is necessarily a broader theory. Where the legal singularity describes radical changes that AI is likely to bring about in the domain of law, the technological singularity is best described as a *general* theory of change. Even though we explain that the advent of AI in the law will have broad repercussions outside of courtrooms and law schools, we anticipate that the shockwaves are going to be felt predominantly in law-adjacent areas. For instance, we expect that the practical elimination of legal uncertainty will mean better legislation, policymaking, and public administration. These areas are highly likely to be affected because of the centrality of legal analysis to their practice. The technological singularity, by contrast, imagines technology as a totalizing force, allowing for "non-biological intelligence" to ultimately merge with our "bodies, brains and environment."[37] The consequences are theoretically limitless; indeed, the technological singularity contemplates upheaval in all contexts where human reasoning takes place. Our claim is comparatively modest, though readers will find that we are careful not to suggest that the implications of our legal singularity are limited to the law.

A second key difference is that the technological and legal singularities are brought about by different mechanisms. The technological singularity depends on our inventing machines that are capable of recursive self-improvement. The conditions for a technological singularity are in fact met only when machines achieve the subtle and creative intelligence that enables them to iterate without human intervention. By contrast, our concept of a legal singularity is a deeply human enterprise. Where recursive self-improvement is the threshold condition for a technological singularity, the threshold condition for the legal singularity – the elimination of legal uncertainty – is already

---

36 European Parliament, *Report on Artificial Intelligence in a Digital Age* (A9-90088/2022), online: < https://europarl.europa.eu/doceo/document/A-9-2022-0088_EN.html>.

37 Jose Luis Cordeiro, "From Biological to Technological Evolution" (2011) 15:1 World Affairs: J of Intl Issues 86 at 89.

technologically possible, yet is frustrated by regulatory, informational, and attitudinal hurdles that we elaborate on in this book. These hurdles, however, are temporary. Advances in AI – and, we hope, the emergence of better and more successful examples of responsible AI use in society – will create significant economic and cultural pressure on legal institutions to absorb these new technologies. How we address these hurdles is what makes the difference between whether our technologized future is one where we achieve greater social, political, and economic equality or whether we will stare down the barrel of what even the most optimistic futurists acknowledge could be a frightening scenario.

b. The Economic Singularity

If the legal singularity and the technological singularity – from which the former draws some inspiration – are conceptually distinct, is there also a relationship between the legal singularity and the emergent concept of the "economic singularity?" The notion of an economic singularity was perhaps best articulated by Nobel Prize–winning economist William Nordhaus in a 2015 National Bureau of Economic Research paper.[38] To Nordhaus, the economic singularity is a threshold after which there would be steep and constantly accelerating economic growth. He acknowledged that "for those with a background primarily in economics," the idea of an AI-enabled singularity "is likely to read like science fiction."[39] He nevertheless gave the idea a rigorous treatment. Building on early ideas by the economists Erik Brynjolfsson and Andrew McAfee,[40] Nordhaus sought to test the economic singularity as a hypothesis and considered seven empirical tests of whether macroeconomic evidence is suggestive of moving in the direction of an economic singularity. Of these diagnostic tests, Nordhaus reported that five were negative, and just two suggested that there could potentially be an economic singularity; however, this would likely occur beyond the year 2100.[41]

---

38 William Nordhaus, "Are We Approaching an Economic Singularity? Information Technology and the Future of Economic Growth" (2015) National Bureau of Economic Research Working Paper No. 21547.

39 *Ibid* at 2.

40 Erik Brynjolfsson & Andrew McAfee, *The Second Machine Age: Work, Progress, and Prosperity in a Time of Brilliant Technologies* (New York: W.W. Norton & Company, 2014).

41 Nordhaus, *supra* note 38 at 23.

Nordhaus's contribution is unique in that it remains largely agnostic about the implications of an economic singularity. More recent works have been particularly attentive to the economic singularity as a long-term possibility. Calum Chace's 2016 book *The Economic Singularity: Artificial Intelligence and the Death of Capitalism* is perhaps the best example of works in this genre. Chace argues that most humans will be superseded by artificial intelligence and alternative means of production, leading to widespread unemployment, and prescribes interventions like a universal basic income in order to provide means for those sacrificed by the labour market and displaced by technology.[42] Along similar lines, Yuval Harari has remarked that the future may witness the "rise of the useless class," numbering in the billions.[43] At the same time, Harari suggests that we may witness a parallel, smaller class of individuals boosted so dramatically by scientific and technological progress that they will be capable of feats previously unimaginable.[44]

Taken together, participants in the debate about an AI future tend to agree that AI presents potential for unprecedentedly beneficial developments but also for dire possible outcomes. In our view, one of the missing elements of the narrative to date is how we can foster and leverage law and legal institutions to avoid or forestall the worst of the possibilities and secure a future state of the world in which we are able to enjoy, as much as possible, the deeply promising benefits of our collective scientific and technological progress. Of course, some legal scholars are doing excellent work to imagine what kinds of safeguards we might implement to ensure that the worst consequences of AI proliferation do not come about.[45] The problem with this literature is that it miscasts law as a static instrument. Put differently, these scholars tend to think of how law *today* might reign in tomorrow's developments. In this book, we recognize instead that law and legal institutions will not

---

42 Calum Chace, *The Economic Singularity: Artificial Intelligence and the Death of Capitalism* (London: Three Cs, 2016).

43 Quoted in Ian Sample, "AI Will Create 'Useless Class' of Human, Predicts Bestselling Historian," *The Guardian* (14 February 2018), online: <https://www.theguardian.com/technology/2016/may/20/silicon-assassins-condemn-humans-life-useless-artificial-intelligence>.

44 *Ibid.*

45 Some excellent examples include Aziz Z Huq, "A Right to a Human Decision" (2020) 106:3 Va L Rev 611; Kate Crawford & Jason Schultz, "AI Systems as State Actors" (2019) 119:7 Colum L Rev 1941; Anupam Chander, "The Racist Algorithm?," Book Review of *The Black Box Society: The Secret Algorithms That Control Money and Information* by Frank Pasquale (2017) 115:6 Mich L Rev 1023.

be unchanged as scientific and technological progress continues. As a social institution that is deeply entwined with politics, economics, and technology, the law will continue to evolve in an increasingly complex relationship with society. The purpose of this book is to explore what this might look like in the future, based on where we find ourselves now.

c. *The Legal Singularity*

Law and legal institutions have been evolving for centuries, in civil law systems and common law systems alike. Civil law systems seek to provide comprehensive legal codes, explicitly setting out the operating system of society through substantive and procedural rules. Civil law systems draw upon a deep reservoir of legal experience; early significant events in civil legal history include the Roman emperor Justinian's effort to compile Roman laws, which John W. Head describes as a "famous exercise in legislation and legal scholarship."[46] Within the civilian tradition, Roman law has exerted a strong influence on subsequent legal developments, including upon the work of Hugo Grotius on the synthesis of ancient Roman law and customary Dutch law in 1631.[47] Grotius's work proved to be an inspiring example, leading to efforts to rationalize and codify laws in civil codes across Europe, which included, among others, Bavaria's 1756 *Codex Maximilianeus bavaricus civilis*, Prussia's *Complete Territorial Code of 1794*, Austria's *1786 Code of Joseph II* and *Complete Civil Code of 1811*, and France's 1804 *Code Napoléon*.[48] Civil codes have proven to be influential also in common law jurisdictions throughout the world.[49] In some ways, civil codes represent an early aspiration to implement a system that can readily provide a guide for answering legal questions, without recourse to the case-by-case analysis demanded by the common law method.

---

46 John W. Head, "Justinian's Corpus Juris Civilis in Comparative Perspective: Illuminating Key Differences Between the Civil, Common, and Chinese Legal Traditions" (2013) 21:2 Mediterranean Studies 91 at 91.

47 Wouter Druwé, "Grotius' Introduction to Hollandic Jurisprudence" in *The Cambridge Companion to Hugo Grotius* (Cambridge: Cambridge University Press 2021) 409.

48 George Mousourakis, "Codification and the Rise of Modern Civil Law" in *Roman Law and the Origins of the Civil Law Tradition* (Cham: Springer, 2014) 287.

49 Jerome Frank, "Civil Law Influences on the Common Law: Some Reflections on 'Comparative' and 'Contrastive' Law" (1956) 104:7 U Pa L Rev 887; see also Joseph Dainow, "The Civil Law and the Common Law: Some Points of Comparison" (1966) 15:3 Am J Comp L 419.

The common law does, of course, place significant demands on judges and jurists to develop the law through the analysis of precedents. This is time consuming and costly. This time and effort is not without its benefits, however. One of the merits of the case-based approach of the common law is its ability to gradually draw out and further develop insights from the experience of many judges across many cases over long periods of time. As Oliver Wendell Holmes pointed out, "The life of the law has not been logic: it has been experience."[50] Experience shows that the bottom-up, case-by-case approach of the common law, exemplified by Blackstone's *Commentaries on the Laws of England*, published in 1765–70, and the top-down, principles-first approach of the civil codes nicely complement each other. Legal scholars and judges frequently study and learn from experiences in other systems.

If the law and legal institutions have been inexorably changing and evolving for centuries, is there any reason to expect this evolution to undergo a significant and sharp qualitative change? Should we expect the evolution of law and legal institutions to be dominated by ongoing incremental changes, or might things proceed by periods of relative stability followed by more abrupt changes?

Those in the "we should expect abrupt change" camp would argue that the path towards legal singularity is likely going to include a series of relatively sudden, important changes to law and legal institutions. Maybe they are right; maybe this time is indeed different. Often, this claim refers to new technologies that are expected to be transformative and then lead to rampant stock market speculation and runaway prices for companies thought to be at the forefront of a new industry – think of the speculative railway mania in the 1840s[51] or the telecom mania in the 1990s that led to the dot-com bust of 2000.[52] Eventually, with the passage of time, society learned that its excitement was, in some ways, an overreaction. In 1987, Robert Solow famously remarked that "you can see the computer age everywhere but in the productivity statistics."[53]

---

50 Oliver Wendell Holmes, Jr, *The Common Law* (Boston: Little, Brown, 1881).
51 William Quinn & John D Turner, "Democratising Speculation: The Great Railway Mania" in William Quinn & John D Turner, eds, *Boom and Bust: A Global History of Financial Bubbles* (Cambridge: Cambridge University Press, 2020) 58.
52 Matthew Richardson & Eli Ofek, "DotCom Mania: The Rise and Fall of Internet Stock Prices" (2003) 58:3 J Fin 581113.
53 Quoted in Jack Triplett, "The Solow Productivity Paradox: What Do Computers Do to Productivity?" *Brookings* (28 July 2016), online: <https://www.brookings.edu/articles/the-solow-productivity-paradox-what-do-computers-do-to-productivity/>.

The gradualists would argue that legal change on the path to the legal singularity is much more likely to be incremental and feel more natural. Frequently, the claims that "this time things are different" are incorrect. Most of the time, future events seem to echo the recent past and give way to what seems like gradual change. From the point of view of the future, we should therefore expect for most to look back at the developments over the next several decades as "inevitable" and as a natural progression from the current status quo. If these expectations are correct, the next several decades are likely to be marked by mostly gradual and ultimately profound changes in our laws, governments, and political institutions. But before we get too far ahead of ourselves, it makes sense to outline what we believe a legal singularity might entail, so that we can identify it as distinct from the more conventional type of slow legal evolution.

The expectation of an attractive legal singularity equilibrium is motivated by the following reasoning. An essential attribute of a fair and just legal system is that it should be as transparent as possible to mitigate unfairness and injustice. If the background conditions are right – i.e., so long as political power, education, information, and opportunity are distributed sufficiently widely and fairly – there is every reason to expect that laws exposed for inspection will tend to be made more just through collective action. It follows that we should aspire to greater clarity in the law, for then we shall have the best chance for securing the most just and fair legal system. It would be possible and, indeed, quite natural to entrust a legal system that has reached a high level of maturity and transparency to generate fair outcomes and to treat individuals in ways that are accepted as normatively appropriate.

One of the significant hurdles associated with our current laws and the legal system is that what the law requires is frequently difficult to ascertain with any reliability; relatedly, because the law is a patchwork that is significantly underspecified, we rely on decision makers – often, but not always, judges – to exercise discretion in order to provide reasonable resolutions to certain kinds of legal uncertainty through *ad hoc* discretionary processes. The challenge with systems that are underspecified and that rely heavily on *ex post* adjudication is that they cannot be clearly defined in advance.

The legal singularity would not *necessarily* result in a fair and just legal system. We contend that it would tend in that direction, since it would satisfy the core dictates of the rule of law. There is a keen academic debate among scholars about whether the rule of law presupposes or requires certain normative content. The traditional view is that the rule of law does not require any specific normative substantive content. On the other hand, it is probable as an empirical matter that, generally, a system of law that satisfies the rule of law criteria will tend to exhibit certain kinds of normative properties that go beyond those identified by Lon Fuller as characteristic of the inner morality of law, which include requirements of legal generality, publicity, prospectivity, intelligibility, consistency, practicability, stability, and congruence.[54] That there is likely to be inner morality of law should perhaps not be surprising, with humans and human societies being as they are; we all share essentially the same biology and, at a high level, will tend to prefer societies and social arrangements that meet our fundamental human needs. With the legal singularity, the consequences of courses of actions and legal arrangements will become much clearer, which will tend to lead (though not inexorably and not necessarily) to an improvement in the content of the law.

The normatively desirable developments associated with the legal singularity (and the accompanying technological and economic singularities) are not inevitable. There are developments that could derail the emergence of the legal singularity and its benefits. Part of the reason we have written this book is to bring attention to the importance of continued evolution in our legal system and institutions so that the technological, economic, and social progress that has so benefited humankind over the past several centuries can continue while we avert potential disaster. Thus, this book aims to provide a vision of how we might experience different possible future courses of the development of law and institutions as we proceed through the twenty-first century. It aims to motivate action and debate by articulating the attractive payoffs of successfully working together to secure safe passage for the realization of the legal singularity. At the same time, it is vital to be wary of the possible challenges for society associated with the sort of fundamental change that will facilitate the emergence of the legal singularity.

The legal singularity, in our view, represents the full development of law's creation, adoption, promulgation, and revision. Relative to the legal singularity, in all current legal systems, laws remain obscure and underdeveloped. In even the most advanced legal systems in the world in 2023, there are many important legal issues with high stakes for

---

54 These eight principles were identified as those associated with the "inner morality of law" in Lon Fuller, *The Morality of Law* (New Haven, CT: Yale University Press, 1964). See also Colleen Murphy, "Lon Fuller and the Moral Value of the Rule of Law" (2005) 24:3 Law & Phil 239 at 240 ("Fuller identifies eight requirements of the rule of law").

life and liberty that arise frequently but that are poorly addressed. At best, in the most advanced legal systems, mechanisms are in place that ensure that legal issues are justiciable by a known institution or decision maker. These mechanisms are frequently used to paper over what really amounts to legal under-specification. By specifying an institution or a decision maker who has the power to decide a particular question, we delegate the power to decide what the law requires to another party in the future. The rule of law, however, requires that the legal system provide guidance prospectively and that the law is clear and understood by those who are subject to it. By these standards, current law falls woefully short.

Why should everyone – not just lawyers and judges – care about these efforts to improve law? Why is the legal singularity relevant to us here and now? The immediate relevance is debatable. The legal singularity is not something that will be achieved overnight, if it will ever be fully realized. It will require decades of effort from potentially millions of professionals in government, in legal practice, in data science, in technology, and beyond. It will also need to draw strength from those who are governed by the laws and who hold the law to account for its fairness and clarity. The legal singularity needs allied forces. To bring the legal singularity into existence will require resources: resources to assemble the law, to digitize the law, to organize and make intermediate steps into marketable products that solve real legal needs and continue to support the movement towards the legal singularity. Many will feel inclined to gainsay the long-run vision and yet can get behind the more incremental and intermediate steps along the path. Those of us who are working to realize the legal singularity will be content to be among a band of visionaries who share the long-term ambition if we can attract sufficient numbers of recruits of good conscience who support the myriad incremental improvements to our legal systems and legal institutions along the way.

III. Hazards Ahead

Central among the hazards that we can see in the future is the risk of not adequately solving what has become known as the *alignment problem*. Brian Christian explains the nature of the alignment problem as follows:

> As machine-learning systems grow not just increasingly pervasive but increasingly powerful, we will find ourselves more and more often in the position of the "sorcerer's apprentice": we conjure a force, autonomous but totally compliant, give it a set of instructions, then scramble like mad

to stop it once we realize our instructions are imprecise or incomplete – lest we get, in some clever, horrible way, precisely what we asked for. How to prevent such a catastrophic divergence – how to ensure that these models capture our norms and values, understand what we mean or intend, and, above all, do what we want – has emerged as one of the most central and most urgent scientific questions in the field of computer science. It has a name: *the alignment problem*.[55]

Making sure that our legal systems and legal institutions do what "we" in human society (setting aside all the issues of who ought to be included in "we" and the various issues in political theory in settling on the preferences of a group) would generally want them to do in new situations and circumstances is, in fact, what our legal systems generally already purport to do (quite imperfectly, of course). If we can harness new technology to improve the capacities and capabilities of our legal institutions at least as quickly as the technologies are creating new potential problems as well as real risks and conflicts, we will have set the stage for the possibility of a safe and effective legal singularity. At the risk of sounding hyperbolic, if we cannot achieve this alignment, we will potentially confront head-on numerous existential threats to humanity. Indeed, one might well claim that the legal singularity is an essential by-product of – or perhaps an invention co-emerging with – a successful solution to the alignment problem.

The alignment problem is a closely related variant of what is sometimes referred to in the literature as the "control problem," with respect to superintelligence. The control problem is concerned with the possibility of humans reining in a superintelligence once that superintelligence has been brought into existence. Nick Bostrom, the Oxford futurist and philosopher, suggests that the control problem can be thought of as having two kinds of potential resolutions. The first kind of solution attempts to *limit* or *contain* the *capabilities* of a superintelligence (generally, controlling in some way what a superintelligence *can* do). With respect to containment, Bostrom suggests that we might try to use (1) isolation or boxing methods (to stop the superintelligence from escaping its confines); (2) incentive methods (to surround the superintelligence with an environment that ensures incentives for safe behaviour, such as other superintelligences as monitors); (3) stunting methods (to limit the resources available to the superintelligence within

---

55 New York: Brian Christian, *The Alignment Problem: How Can Machines Learn Human Values?* (New York: W.W. Norton & Company, 2020) at 18.

safe bounds); or (4) tripwires (to shut down the superintelligence in the event that certain diagnostic tests suggest danger).[56]

The second kind of solution to Bostrom's control problem sets out to control the *motivations* of a superintelligence (generally, what it *wants* to do). This motivation-selection kind of solution could involve (1) direct specification of motivations (raising issues of being "careful what we wish for");[57] (2) domesticity, whereby the system is designed to pursue only severely limited goals; (3) "indirect normativity," in which the system infers principles or values based on training information; and (4) augmentation, in which a system starts with human values and capabilities and then builds upon that basis into a superintelligence.

Regardless of whether one would like to refer to the challenge as being one of "alignment" or "control," further development of artificial intelligence and machine learning has the potential to lead to adverse outcomes for humanity. As Bostrom writes, "This is quite possibly the most important and most daunting challenge humanity has ever faced. And – whether we succeed or fail – it is probably the last challenge we will ever face."[58] As Stuart Russell remarks in his 2019 book on the importance of developing "provably beneficial" artificial intelligence, "We cannot predict exactly how the technology will develop or on what timeline. Nevertheless, we must plan for the possibility that machines will far exceed the human capacity for decision-making in the real world. What then?"[59]

IV. Our Story and Objectives

The story of our interest in the legal singularity begins with a Toronto-based company called Blue J. Co-author Benjamin Alarie, a law professor with the University of Toronto Faculty of Law, founded the company with academic colleagues Anthony Niblett and Albert Yoon. The motivation: legal research was woefully inefficient, and answers to legal questions were unnecessarily imprecise. When attempting to answer complex legal questions, even the most capable lawyers could, at best, review only a sampling of relevant data – perhaps only a relatively small

---

56 Nick Bostrom, *Superintelligence: Paths, Dangers, Strategies* (Oxford: Oxford University Press, 2014) [Bostrom, *Superintelligence*].
57 Nick Bostrom, "Ethical Issues in Advanced Artificial Intelligence," n.d., online: <https://nickbostrom.com/ethics/ai>.
58 Bostrom, *Superintelligence, supra* note 56 at vii.
59 Stuart Russell, *Human Compatible: Artificial Intelligence and the Problem of Control* (New York: Penguin Books, 2020) at xi.

number of cases in any depth, along with the applicable statutes and regulations – when working under real-world time pressures. Focusing first on tax and then employment law, Blue J has built and developed software that used machine learning to predict the answers to legal questions. As the company grew, co-author Abdi Aidid joined and led the team of lawyers and researchers who built and expanded the platform. By the time work began on this book in early 2019, Blue J had thousands of users in hundreds of organizations, including in government, law firms, public-interest organizations, and academic institutions. At the same time, a wider community of legal technology firms were emerging and becoming established, including companies using AI to perform lawyerly tasks like due diligence, contract review, and even memorandum drafting.

Early in the Blue J journey, Professors Alarie, Niblett, and Yoon convened an academic symposium at the University of Toronto Faculty of Law that culminated in a focus feature in the *University of Toronto Law Journal* titled "Artificial Intelligence, Big Data and the Future of the Law." As part of the journal's special edition, Alarie published a brief essay arguing that advances in technology are substantially likely to bring about a legal singularity, which the essay likened to a Rawlsian reflective equilibrium.[60] That essay is an early sketch of some of the ideas that we elaborate here.

Though the article was just thirteen pages, the reaction to it was swift. The piece generated intense reaction – and criticism – from all corners of law's epistemic community. Esteemed scholars such as Jennifer Cobbe, Simon Deakin and Christopher Markou, Lance B. Eliot, and Robert F. Weber published thoughtful rejoinders to the concept of the legal singularity.[61] Taken together, these criticisms tended to take the form of either (1) disbelief that the legal singularity could ever *actually* take place; or (2) concern that the legal singularity would portend some social consequences that we could not adequately account for. It became immediately apparent that the legal singularity was a fertile concept that serious thinkers were interested in engaging with. Equally clearly, it needed a more thorough academic treatment to serve as its intellectual foundation.

The reaction to the essay foretold a problem that we have seen repeatedly: concerns about an AI future are pronounced in the legal

---

60 Benjamin Alarie, "The Path of the Law: Towards Legal Singularity" (2016) 66:4 UTLJ 443.

61 Some of these responses are collected in Deakin & Markou, *supra* note 1.

community, sometimes even manifesting as outright panic. There are at least two explanations for this reaction. The first is a familiar one: the legal profession is notoriously conservative. Whether or not individual lawyers themselves are change resistant is largely beside the point. As in every professional community, some are on the cutting edge of new technologies while others will overstate the threat or dismiss the value of change altogether. But the fact remains that little about the profession has been changing for many decades. For illustrative purposes, imagine yourself transported back to a law office in England in the year 1900. You would see those lawyers performing largely the same tasks as modern lawyers: reading law books, drafting documents, negotiating settlements, preparing for arguments in court, and so on. To the extent that there are differences in legal practice today, these tend to be differences of degree, not kind. For instance, modern lawyers work with considerably more abundant substantive law than the lawyer of 1900 would have done, but the modes of reasoning and analysis and techniques of interpretation are largely the same. Indeed, the well-trained lawyer of 1900 would likely have little problem handling today's legal challenges (assuming they first learn to use a computer).

The conservatism we lament here is more of a feature of the legal profession than a bug, so to speak. As far back as 1948, scholars such as Edgar Bodenheimer observed that, "[b]y and large, it can be said that judges and lawyers ... have rarely been the primary architects of basic legal change."[62] To Bodenheimer, conservatism is inherent in the law's dispute resolution function, as law is a "device for the neutralization of tensions," that "strive[s] with all its might to maintain and protect it against disturbances and disruption."[63] Technological advances that present themselves as disruptive may then provoke the same strong antibody response that, in other contexts, enables the law to serve its vital social stabilization function. Others have observed that the nature of the legal profession – its reliance on judicial precedent and its institutional appeals to authority – makes this conservatism inescapable.

A second explanation for the legal community's trepidation about AI is a more charitable one: lawyers, collectively, share a professional commitment to the rule of law. Any event touted as "revolutionary," even if it promises to be a friendly revolution, might raise questions about whether it would undermine systems that the public relies on

---

62 Edgar Bodenheimer, "The Inherent Conservatism of the Legal Profession" (1947) 23:3 Ind LJ 221 at 222.
63 *Ibid* at 231.

to dispense justice and ensure order and stability. We anticipate and address these concerns in this book, asking ourselves throughout: how can we ensure that we harness machine intelligence for our benefit, for the benefit of our legal institutions, and for the benefit of future generations?

Our goals with this book are threefold. The first is to firmly root the legal singularity in the popular imagination as an idea that we collectively must address to ensure that the world's legal systems undergo changes that are in alignment with humanity's interests as artificial intelligence and machine learning continue to improve. If managed deftly, these technological developments in artificial intelligence and machine learning can and will lead to astounding improvements to social justice and distributive justice, and will contribute to widespread human flourishing. This is, of course, an optimistic and ambitious vision. Others have pointed out less rosy possible scenarios; our view is that those scenarios are avoidable if efforts are undertaken now to help to navigate towards positive outcomes. Realizing a stable, safe, and normatively desirable legal singularity will require deliberation, experimentation, wisdom, knowledge, and the cumulative efforts of governments, academia, and industry over the coming years. There will be problems. There will be dead ends. There will be experimentation, failures, and more experimentation. Ultimately, there will be significant progress. The good news is that many efforts are being undertaken even as we write. With this book, we aspire to echo and amplify those who seek to leverage technology as a means of improving law. To this, we add our own vision of how technology, ambitious problem-solving, and responsible stewardship will guide law towards the legal singularity.

Our second aim is to press the point that technology-based changes to our legal systems are *not* simply a possibility to be discussed on a theoretical level by the intellectually curious. It is tempting for many in the legal profession to want to assume that we could simply press "pause" on technological progress and the concomitant evolution of our legal systems until a sufficiently widespread level of practical confidence and psychological comfort is reached. Many would prefer to defer serious consideration of the uncomfortable topics that are explored in this book until they are first convinced that (1) the status quo is unsustainable; (2) the kinds of changes that are being driven by technological advances have been thoroughly tested and designed with normative and conceptual coherence; and (3) an implementation plan has been devised to accommodate these changes in a manner that will be minimally disruptive to the existing legal order. These instincts are understandable. Unfortunately, the context in which law functions and operates is changing too quickly. While we will not address in any depth the domain-specific technological changes that are transforming various industries, to ignore them when considering the future of law would be blinkered. Law does not exist in a vacuum.

Consider some examples of technological progress that are expected on the near horizon in the 2020s. In biotechnology and health care, efforts are afoot to extend human lifespans through various technologies, including gene editing using CRISPR and treatments of blood plasma.[64] DeepMind's machine-learning breakthroughs on protein folding in 2020 portend additional thrilling discoveries in medicine during the rest of the decade.[65] With respect to energy and transportation, we have seen radical reductions in the cost of solar energy in the past few decades, and developments with respect to harnessing geothermal and fusion energy are promised in the future. It is expected that the 2020s will be the decade in which electric vehicles replace internal combustion automobiles in many countries; California and numerous other jurisdictions are requiring all new cars purchased after 2035 to have zero emissions. Many billions of dollars are being invested in improving artificial intelligence and machine learning, harnessing continued exponential improvements in computing power, and pairing those with ever wider and deeper pools of data. And, of course, quantum computing is increasingly appearing to be viable, with difficult to predict implications. These developments are not waiting for lawyers and judges to become psychologically comfortable with the need for legal change; they are happening now.

Our third and final aim with this book is to join the emerging international movement in academia, government, the judiciary, and civil society, and among actors in the legal system more generally, to secure the safest, wisest, and most effective path to the legal singularity. The forces driving us towards legal singularity are persistent and powerful: there is no "off" switch to the internet; computing power looks to continue its exponential growth. We aim to help ameliorate two categories of risks. The most obvious are the risks associated with

---

64 Lucas B. Harrington et al, "A Thermostable Case with Increased Lifetime in Human Plasma" (2017) 8:1 Nature Communications 1424.

65 Ewen Callaway, "'It Will Change Everything': DeepMind's AI Makes Gigantic Leap in Solving Protein Structures," *Nature* (30 November 2020), online: <https://www.nature.com/articles/d41586-020-03348-4> [https://doi.org/10.1038/d41586-020-03348-4].

unforeseen consequences of the direct uses of the underlying technologies themselves. We contend that as technology continues to progress, the law must also increase in its sophistication to effectively meet this first category of potentially existential risk – the alignment or control problem associated with AI, as popularized by Brian Christian and Nick Bostrom. This first consideration gives rise to a second, less obvious, category of dangers: the potential risks associated with using new technologies within the legal system itself on the path to the legal singularity. The shape of an eventual legal singularity can undoubtedly be influenced for the better by careful monitoring, concerted action, and thoughtfulness (or, for the worse, by the abuse of technology to oppress or suppress populations). It is in our collective interest to work to forge and secure the best-possible path to legal singularity.

V. Orienting Ourselves

Law is sophisticated by both historical and contemporary standards, as we see and understand it here from our vantage point in Toronto in 2023. Canada's legal system has a constitutionalized bill of rights in the *Charter of Rights and Freedoms*; strong administrative institutions that – despite grumbling around tax time in April each year – have earned the respect of Canadians; and a professional, competent, and independent judiciary at the federal and provincial levels. Moreover, leaders of our federal, provincial, territorial, municipal, and Indigenous governments across the decades have fared reasonably well in public opinion. And, despite some high-profile examples to the contrary, our leaders have generally been relatively resistant to corruption and have conducted themselves in ways that have tended to contribute to the perceived integrity of our institutions. All things considered, Canada's legal system and its political, social, economic, and administrative institutions are, from a comparative historical perspective, performing well in 2023.

Of course, Canada is not alone in having reasonably good laws and institutions. Similar claims could be advanced about the legal systems and the institutions in the thirty or so countries at the top of the United Nations' human development index (HDI). These countries have well-developed legal systems and institutions that support their populations with relatively high life expectancy at birth, provide for substantial educational opportunities for their children, and facilitate what are relatively high levels of per capita gross domestic product.

The top position in the 2020 HDI rankings was held by Norway, with an HDI of 0.957.[66] Canada was sixteenth, with an HDI of 0.929,[67] just behind Belgium and New Zealand (tied for fourteenth position, with HDIs of 0.931),[68] and just ahead of the United States, which stood seventeenth, with an HDI of 0.926.[69] Estonia and Italy rounded out the top thirty, tied with an HDI of 0.892.[70] While the suitability of the methodology for the HDI is not beyond debate, it is a reasonable proxy for the quality of life supported by a country's legal system and institutions. To be among the top thirty countries on the HDI is an indication that a country has been able to establish and maintain laws and institutions that support human well-being.

Perhaps, however, those of us living in countries that are currently near the top of the HDI should not be so quick to congratulate ourselves on our laws and legal institutions. Compared to law in the future (or at least compared to what we ought to aspire to), the law and legal institutions in Canada (and indeed throughout the countries at the top of the HDI rankings) in the early 2020s are poorly understood by those to whom they apply. The laws are too complex, riddled with inconsistencies and internal contradictions, and are ineffective in remedying many types of significant social injustices. Are they functional? Reasonably so. Are they better than laws and legal systems that have typically been in place over recorded history? Probably. Are they optimal? Absolutely not. There is massive room for improvement.

Some would argue that even in our "best" legal systems, the law and our legal institutions are, in many instances, themselves responsible for

---

66 "Norway," *Human Development Report 2020 – The Next Frontier: Human Development and the Anthropocene*, online: <https://hdr.undp.org/sites/default/files/Country -Profiles/NOR.pdf>.

67 "Canada," *Human Development Report 2020 – The Next Frontier: Human Development and the Anthropocene*, online: <https://hdr.undp.org/sites/all/themes/hdr_theme /country-notes/CAN.pdf>.

68 "Belgium," *Human Development Report 2020 – The Next Frontier: Human Development and the Anthropocene*, online: <https://hdr.undp.org/sites/all/themes/hdr_theme /country-notes/BEL.pdf>; "New Zealand," *Human Development Report 2020 – The Next Frontier: Human Development and the Anthropocene*, online: http://hdr.undp.org /sites/default/files/Country-Profiles/NZL.pdf>.

69 "United States," *Human Development Report 2020 – The Next Frontier: Human Development and the Anthropocene*, online: <https://hdr.undp.org/sites/default/files /Country-Profiles/USA.pdf>.

70 "Estonia," *Human Development Report 2020 – The Next Frontier: Human Development and the Anthropocene*, online: <https://hdr.undp.org/sites/all/themes/hdr_theme /country-notes/EST.pdf>; "Italy," *Human Development Report 2020 – The Next Frontier: Human Development and the Anthropocene*, online: <https://hdr.undp.org/sites /default/files/Country-Profiles/ITA.pdf>.

producing, generating, or perpetuating injustice; indeed, numerous examples exist of precisely such outcomes. This statement should not be read as an indictment of the current state of the law in Canada or in other developed countries. On the contrary, to reiterate the point, the current state of the law among the top thirty or so most-developed countries is about as strong as it has been in recorded history. The key point is that, despite the effectiveness, competence, and, indeed, often heroic and successful efforts of individuals in contemporary legal systems, there are nevertheless serious limitations of communication, technology, information, administration, and access to justice that affect our legal systems and legal institutions. We could do better. As it stands, our laws are, too frequently, poorly designed, with significant gaps, inconsistencies, and uneven enforcement. Actors in our legal systems are often forced by circumstance to make decisions without enough time, data, information, or feedback for those decisions to stand a reasonable chance of being optimal. Heroic one-off efforts are insufficient. And the challenges are likely to continue to mount. The stresses that will be imposed on our laws and legal institutions by accelerating technological changes in the coming years will test the dynamism and resilience of the legal systems that we often celebrate as among the best at promoting human well-being.

Individuals in the year 2100 will, we expect, recollect in astonishment how populations in even the most developed countries in the 2020s tended to quietly accept the current limitations associated with their laws and legal systems (even though this acceptance is often grudging). They will marvel at our ability to muddle through using the slow and laborious methods that we currently take as unavoidable for making policy and for teaching administering, and reforming law. We expect that this reaction of observers in the future will be like the difficulties with which we imagine human populations of the year 1450 coping without the printing press, electrification, telecommunications, reliable sanitation systems, the internal combustion engine, antibiotics, radio, recorded music, aircraft, or any number of modern conveniences. If developments in the next several decades continue along their current path, then law in the future will be radically better than it is now. To repeat: we are on the path to legal singularity.

We are not historical determinists. We do believe, however, that in the twenty-first century we are witnessing the emergence of new legal orders that are more responsive and adaptable and, therefore, more stable. The forces that are currently leading to significant improvements in artificial intelligence, such as rapidly decreasing costs of computation, productive investments in research into algorithms and machine-learning techniques, and an explosion of data collected through an increasing variety of sensors and methods are likely – if managed well – to lead to radical positive impacts in the substance and the process of the law and our legal institutions. We contend that it is reasonable to expect that law's rate of change will increase, undergoing a mostly gradual transformation, and will ultimately reach an equilibrium that will manifest as a functionally complete and mature system of laws and legal regulation that enjoys widespread acceptance. The most significant catalyst for this change in law will be the continued development of systems that rely on improvements in computation and methods of feedback, inference, and learning, leading to continuous improvement and course correction.

VI. Towards the Legal Singularity

Owing to our positions as academics *and* legal technologists, this book is neither solely an academic work nor a blueprint for further technological growth. Instead, we offer a framework for future discussion and elaboration among all members of law's epistemic community: the scholars who embrace legal technology or question it; the lawyers who think it augments their practice or threatens it; and the judges, law students, and engaged citizens who are wondering how the future might look.

We are at pains to explain that we do not need to predict the specific manner of the development of law and legal technology; moreover, we readily concede that we are not up to the task. Instead, we can take note of well-established and well-documented improvements in computing power, data, and algorithms, in order to foretell a time when the implications and most likely consequences from different possible laws and policies will be capable of being accurately forecasted. It is nevertheless reasonable to claim, as we do, that the law can be made vastly clearer and better with massively more data, improved algorithms, and essentially costless computing power. We note, for example, that a single gaming console, such as Sony's PlayStation 5, has about ten times the computing power that the world's fastest supercomputer did in December of 1996.[71] That computer – ASCI Red – cost US$46 million

---

71 Jay Peters, "PlayStation 5: Everything You Need to Know about Sony's Newest Consoles," *The Verge* (12 November 2020), online: <https://www.theverge .com/21450334/playstation-5-ps5-sony-news-price-features-specs-hardware -games>; Frank Pelligrini, "Computing Reaches Record Speed," *Time* (17 December 1996), online: <https://content.time.com/time/nation/article/0,8599,7402,00.html>; see also Greg Henry & Timothy G. Mattson, "The Performance of the Intel TFLOPS Supercomputer," (1997) Intel Tech J 1.

at the time of its construction, a cost that translates to about CA$104 million in 2022 terms; a PlayStation 5 today carries a retail price of CA$649.99.[72] Doing the math suggests that the hardware to run one computational operation now costs only about *one-millionth* of what it cost just twenty-five years ago. And this does not factor in the other massive improvements in computing, including reductions in size, lower power consumption, better networking connectivity, lower operating costs, and so on.

Humans and our relationships are not changing as quickly. Just as Shakespearean dramas remain illuminating and worthy of time, attention, and study, the legal problems associated with our society remain fundamentally unchanged. Even where technology requires new policies and regulations, we would argue that these challenges are not likely to become a million times more complex over twenty-five years. We argue that the exponential growth in AI and machine learning is likely to overtake in capacity the demands for more legal complexity as technology becomes more sophisticated.

The legal singularity may strike many people as science fiction; it may be too "out there" for today's judges and lawyers who, for example, on any given Tuesday afternoon witness firsthand the messiness of the real world in their day-to-day interactions with the public, paperwork, litigants, police, administration, courthouse staff, sheriffs, and the routine, mundane aspects of the legal system. Perhaps many judges and lawyers will dismiss the legal singularity as ivory tower dreaming. But, just like any long-term movement for greater social justice and improvement in the human condition, the understanding that the legal system and legal institutions are capable of significant improvement using new technologies and new institutional arrangements will become easier as improvements take hold and exhibit increasing positive momentum. Nothing motivates like a bold and difficult objective that appears to be just barely within reach. Even the articulated conviction that significant movement on the path towards legal singularity is happening is likely to be motivating for many.

What does this mean for those who are inclined to be supportive? Be prepared to listen patiently to interest-group resistance without being unduly persuaded by all the reasons why we cannot do better than we

---

72 Jim Ryan, "PS5 Price to Increase in Select Markets Due to Global Economic Environment, Including High Inflation Rates" (25 August 2022), online (blog): <https://blog.playstation.com/2022/08/25/ps5-price-to-increase-in-select-markets-due-to-global-economic-environment-including-high-inflation-rates/>.

currently are; to repeat: there is massive room for improvement in our legal systems. All along the journey towards the legal singularity, there will be difficult resistance. The legal singularity will run up against those whose livelihoods (at least as they now know them) depend upon the failure or significant delay of the legal singularity. We should expect this and yet acknowledge and appreciate that those who point out challenges are often correct. It is inevitable that we will encounter myriad genuine and difficult problems along the way. Ultimately, the legal singularity will be achieved through a combination of technological progress, relentless troubleshooting, inventiveness, perseverance, and resourcefulness. It will be supported by the demands of the public for transparency, fairness, and clarity. We will collectively demand a legal system that is manifestly capable of being trusted.

Despite the above claims, it is probable that the legal singularity project will never be perfectly realized. Indeed, the legal singularity vision is one of a legal system that is in a dynamic, normative equilibrium, one that is constantly ebbing and flowing to accommodate and anticipate changes and developments in society. It will need to be robust and capable of absorbing shocks. It will need to be well maintained and constantly monitored for healthy vital signs. Like the power grids of today that supply stable electricity, or the cloud infrastructure that powers and supports the online world, an entire industry of talented and dedicated individuals will be devoted to addressing issues, troubleshooting, and doing preventative maintenance on the systems that sustain and support the realization of the legal singularity. The vision is *not* one of an autonomous legal system that is self-executing and entirely free of the influence of humans. The vision of legal singularity is one, instead, of elevating the capabilities and ambitions of our laws and legal institutions to the highest practical level by leveraging technology, human ingenuity, and our collective moral imagination. We are on the path to legal singularity.

Chapter Two

The Nature of Legal Information

I. Introduction

"If it is law, it will be found in our books. If it is not found there, it is not law." So spoke Lord Camden from the King's Bench in the famous 1765 case of *Entick v Carrington*.[1] The case concerned one John Entick, a pamphleteer and occasional writer for the London-area publication *The Monitor*. Entick was a fierce critic of his government's conduct during the Seven Years War and, pursuant to a warrant issued by a British cabinet minister, he was arrested on accusations of sedition and his property searched by royal messengers.[2] After his release, Entick sued the chief royal messenger, Nathan Carrington, and his accomplices for trespass.[3] The question before the Court was a rather routine one: did the warrant constitute valid authority for the search?[4]

In a judgment that was later heralded by the US Supreme Court as "the true and ultimate expression of constitutional law,"[5] Lord Camden said, quite simply: no.[6] The case became famous in the annals of legal history for being the quintessential "precedent about precedent," establishing that the executive could not search someone's home or seize property

---

1 *Entick v Carrington*, [1765] EWHC J98 (KB), (1765) 19 Howell's State Trials 1029, 95 ER 807 at 1066 [*Entick*]; see also Richard Moules, "Judicial Review of Prerogative Orders in Council" (2009) 68:1 Cambridge LJ 14.
2 *Entick*, *supra* note 1 at 1031.
3 *Ibid* at 1029.
4 *Ibid* at 1045.
5 *Boyd v United States*, 116 US 616 at 626–7 (1886) [*Boyd*].
6 *Entick*, *supra* note 1 at 1074.

unless authorized to do so by statute or common law.[7] The decision had significant ramifications throughout the Anglo-American legal world, particularly in the United States; as Richard Epstein writes, *Entick* so influenced the American founders that the ultimate text of the Fourth Amendment was "clearly an effort to mimic in the Bill of Rights the protection that Lord Camden offered in *Entick*."[8] We know that Entick prevailed in the case,[9] and we have often repeated Lord Camden's famous *dictum* that law must be found in our books.[10] Unfortunately, we know little else for certain.

It is one of the great ironies of legal history that there is no definitive text of the decision in *Entick*. To put it plainly, the very case announcing that law must be found in our books *cannot itself be found in any reliable form*.[11] Subsequent courts relied on two different versions of the case.[12] But even with this contested provenance, Lord Camden's famous pronouncement is something every first-year law student knows to be true: the law – and by extension, legal analysis – is more or less limited to what you can find in legal texts. The fact of the missing *Entick* decision points to a second truth: our access to those legal texts is hardly guaranteed.

In this chapter, we discuss the centrality of legal information to how we currently practise, analyse, and make law. The discussion is divided into three main sections. In section II, we explore the centrality of information to legal practice and analysis, describing how law functioned before the emergence of legal texts, the impact of codification, and the resulting information environment. In section III, we explain how the history of legal information is best characterized as having three distinct eras: the analogue era, the digital era, and the emerging computational era. In section IV, we conclude by looking at the current state of legal information and discuss some of the considerations that have, thus far, constrained the growth of computational legal analytics.

---

7 Orin Kerr, "Legal History Bleg – Identifying the Most Important Version of *Entick v. Carrington*" (25 September 2012), online: *The Volokh Conspiracy* <https://volokh.com /2012/09/25/legal-history-bleg-identifying-the-most-important-version-of-entick -v-carrington/>.

8 Richard A. Epstein, "'Entick v Carrington' and 'Boyd v United States': Keeping the Fourth and Fifth Amendments on Track" (2015) 82:1 U Chicago L Rev 27 at 32.

9 *Entick, supra* note 1 at 1074.

10 *Ibid* at 1066.

11 *Ibid* at 1029.

12 See, e.g., *Boyd, supra*, note 5; *US v Jones*, 565 US 400 (2012).

II. The Centrality of Information to Law

a. Law before Text

There is a close relationship between what we call the "law" and "legal information." At its core, law is a text-based system. Though lawyers might identify many activities as core to their professional identities (think: oral advocacy or strategic negotiations), common law and civil law legal systems are based on textual components: codes, constitutions, statutes, regulations, agreements, conventions, treaties, and case law.[13] Lawyers are trained to read and synthesize these materials, to make arguments based on them, and to render advice based on what can be found in authoritative texts. A universe of secondary sources supports this goal; lawyers consult treatises, academic articles, and other materials to guide their interpretation of the primary sources. This basic insight – that laws tend to be written and that legal authority is derived from text – is an obvious statement that many lawyers take for granted, yet it is the result of centuries of practice and concerted effort to codify and publicize society's rules.[14] Even areas of law that are not well specified and depend on norms and established practices (for instance, customary international law) have, at a minimum, secondary texts that provide some interpretation and interpretive guidelines.[15]

But this was not always the case. Ancient societies rarely codified their laws; among other reasons, codification was costly, given that the best available technology was manual transcription. Historians trace the first formal compilation of laws to King Ur-Nammu of Sumer (circa 2100 BCE).[16] The text, written in cuneiform, consisted of conditional laws that announced the legal ramifications of certain conduct.[17] Perhaps the most well-known codification effort occurred several centuries later, around 1754 BCE, when the Code of Hammurabi announced the principle of

---

13 See generally Robert C Berring, "Legal Information and the Search for Cognitive Authority" (1999) University of California at Berkeley School of Law Working Paper No 99-1 at 3–4, online: <https://papers.ssrn.com/paper.taf?abstract_id=184050> [https://doi.org/10.2139/ssrn.184050; Berring, "Legal Information"].
14 See generally Robert C Berring, "Legal Research and Legal Concepts: Where Form Molds Substance" (1987) 75 Cal L Rev 15 [Berring, "Legal Research"].
15 See, e.g., International Law Commission, *Report of the International Law Commission*, UNILCOR, 70th Sess, UN Doc A/73/10 (2018) at 119; International Law Commission, *Formation and Evidence of Customary International Law*, UNGAOR, 68th Sess, Supp No 10, UN Doc A/CN.4/659 (2013).
16 Samuel Noah Kramer, "The Oldest Laws" (1953) 188:1 Scientific American 26.
17 JJ Finkelstein, "The Laws of Ur-Nammu" (1968) 22:3/4 J Cuneiform Studies 66; see also J.J. Finkelstein, "Sex Offenses in Sumerian Laws" (1966) 86:4 J Am Oriental Society 355.

retributive justice we now know as the *lex talionis*, or "an eye for an eye."[18] Other major codification efforts, including the Justinian Code[19] and the Magna Carta,[20] were notable historical documents but were largely exceptions to what were otherwise informal legal traditions.

The most substantial change in the world of legal information came with the advent of the printing press in the fifteenth century. As Richard J. Ross explains, it did not take long for lawyers to understand the significance of widespread dissemination.[21] Lawyers in sixteenth-century England, for instance, vigorously debated the virtues and drawbacks of printing. According to Ross, advocates "prophesied national unity, godliness and social harmony flowing from the legal press," while detractors worried that freely available legal materials would be misinterpreted by a public that was not trained in legal methods.[22] The prospect of publication appealed to lawyerly self-interest: many recognized that embracing the legal press – either by writing treatises or by having their advocacy documented in published decisions – meant increased professional status and perhaps even an elevated place in the history of the law.[23]

There are at least four significant distinct developments that resulted from the proliferation of legal presses. The first and most significant is the advent of modern legal precedent. The principle of *stare decisis* – that courts are bound to follow the reasoning of prior superior courts in similar cases – existed before legal publication, but more complete records of recent case law made rigorous citation more possible. As Frederick Schauer explains, "citation practice is intimately connected with the authoritative core of the idea of law."[24] Put differently, legal arguments derive their authority from reference to specific examples of historical case law. Just as advocates invoke these examples, judges cultivate legitimacy by rooting analyses in the reasoning and legal manoeuvres of previous courts. As the publication of judicial decisions became more widespread, judges also embraced

---

18 Peter Tiersma, "Writing, Text, and the Law" (2005) Loyola Law School Working Paper No 2005-31 at 3–5.
19 Joseph H Drake, "The Justinian Codification Commission of 528 A.D." (1928) 27:2 Mich L Rev 125.
20 David Carpenter, "Magna Carta 1215: Its Social and Political Context" in Lawrence Goldman, ed, *Magna Carta: History, Context and Influence* (London: University of London Press, 2018) 17.
21 Richard J Ross, "The Commoning of the Common Law: The Renaissance Debate over Printing English Law, 1520–1640" (1998) 146:2 U Pa L Rev 323.
22 *Ibid* at 324.
23 *Ibid* at 329.
24 Frederick Schauer, "Authority and Authorities" (2008) 94:8 Va L Rev 1931.

the self-conscious role of precedent-producer; as the *function* of judicial opinions changed, so too did the *form*, and judges wrote with a view to posterity and announced legal rules more openly.[25]

Second, the proliferation of legal publications created conditions for law as a public affair. The publication of statutes, regulations, and case law took legal decision-making from the domain of narrow professional community concern to public interest politics.[26] Improved public understanding of the law meant, in theory, increased potential for public debate about its content. Later legal philosophers correctly recognized that, even though legal texts enhanced the possibility for more public engagement with law, this promise went largely unrealized because of fragmented sources and barriers to access.[27] Jeremy Bentham, for instance, famously described publicity of laws as "the very soul of justice," arguing that it was a critical tool of good governance. Bentham proposed revising and recodifying all laws under a single text – or "comprehensive body of law" – as assurance that citizens had a single, accessible source of their rights and obligations.[28] Bentham's proposal was an early recognition that the mechanisms for publicizing and distributing legal materials were inadequate, despite the promises of codification and publication.

Third, codified laws and published case law facilitated the emergence of more rigorous legal education. The practice of law prior to legal publication involved on-the-job vocational training in the tools of the trade, including advocacy techniques and instruction about the prevailing legal doctrines.[29] To be certain, the apprenticeship method remained the dominant mode of legal education through the late eighteenth century, but the proliferation of published legal materials increased the complexity of the discipline.[30] Lawyers were eventually required to master leading cases and learn core concepts as documented in treatises.[31] Just as the law became a more serious field of study for students, it became a serious field of inquiry for scholars: legal presses' demand for books meant more lawyers stepping into their roles as reporters of legal subject matter, and emerging cultures of peer review and criticism meant more concerted efforts to advance new ideas.[32]

---

25 Tiersma, "Writing, Text and the Law," *supra* note 18 at 21–4.
26 Berring, "Legal Research," *supra* note 14 at 18.
27 Anthony D'Amato, "Legal Uncertainty" (1983) 71:1 Cal L Rev 1.
28 Jeremy Bentham, *Legislator of the World: Writings on Codification, Law, and Education*, ed by Philip Schofield & Jonathan Harris (Oxford: Clarendon Press, 1998) at 245.
29 Mark T. Flahive, "The Origins of the American Law School" (1978) 64:12 ABA J 1868.
30 Berring, "Legal Information," *supra* note 14 at 15.
31 See, e.g., *ibid* at 7; Ross, *supra* note 21 at 448.
32 See, e.g., D'Amato, *supra* note 27 at 11.

Fourth and finally, codification and the availability of legal texts created the modern legal profession. As Ross explains, lawyers reading the same texts cultivated a "group identity" that existed "beyond the ambit of the personal contact and spoken word" of the court.[33] Put differently, the profession became increasingly drawn together through the cultivation and development of a common corpus of knowledge. Where lawyers in the pre-publication period formed epistemic communities of their own, these remained largely regional and full of local practice eccentricities. The advent of legal publication meant some measure of standardization.[34]

Here, it is important to pause and note that we are largely describing the European civil tradition and the Anglo-American common law world. Even within those systems, though, there are influential legal traditions that do not take text as a central medium for communicating legal information. As John Borrows explains of Indigenous legal traditions in Canada, legal principles, and the types of information that common law lawyers might call "precedent," are often expressed orally or demonstratively. This often means that the values that are germane to legal decision-making are narrated, passed down through generations and take the form of historically informed customary knowledge.[35] That these principles are not necessarily "written down" does not, of course, say anything about the depth of the principles and their importance to the legal systems they underpin. Put simply, codified, documented laws do not mean inherently more sophisticated laws. Similarly, there are religious traditions with well-developed, complex jurisprudence that rely to a significant extent on oral transmission. As one example, Ahmed Souaiaia explains that, in the key developmental period of Islamic law, "written documents were early considered relatively subordinate to the oral literature and practices that actually shaped the classical body of Islamic law."[36] A major challenge for future developers of computational legal tools will be determining the best ways to absorb oral legal information into systems that, up to this point, have demanded text as input data. The extent to which this is achievable or normatively desirable remains an open question that it is beyond our ambit to answer.

---

33 Ross, *supra* note 21 at 447–8.
34 *Ibid.*
35 John Borrows, "Indigenous Legal Traditions in Canada" (2005) 19:1 Wash UJL & Pol'y 167 at 189–92.
36 Ahmed Souaiaia, "On the Sources of Islamic Law and Practices" (2004) 20:1 JL & Religion 101 at 103.

b. Prediction and Law's Information Environment

Frederick Schauer and Virginia Wise once explored the distinction between legal and non-legal information by asking two questions: (1) Would a given source have been "available on the shelves of a typical federal, state, county, municipal, or law school law library in, say, 1970?" and (2) Would a given source be subjected to "criticism if a first-year law student had included the source in a moot court brief written for internal, first-year, training purposes?"[37] To Schauer and Wise, legal information included only those texts that made authoritative statements about the law and were backstopped by the imprimatur of a judge, a legislative body, an administrative agency, a law commission, or perhaps a well-established legal scholar.[38] John Furlong's well-known definition of legal information covers much of the same ground: to Furlong, legal information includes "all official statements of law together with interpretations and commentaries."[39] Though the Schauer-Wise and Furlong definitions have been criticized as being imprecise,[40] both convey a foundational understanding of legal information as consisting of texts *about the law*. Both definitions are also helpful for distinguishing legal information from other sources that might bear on legal outcomes. For instance, dispute resolution usually involves evidence, including materials shared by the litigating parties as well as materials produced through adjudicatory processes (such as witness transcripts, for instance). Schauer and Wise and Furlong helpfully distinguish these from "legal information," because such sources are not strictly *about the law*, despite being important inputs for legal decision-making.

Still, all these definitions tend to suffer from the same shortcoming: they fail to explain what legal information is *for*. Other fields that consider information a central component tend to have more purposive definitions. In the computer science literature, for instance, scholars describe information as "processed data on which decisions and actions

---

37 Frederick Schauer & Virginia J Wise, "Nonlegal Information and the Delegalization of Law" (2000) 29:1 J Leg Stud 495 at 497–500.

38 *Ibid*.

39 John Furlong, "Legal Information" in John Feather & Paul Sturges, eds, *International Encyclopedia of Information and Library Science* (London: Routledge, 2003) 363 at 363.

40 See, e.g., Robert C. Richards Jr, "What Is Legal Information" (Boulder Summer Conference on Legal Information, 2009) [unpublished], online: <https://papers.ssrn.com/sol3/papers.cfm?abstract_id=2378143>.

are based."[41] The benefit of this sort of purposive definition is two-fold. First, it allows for degrees of informativeness. Second, it allows for the analysis of informational hierarchies in ways that are attentive to how the information is used, rather than through more nebulous markers such as prestige and tradition. In the legal profession, this is especially important: advocates need to draw distinctions between precedents that are effective and other sources that, through received wisdom, might have garnered status but are nevertheless not particularly helpful.[42]

In this book, we build on the Schauer-Wise and Furlong definitions, describing "legal information" as information that is used to inform *legal prediction*. Put differently, legal information is that which sheds light on how legal concepts are interpreted and applied and, therefore, how legal questions in the real world are likely to be resolved. Our understanding of legal information as input for legal prediction is premised on the view that a lawyer who can recite from legal authorities, can quote verbatim appropriate sections of the civil code, or describe the relevant judicial doctrine still might not be said to *know* the law unless they can also predict how a future court is likely to apply that information. Of course, clients intuitively understand this. A criminal defendant does not come to a lawyer asking about which specific legal standards apply to their sentencing; instead, they want to know how much time they are facing. Likewise, a corporate client seeking US federal income tax advice is not necessarily interested in a description of the two-part test of, say, the economic substance doctrine; instead, they want to know whether their company's transactions will be deemed compliant and whether the claimed tax benefits will be respected if they are subsequently challenged by the Internal Revenue Service. Whether in litigation or transactional settings, the quality of a lawyer's advice depends on how well they can anticipate outcomes.

This conception of legal practice as the art of prediction is hardly new. In his seminal 1897 article "The Path of the Law," Oliver Wendell Holmes famously described the law as "systematized prediction"[43] and "the prophecies of what the courts will do in fact, and nothing more pretentious."[44] To Holmes, even basic assertions of legal rights require one to foresee court outcomes. For instance, for an individual to say

---

41 Estifanos Tilahun Mihret, "Lecture I – Introduction to Emerging Technologies" (presentation at the Computer Science Department, Mettu University, 2021) at 4.
42 See, e.g., Schauer, *supra* note 24 at 1935–40.
43 Oliver Wendell Holmes Jr, "The Path of the Law" (1897) 10 Harv L Rev 457 at 458.
44 *Ibid* at 460.

"I own property" is really for that individual to assert that they are confident that a future court will endorse their view of their own property rights.[45] The "prediction theory of law," as it came to be called, works on two levels. At the first level, it articulates a minimum standard of professional responsibility. A lawyer who merely advises the court of what the law says and advocates for the logical application of pre-existing rules is not doing a complete job. Instead, the responsible advocate advises their client of risks based on their sound appraisal of the likely distribution and incidence of negative outcomes, conditional on what the law ostensibly says.[46] At a second level, the prediction theory of law specifies what the content of the law *actually is*.[47] Laws are dense and, occasionally, take the form of over-inclusive statements; conceiving of law as consisting of the information that accurately facilitates prediction helps to separate signal from noise.

Understanding legal information as inputs into a prediction process allows us to think of it along a continuum of predictiveness, rather than in binary states of information/non-information. Schauer and Wise, by contrast, exclude content because of its form, even if that content is self-evidently about the law; for instance, a law review article by an American legal scholar counts as legal information, whereas an essay by the same scholar in the *Journal of Philosophy* or *Econometrica* would be considered non-legal information.[48] Identifying legal information by the extent of its predictiveness is attentive to the actual content of these texts rather than their site of publication. Thus, articles from publications outside the legal profession might well constitute valuable legal information, to the extent that they offer insights into how the law is likely to be interpreted, analysed, and applied. Given the trend towards more interdisciplinary legal scholarship, it is virtually certain that *some* of these sources will have explanatory capacity similar to a law review article.[49]

To help illustrate this point, consider the continuum in figure 2.1. Here, predictiveness generally tracks what we call "authoritativeness" in traditional legal analysis. At the far right of the continuum are the

---

45 *Ibid.*
46 *Ibid* at 467–70.
47 *Ibid* at 460.
48 Schauer & Wise, *supra* note 37 at 498–9.
49 See, e.g., William B Eldridge & Sally F Dennis, "The Computer as a Tool for Legal Research" (1963) 28:1 Law & Contemp Probs 78.

	Other	Non-legal interpretive sources	Legal interpretive sources	Secondary statements of law	Primary statements of law	
Less predictive						More predictive

Figure 2.1. Classifying sources as legal information based on predictiveness

texts we refer to as "primary statements of law": cases, statutes, regulations, and other documents that themselves have the force of law. In other words, these texts are authorities. Joseph Raz famously explained that authority is that which "requires one to let authoritative directives preempt one's own judgment."[50] Lawyers' analyses are usually correct only to the extent that they are consistent with these texts. Importantly, authoritativeness does not mean that the content of these texts is uncontested; indeed, it is in the nature of legal argument for lawyers to challenge the applicability of given authorities by construing the content of those authorities to their client's benefit. The second category, "secondary statements of law," comprises chiefly the type of content available in legal dictionaries, encyclopedias, restatements, and doctrinal treatises. The legal treatise best typifies this category; as Angela Fernandez and Markus Dubber explain, legal treatises are "methodical discussion or exposition" of specific legal principles, and, though decision makers are not bound to follow a given treatise's expression of the law, some have grown to have comparable influence to more authoritative legal information.[51] Herbert Hovenkamp's *Antitrust Law*, for instance, is a staple of US antitrust litigation, so much so that Justice Breyer said that advocates are better off having "two paragraphs of [the] treatise on their side than three Courts of Appeals or four Supreme Court justices."[52]

The next category, "legal interpretive sources," refers to texts that do not serve the principal aim of announcing the law but help to analyse and interpret its application and implications. Academic literature exemplifies this category, but it also includes works that might

---

50 Joseph Raz, "Introduction" in *Authority* (New York: New York University Press, 1990) at 5.

51 Angela Fernandez & Markus D Dubber, "Introduction: Putting the Legal Treatise in Its Place" in Angela Fernandez & Markus D Dubber, *Law Books in Action: Essays on the Anglo-American Legal Treatise* (Oxford: Hart Publishing, 2012).

52 Stephen Breyer et al, "In Memoriam, Phillip E Areeda" (1996) 109:5 Harv L Rev 889 at 890.

be traditionally viewed as treatises – such as, for example, *Corbin on Contracts* – that also serve the purpose of contextualizing and advancing a view of certain primary statements of law.[53] The fourth category, "non-legal interpretive sources," generally refers to materials such as scholarship from cognate disciplines that are known to influence legal analyses. The predictiveness of such texts depends highly on the context. In antitrust and competition law, for instance, the work of the "Chicago School"[54] – a group of highly influential economists at the University of Chicago – "shaped government enforcement" and even "came to shape Supreme Court doctrine" on notable antitrust matters, particularly cases that concerned predatory pricing, throughout the 1970s and 1980s.[55] Indeed, this subcategory of scholarship enabled courts to break from the historical case law.[56] In that specific context, the ordering of the predictiveness continuum is challenged; primary statements of law represent realities that are in flux, and the normative positions of scholars who are not making traditionally "authoritative" statements might better forecast court outcomes.

Note that the predictiveness continuum eschews the traditional characterizations of authority as "binding" or "persuasive." These traditional characterizations are too narrow to accommodate the many uses of legal information. As an initial matter, the language of binding /persuasive assumes legal information is being marshalled primarily for the benefit of an adjudicator. The profession includes many lawyers who do not typically appear before judges but nevertheless use their training to render advice, structure transactions, and provide other counsel outside the context of traditional litigation. These lawyers will want to rely on law that is binding but, because they are not principally tasked with constructing arguments, have less of an immediate interest in whether that text is persuasive.

The modern lawyer's task is not simply to read and recite the legal information they consult, of course. Even as they form the basis for arguments and the source material for legal advice, legal texts are interpreted according to the – occasionally imprecise – norms and customs of the legal profession.[57] Sources also vary in their authoritativeness. In

---

53 Friedrich Kessler at al, "Corbin on Contracts," Book Review of *A Comprehensive Treatise on the Rules of Contract Law* by Arthur Linton Corbin (1952) 61:6 Yale LJ 1092.

54 Herbert J. Hovenkamp & Fiona Scott Morton, "Framing the Chicago School of Antitrust Analysis" (2020) 168:7 U Pa L Rev 1843.

55 Lina M. Khan, "Amazon's Antitrust Paradox" (2017) 126:3 Yale LJ 710.

56 *Ibid* at 726–30.

57 Lawrence M Friedman, "Some Comments on Legal Interpretation" (1988) 9:1 Poetics 95.

the case of primary statements of law, authority tends to be easier to establish; common law lawyers observe the principles of *stare decisis*, while civil law lawyers recognize the primacy of the civil code.[58] Many jurisdictions maintain official case reports providing official versions of court decisions. For secondary legal information, such as treatises, there remain few-to-no identifiable rules for determining how authoritative one source may be over another, and even less guidance about whether courts will accept arguments based on secondary texts.[59] Instead, lawyers learn the appropriate cues through experience. Indeed, lawyers steeped in law's traditions know a credible source from one that, though it might contain the right information, is held in lower esteem by the professional community.[60]

III. Analogue, Digital, Computational

Legal information can be characterized as having three eras: analogue, digital, and computational. The analogue era describes a time as recently as twenty years ago in which legal research principally involved navigating the stacks of brick-and-mortar law libraries, perusing bounded, physical volumes. The second, the digital era, is best described as a "platforming" of analogue materials: hard-copy law library collections were digitized and collected in electronic databases. The result – computer-assisted legal research – enables legal researchers to find relevant sources by conducting keyword searches.[61] The history of the analogue and digital eras of legal research are important to recount because they demonstrate that, historically, legal information has been in the service of legal prediction.[62]

At the core, legal research is a quest for understanding what the law requires. The purposes for seeking this understanding are manifold.

---

58 H Campbell Black, "The Principle of Stare Decisis" (1852) 34:12 Am L Register 745; see also Jack Knight & Lee Epstein, "The Norm of Stare Decisis" (1996) 40:4 Am J Pol Sci 1018.

59 Schauer, *supra* note 24 at 1940–52.

60 See, e.g., Berring, "Legal Information," *supra* note 13 at 5.

61 William G Harrington, "What's Happening in Computer-Assisted Legal Research?" (1974) 60:8 ABA J 924; see also James A Sprowl, "Computer-Assisted Legal Research: An Analysis of Full-Text Document Retrieval Systems, Particularly the LEXIS System" (1976) 1:1 Am Bar Found Res J 175.

62 A version of this three-stage timeline was included in Benjamin Alarie, Anthony Niblett & Albert Yoon, "How Artificial Intelligence Will Affect the Practice of Law" (2018) 68:1 UTLJ 106.

It can be to guide planning in personal, government, and/or business contexts. In case of conflict, it can be to strive to adequately resolve issues between disputing parties, both for the judge and the litigants themselves. For academics, it can be simply to better understand the law. Or legal research may inform efforts to seek changes to law as an affected party out of private interest, or to explore possible changes as a maker of public policy. Whatever the reason for engaging in legal research, a central aspect of this work can be characterized as legal prediction leading to legal understanding.

Today, we are in the early days of the third era of legal information – the computational. Where the digital era merely platformed the same kind of information as was available in the analogue era, computational legal tools use artificial intelligence to synthesize abundant sources of legal information with great speed, low cost, and high accuracy. A key feature of this computational era has been the birth of predictive legal technology tools, which treat law as data and use statistical techniques to model likely outcomes based on sources of relevant legal information. The computational era is so important to the legal singularity that the entirety of the next chapter is dedicated to it. For now, we explore the history of the analogue and digital eras, to set the stage for the computational era discussion that follows.

a. The Analogue Era

As important legal information – such as judicial decisions and legislative acts – settled into published volumes, printed hard-copy materials earned a critical role in the practice of law. This period – which we call the analogue era – was characterized by brick-and-mortar libraries and the use of traditional research materials such as books, case reports, law journals, loose-leaf services, legal indices, and hard-bound legislation.

The books that were available to judges, lawyers, and litigants both enabled and constrained the scope of legal practice. Here, access to books was everything: lawyers with extensive collections had more information upon which to base their advice and advocacy.[63] But, like Abraham Lincoln, whose own practice of law was limited to however many books he was capable of "carrying on his horse," judges and lawyers were limited throughout the analogue era by the cases that they

---

63   *Ibid* at 113.

could access.[64] New, distinct problems arose when the number of such books began to grow. Writing in 1909 for the *Law Library Journal*, John B. West – the founder of Westlaw Publishing – explained the concerning situation:

> No one who has to do with the profession in connection with the purchase or use of books, can fail to notice the continual complaint of increasing cost, of lack of shelf room, of consuming citations and other complications arising from multiplicity of reports. The problem presents itself in an increasingly serious way from year to year as the number of courts and the number of decisions continually increase.[65]

In response, legal publishers developed techniques to centralize information and make materials more easily retrievable. Among them was the well-known West American Digest System, which even today forms the basic infrastructure of the Thomson Reuters–owned digital publishing giant Westlaw. Emerging in 1887, early versions of the system functioned like indexes, with digests organizing collections of "headnotes" – short abstracts outlining major points of law.[66] One of West's great contributions to the information environment of the law was the introduction of the Key Number System, a methodology that classified legal topics covered in case law into numbered categories and subtopics[67] (for example, 331k18 is the key number that refers to information about avoiding contractual releases for reasons of duress; the number 331 stands for the digest topic "Release," while the number 18 stands for the subtopic "Duress").

The value of these centralization efforts was considerable. To better understand the practice of law during the analogue era, imagine a criminal defence lawyer in 1968 New York working on a case reminiscent of *Entick*. Her client, an activist in the state's civil rights community, had his property searched by local police and was ultimately arrested for engaging in a criminal conspiracy. Our lawyer, with years of experience and training under her belt, quickly identifies the possibility that

---

64 Oliver Goodenough, "The State of the Art of Legal Technology Circa 2015" (keynote speech at Codex Future Law, 2015), online (video): YouTube (Stanford Law School) <https://youtu.be/peU756mYfjQ>.

65 John B West, "Multiplicity of Reports" (1909) 2 Law Libr'n J 4 at 4.

66 Olufunmilayo Arewa, "Open Access in a Closed Universe: Lexis, Westlaw, Law Schools, and the Legal Information Market" (2006) 10:4 Lewis & Clark L Rev 797 at 816.

67 Berring, "Legal Research," *supra* note 14 at 24–25.

the search may have been unconstitutional because of a defective warrant, and she wants to present these arguments at her client's upcoming hearing in federal court. She also knows that American courts adhere to the principle of *stare decisis* – the legal doctrine that binds courts to follow historical precedent when adjudicating similar cases.[68] For her arguments to be accepted by the court, she needs to support them with legal information.

Consider our lawyer's uphill battle. Her search for supporting legal information involves finding signals among a cacophony of background noise. This would have been both time consuming and expensive. As W. Ronald Robins observed about the United States *back in 1986*:

> The volume of jurisprudential reference material staggers the imagination. There are approximately 2.3 million reported cases, 1.5 million statutory sections, an untold number of administrative agency rulings and regulations. To this already formidable backlog of materials we are adding tens of thousands of new cases and statutes each year. The literature of law, along with the literature of most professions, has been caught up in a national "information explosion." Not only is the body of legal materials increasing at an alarming rate, but also the rate of increase is increasing.[69]

Our lawyer's first step, then, would be to consult a secondary source – either a legal encyclopedia or treatise with information about criminal law and criminal procedure. Ideally, these sources would direct her to more helpful primary material, such as a relevant case matching her client's situation. More likely than not, the encyclopedia or treatise would have pointed her to multiple cases that she would have to examine closely. Assuming she did not own an extensive personal library of case reporters, which, in 1968, would have cost a significant amount for just one copy of that year's federal volume,[70] she must venture to a law library to read the cases. Her task is further complicated by the amount of cross-referencing she would have to do to determine that the cases she is reading are still acceptable precedent and have not been superseded by conflicting cases or new legislation.

---

68 Schauer, *supra* note 24 at 1940.
69 W Ronald Robins, "Automated Legal Information Retrieval" (1986) 5 Hous L Rev 691 at 691.
70 Patrick E Kehoe, "A Beginning Level Library Collection of United States Law" (1976) 3:4/6 Revista Chilena de Derecho 233 at 237–9.

Only once she has confirmed that the cases that she would like to reference meet this minimum standard will she then proceed to the heavy lifting of determining how the law is interpreted and applied in those cases and whether they serve her client's best arguments. Imagine that our lawyer, a skilled researcher, finds two recent cases – a 1961 case called *Klein* from the Southern District of New York and a well-known 1961 case from the Supreme Court of the United States called *Mapp* – upon which she could argue for the defectiveness of the search warrant.[71] Armed with those cases and some more general research about requirements for federal search warrants, she presents her arguments in court. Even assuming her arguments are persuasive on their own merits, our lawyer must hope that her opposing counsel, the relatively well-resourced federal government, did not have such superior access to case law that they were able to identify case law that clearly contradicted *Klein* and *Mapp*. Given the number and complexity of the steps involved in the lawyer's research and the exponential growth of relevant legal material, it is not hard to imagine just how drawn out the process could become. Our lawyer's ability to accurately and confidently forecast the case's outcome for her client is necessarily limited by the legal informational tools available to her.

b. The Digital Era

Just as lawyers suffered the high costs of legal research in the analogue era, so too did legal publishers. Supplying a constant stream of lengthy printed material that required the investment of time and energy by various legal professionals (e.g., judges, lawyers, academics) was expensive during this period.[72] It remains quite expensive today, too: in 2017, *Maclean's* reported that the average cost of books for a student in a law program was over CA\$850.[73] Although law libraries during the analogue era aimed to house as many relevant materials as possible for their patrons, printing, shipping, and storing bound materials required significant resources.[74] The fact that the market for law books was effectively limited to law students, lawyers, and academics all but

---

71 *Pugach v Klein*, 193 F. Supp. 630 (1961); *Mapp v Ohio*, 367 U.S. 643 (1961).
72 Arewa, *supra* note 66 at 802–4.
73 Mark Brown, "The Heavy Cost of Books, by School and by Program," *Maclean's* (4 December 2017), online: <https://www.macleans.ca/education/most-expensive-books/>.
74 Morris L Cohen, "Computerizing Legal Research" (1973) 14:1 Jurimetrics 3.

guaranteed that prices would be high and inflexible. As a result, access to the best and most up-to-date material was reserved for those wealthy enough to afford it – which often meant private law schools and the wealthiest lawyers and firms.

The next stage, the digital era, was marked by the development of legal research tools that harnessed the power of what we would today consider basic computing. The emergence of online databases like Westlaw and Lexis (whose development we discuss later in this section), beginning in the 1970s, created opportunities for faster and potentially more economical legal research.[75] These developments were consistent with rapid change across all information-heavy industries, as everything from banking to manufacturing to aviation developed new processes around storing, retrieving, and processing information using computers. At the same time, all corners of the legal profession grappled with how best to present and navigate the explosion of legal information that occurred towards the end of the analogue era. By the middle of the 1970s, mass commercial digital legal research technology was available. Instead of sifting through endless stacks of books in the library for hours and hours, lawyers soon had at their fingertips all that text and could search through it using computers in minutes.[76]

One of the first efforts to digitize legal research was Robert Morgan's "points of law" method, developed in 1957.[77] Morgan, a business law professor at Oklahoma State University, attempted to index all legal information. His approach involved surveying an entire field of law – like torts, for instance – and assigning a unique code to each legal concept (i.e., the "point of law") in the field. The concept of *trespass*, as an example, would have a unique code number. Morgan would code all legal materials about trespass with the same number. A user, then, could navigate to the index, find the code number for trespass, and review all material associated with that coded number. Morgan's system enabled searches for the point of law by name or code number.[78] Morgan predicted that his

---

75 Robert J Munro, JA Bolanos & Jon May, "Lexis v. Westlaw: An Analysis of Computer-ized Research" (1979) 65:2 ABA J 269.

76 See, e.g., Katrina Fischer Kuh, "Electronically Manufactured Law" (2008) 22:1 Harv JL & T 223 at 241–6 for a comparison of analogue and digital research processes.

77 Allen Harris, "Judicial Decision Making and Computers," (1967) 12:2 Vill L Rev 272 at 283; see also John C. Lyons "New Frontiers of the Legal Technique" (1962) 3:4 MULL Mod Uses Logic L 256 at 256–67.

78 Robert T Morgan, "The 'Point of Law' Approach" (paper delivered at the Special Committee of Electronic Data Retrieval, 1961) (1962) 3:1 MULL Mod Uses Logic L 44 at 46.

computerized legal research would have two dramatic effects on the legal profession. First, he believed that simple retrievability of legal information would encourage settlement. In his view, parties litigated disputes in part due to disagreements about the content of the law, which could well be caused by differential access to vital legal information.[79] Second, he believed that computerized legal research would improve the quality of lawyering. "[I]f both sides have all the law, and the courts of record can obtain this information gratis," Morgan explained, "then the person who relies solely on his personality and his opponent's reluctance to do thorough research would be out of business."[80] To Morgan, the points-of-law approach promised to help legal practice become more about the legal merits of a dispute and less about a lawyer's individual charisma or resources.[81]

We invite readers to keep Morgan's predictions in mind. As this book progresses, we will explain how and why these predictions have remained merely hypothetical even to this day but are likely to materialize during the computational stage of legal information. Morgan's own efforts were cut short by his untimely death in 1962, just as he planned to develop computerized tools for comparing legislative changes.[82] Scholars have suggested that Morgan's points-of-law approach, if further developed, would likely have accelerated the onset of computational legal tools.[83]

Morgan's efforts were not the only early significant moves towards computerizing legal research. John Horty of the University of Pittsburgh, widely considered a pioneer in the application of computers to legal research, developed a sophisticated computerized system for retrieving health laws from across the United States.[84] Horty's work was prompted by his frustration with traditional research methods, which he found to be unhelpful for cross-jurisdictional statutory work.[85] His solution was an elegant one: with his team, he developed

---

79 *Ibid* at 47.
80 *Ibid* at 47–8.
81 *Ibid* at 47–8.
82 Robert A Wilson, "Minutes of the Annual Meeting of the Special Committee on Electronic Data Retrieval of the American Bar Association August 8, 1962" (1962) 3:4 MULL Mod Uses Logic L 267 at 267–9.
83 See, e.g., Eldridge & Dennis, *supra* note 49 at 86; Anatole Jarmolych, *A Computerized Interactive System for the Retrieval of Case Law* (Master of Science Thesis, MIT, 1969) [unpublished] at 51.
84 Robins, *supra* note 69 at 708.
85 John F Horty, "The 'Key Words in Combination' Approach" (1962) 3:1 MULL Mod Uses Logic L 54 at 55.

keyword searching using natural language. Statutes were typed into computers verbatim and recorded on magnetic tape.[86] To perform a search in this system, a lawyer would come up with all the words they wanted to appear in the search results. Unlike modern keyword searching, the lawyer would need to manually enter all permutations of the words, including plurals and alternate spellings, as well as synonyms. A specially created thesaurus would aid the lawyer in this task. Similar work was being undertaken in Canada throughout the period. Two examples include the University of Montreal's DATUM (Documentation automatique des textes juridiques de l'Université de Montreal) project, which boasted a bilingual legal database of around 140 million characters of case law, and Queen's University's QUIC/LAW (an acronym for Queen's University Institute for Computing and Law). The latter project, a partnership with IBM, used statistical probabilities "and used term weighting as a basis for selection and output relevance ranking."[87] The system displayed the results in order by relevance, putting the most relevant results first. QUIC/Law, which later became QL Systems, was ultimately purchased by LexisNexis in 2002.[88]

Throughout this period, members of the legal profession were calling for more computerization of legal information. Morgan's points-of-law approach, Horty's work at the University of Pittsburgh, the DATUM Project, and QUIC/LAW are simply examples of an emerging movement in the legal profession towards meaningful computerization. The movement was an intellectual one, too; as early as 1963, members of the profession were debating design principles for computerized research tools and theorizing about the prospective impact of these emergent techniques. A 1963 article in the interdisciplinary legal journal *Law and Contemporary Problems* by William B. Eldridge of the American Bar Foundation and Sally F. Dennis of IBM shows most clearly how ambitious this movement was.[89] Eldridge and Dennis, observing that legal information was growing in volume, articulated a set of five characteristics for the "ideal law-finding system."[90] First, they proposed that the ideal system would be language-based, rather than subject-based. Second, it would have a built-in capacity "for automatic, large-scaled

---

86 *Ibid* at 56–8.
87 Charles Bourne & Trudi Bellardo Hahn, *A History of Online Information Services, 1963–1976* (Cambridge, MA: MIT Press, 2003) at 313.
88 *Ibid*.
89 Eldridge & Dennis, *supra* note 49.
90 *Ibid* at 94–5.

reorganization and updating."[91] Third, the ideal system would accommodate a wide variety of possible searching strategies. Fourth, Eldridge and Dennis proposed that the ideal system should aid the user by filling in potential blanks in research. Fifth, the ideal system should have the capability to perform semantic and syntactical analysis to clarify the meaning of legal texts. Eldridge and Dennis hypothesized that the system would develop a sense of the meaning of the words by "reading" extensively, writing that the system "cannot know anything about a word that it has seen only once, but as it experiences the word repeatedly in different contexts, it begins to 'catch on' to its meaning."[92] Readers who are familiar with artificial intelligence techniques will recognize that Eldridge and Dennis were describing – perhaps unwittingly – a form of what we would today call natural language processing.

IV. The New Information Environment

a. Impact of Digitalization

These developments – early as they were – laid the foundation for the transition from paper-based, analogue materials to computerized legal research. In addition to the self-evident ways in which digital legal research made the mechanical process of information retrieval easier, the predominance of digital research databases had at least four major impacts: (1) increased expectations; (2) a new relationship to legal precedent; (3) an improved capacity to make legal predictions; and (4) improved public engagement with case law.

To elaborate, first, along with computerization came increased expectations. Good lawyering meant good, thorough legal research, and clients grew to expect that their lawyers would be using electronic resources to maximize their effectiveness. Law firms benefited from these greater expectations, too. As Robert C. Berring explains, Westlaw, Lexis, and other digital research databases promoted their products to firms as "disbursable" – in other words, chargeable to clients.[93] Unlike the ability to read and comprehend books, which was rightly viewed as a minimum competency that lawyers could not use to distinguish themselves from other lawyers (or charge their clients extra for),

---

91 *Ibid* at 95.
92 *Ibid* at 99.
93 Robert C Berring, "Chaos, Cyberspace and Tradition: Legal Information Transmogrified" (1997) 12:1 BTLJ 189 at 197.

digital research tools enabled firms to market themselves as technologically savvy or particularly adept at navigating the new information environment.

Second, lawyers' relationship to legal authorities changed significantly due to the inundation of digital legal information. Prior to the advent of computerized legal research, lawyers were making arguments based on relatively sparse precedent and from first legal principles. This required a lot of skill: given that advocates on both sides of an issue were working with the same core cases, there was a premium placed on a well-crafted argument. As digital tools enabled lawyers to find more case law, it became considerably easier to identify helpful (and unhelpful) precedent, and the new, higher-resolution search functionality enabled lawyers to select for specific facts and case outcomes. This became especially true in areas of law with frequent litigation: a personal injury lawyer, for instance, would be much more likely to find a helpful case matching their client's injury in the digital than the analog era, when resource and information constraints might have forced them to analogize from more general negligence cases.

Some scholars question whether increased case-law access was a net benefit to the profession. Berring, for instance, explains that the availability of more precedents might have created the unintended consequence of undermining precedent altogether.[94] Take, for instance, the ability of digital-era lawyers to find cases by searching for keywords in a research database. To Berring, this makes it more likely that researchers will obtain a given legal text without a sense of where it fits into a broader legal-epistemological structure. The classification and indexing systems of old, by contrast, forced researchers to understand where a given text sat in its broader doctrinal and conceptual context. In Berring's view, the equal retrievability of important and unimportant cases without context "dilutes the authority of the cases that really do matter."[95] M. Ethan Katsh makes a similar argument: prior to digital research tools, the legal profession was invested in the helpful myth of law's structure, which is less possible in an information environment where numerous cases stand for the same proposition and are effectively treated like data points.[96]

---

94 Robert C Berring, "The Heart of Legal Information: The Crumbling Infrastructure of Legal Research" in Richard A Danner & Frank G Houdek, eds, *Legal Information and the Development of American Law* (St Paul: Thomson/West, 2007) 272 at 289.

95 *Ibid.*

96 M Ethan Katsh, "Communications Revolutions and Legal Revolutions: The New Media and the Future of Law" (1984) 8 Nova LJ 631 at 658–9.

But as Berring[97] and Katsh[98] acknowledge, the notion that law fits neatly into the categories available in the analogue-era indexes is itself an overstatement, if not an outright myth. Analogue-era research tools – and many digital databases, in fact – presume a greater degree of structure than is inherent to the law.[99] Granted, the suggestion of structure serves a valuable communication purpose: categories act as information signals by suggesting a degree of sameness between information in the category and discontinuity from information outside of it. However, treating categories as strict, bounded boxes understates the fuzziness inherent in law's conceptual boundaries. To the extent that keyword searching extracts legal information from its nested categories, it does so with specific reference to the *content* of a given text. A researcher looking for case law clarifying interpretive rules for proximate cause, for instance, can do so by searching for the terms most likely to appear as part of the analysis. Researchers then use the profession's interpretive resources to situate the legal text. The rules of *stare decisis* demand that the researcher "zoom out" from the case, so to speak, and consider the relevant procedural posture and the decision's positionality in the wider universe of precedent. To the extent that Berring's and Katsh's critiques are motivated by concern that the ease of digital information retrieval through keyword searching will make researchers less attentive to the broader context of the legal information that these searches yield, the profession's own research standards act as a sufficient backstop.

In addition to raising research expectations and changing lawyers' relationship to precedent, we note a third impact of computerized legal research: an improved capacity to make predictions. Taking the Holmesian view, forecasting case outcomes not only characterizes the practice of the law, but defines its content and parameters, as well.[100] With the advent of computerized legal research, the universe of possible case law would be knowable to litigating parties. Whereas in the analogue era, lawyers' differential access to physical texts meant that advocates might bring entirely different precedents to a dispute, comprehensive digital legal databases made it much more likely that lawyers – and,

---

97   Robert C Berring, "Collapse of the Structure of the Legal Research Universe: The Imperative of Digital Information" (1994) 69:1 Wash L Rev 9 at 14.

98   M Ethan Katsh, "Law in a Digital World: Computer Networks and Cyberspace" (1992) 38:2 Vill L Rev 403 at 405 [Katsh, "Law in a Digital World"].

99   *Ibid.*

100 See generally Martin P Golding, *Legal Reasoning, Legal Theory and Rights* (London: Routledge, 2007).

indeed, judges – would come across the same precedent. For a lawyer trying to predict a case outcome, this meant a reduced chance of a case being decided based on precedents that they would be unaware of. This is a long-held aspiration. Then US Assistant Attorney General Lee Loevinger advocated for computerized legal research precisely for this reason, writing in 1963 that computer case repositories would provide "somewhat greater assurance in forecasting the judicial decision than if ... [the lawyer] must take account of the possibility that the judge has discovered a different set of precedents than the lawyer was aware of when presenting the case."[101] Though parties having increased access to equal precedents might make prediction an easier task than it would have been in a pure physical text–based system, the quality of those predictions will still depend on lawyers' ability to synthesize the sources and reconcile that data against their knowledge of judges' historical decision-making. It turns out that technological developments now make such prediction possible without over-relying on individuals' limited forecasting abilities – more on this later.

Fourth, digital legal research databases created conditions for increased public engagement with legal information. Yet, as we discuss in the next section, this information has not always been easily accessible and tends to live behind expensive, subscription-based paywalls. Nevertheless, the digitization efforts discussed above made it such that some predictive legal information could be found on the internet, including in not-for-profit databases such as Justicia and the Cornell Legal Information Institute (LII). As we discuss in the next section, the online nature of this information has also led to questions about trustworthiness and veracity that the legal profession must address to improve access to justice.

b. Access to Data and Access to Justice

The shift from the analogue era to the digital era was an obvious advancement. But the current state of access to legal information remains, in a word, abysmal. Some of the barriers that existed during the analogue era remain, and legal information is expensive to access and exceedingly difficult for non-professionals to interpret.[102] The difference now is that there is no longer an excuse for these limitations.

---

101   Lee Loevinger, "Jurimetrics: The Methodology of Legal Inquiry" (1963) 28:1 L and Contemp Probs 5 at 34.
102   Arewa, *supra* note 66 at 828–36.

When law was contained in bounded, physical volumes, the profession could justify its limited distribution by referencing the logistical challenges in disseminating the information. Today, there is no such barrier to open access, except unwillingness – unwillingness on the part of governments to make access widespread, but also unwillingness on the part of the legal profession to prioritize access to information and agitate for it.

Few governments in common law jurisdictions make complete collections of legal information widely available. Among primary statements of law, only statutes and regulations are presumptively accessible, though often on government websites that are difficult to search and outdated, compared to modern webpages.[103] Case-law data can be especially difficult to access. The United States provides one particularly byzantine example. State court decisions are released at the discretion of individual courts.[104] Predictably, this has led to absurd results: in Florida and Texas, for instance, case law from courts in one county might be posted on a webpage, whereas case documents from another court in a neighbouring county are available only in paper form and upon request. The result is that those with the resources to do the legwork of retrieving the case data will tend to have the most robust collections. Unsurprisingly, lawyers seeking completeness have few alternatives other than the traditional legal information giants like Lexis and Westlaw.

The stakes of inadequate access to legal information are high. As Deborah L. Rhode observed, adversarial litigation systems are built on the assumption of symmetry between parties, including equal access to information.[105] Lawyers without access cannot zealously advocate for their clients and, as we discussed above, are in a poor position to predict case outcomes. Self-represented litigants are even further behind and face the double uncertainty of navigating complexity and incompleteness.

Even outside the dispute-resolution context, open access to legal information is a necessary precondition to a well-functioning legal system.

---

103   Daniel Martin Katz, Ron Dolin & Michael Bommarito, *Legal Informatics* (Cambridge: Cambridge University Press, 2021) at 478–80.

104   See generally Melissa M Serfass & Jessie L Cranford, "Federal and State Court Rules Governing Publication and Citation of Opinions" (2001) 3:1 J Appellate Practice and Procedure 251.

105   Deborah L Rhode, "Legal Ethics in an Adversary System: The Persistent Questions" (2006) 34:3 Hofstra L Rev 641 at 649.

Peter W. Martin identifies five justifications for open access to law: (1) to assure fairness in judicial proceedings; (2) to ensure that the public can engage in informed discussion and criticism of "government affairs"; (3) to foster "public education about, and confidence in, the functioning of the legal system"; (4) to allow for the public to check the judiciary; and (5) to provide "an outlet for 'community concern, hostility and emotion' in cases that are in the public eye."[106] Taken together, these five justifications have a common theme: open access promotes healthy scrutiny of, and engagement with, the legal process. Yet neither legislatures nor courts themselves have made open access a priority. Even data that are made electronically available to the public have unnecessary barriers. The Public Access to Court Electronic Records platform (PACER) in the United States, for instance, electronically compiles all federal court filings but requires that users pay to access many of the documents.[107]

Even if enterprising researchers succeed in getting their hands on scarce rare structured legal data (e.g., court statistics), these data are plagued by further limitations, usually the result of the judiciary's protectionist impulses. For instance, University of Toronto law professor Albert Yoon contends that "courts have been loath to link the identities of their judges to their decisions."[108] Consider the example of the US Federal Judicial Center's (FJC)'s Integrated Data Base (IDB), a public repository of data about civil and criminal cases. The FJC has declined to associate judges' identities with their decision records. Consequently, researchers are prevented from "analyzing the data to observe how differences in case outcomes vary by individual judge."[109] This aversion to scrutiny is not unlike the reaction to judicial analytics in France, wherein Article 33 of the French *Justice Reform Act* made it a criminal offence to use "personally identifiable data concerning judges ... with the purpose or result of evaluating, analyzing, or predicting their actual or supposed professional practices."[110] Violating the ban on judicial analytics in France carries a penalty of up to five years' imprisonment.

---

106   Peter W Martin, "Online Access to Court Records: From Documents to Data, Particulars to Patterns" (2008) Cornell Legal Studies Research Paper No 08-003 at 2.
107   *Ibid.*
108   A Yoon, "Technological Challenges Facing the Judiciary," in David Freeman Engstrom, ed, *Legal Tech and the Future of Civil Justice* (Cambridge: Cambridge University Press, 2023) (forthcoming).
109   *Ibid.*
110   Jason Tashea, "France Bans Publishing of Judicial Analytics and Prompts Criminal Penalty," *ABA Journal* (7 June 2019), online: <https://www.abajournal.com/news/article/france-bans-and-creates-criminal-penalty-for-judicial-analytics>.

c. An Open Source Movement?

Given that modern barriers to accessing legal information are largely the result of deliberate policy choices and not technological or logistical constraints, it seems like little will change unless attitudes do. Indeed, the predominance of Lexis and Westlaw depends almost entirely on legislative inaction. As numerous scholars have observed, legislatures can fund digitization and open access, but simply choose not to.[111] Judiciaries are also capable of releasing court data – particularly docket data – but have not made a concerted effort to do so in a way that promotes access and easy retrieval. Olufunmilayo Arewa tracks the absurd results that this state of play occasionally produces: the same Ohio Bar Association that developed the public interest automation project that would go on to birth Lexis has recently partnered with digital database Casemaker to provide a lower-cost legal research alternative to – among others – Lexis.[112]

Throughout common law jurisdictions, open access databases following the Legal Information Institute (LII) model have emerged (such as the Canadian Legal Information Institute and the British and Irish Legal Information Institute).[113] Similarly, projects aimed at promoting access for academic researchers, like the Harvard Caselaw Access Project (CAP), have improved the information environment. There are limits, however; the Harvard CAP data are prohibited for commercial use, and eligible researchers must obey the terms of a collaboration agreement with a company recently purchased by LexisNexis.[114]

In any case, none of these important efforts have been successful in inculcating the open access ethos that the legal profession sorely needs. Bottom-up pressure from those who wish to gain access to legal data – namely technologists, academic researchers, and public-interest organizations – continues to put the onus on legislators. In the meantime, however, researchers have made advances even within the constrained information environment. We turn to the advent and rise of computational law in the next chapter.

---

111 Arewa, *supra* note 66 at 834–5.
112 *Ibid* at 835.
113 *Ibid* at 837.
114 "About: Caselaw Access Project," n.d., online: <https://case.law/about/>.

Chapter Three

The Computational Era in Legal Information

I. Introduction

As we discussed in chapter 2, the advent of digital research databases enabled the legal profession to move from the analogue era (characterized by physical texts and bricks-and-mortar libraries) into the digital era (characterized by the use of personal computers for information retrieval). Though this change has had substantial impact on lawyers' and researchers' practices, the chief contribution of the digital era was the creation of new mechanisms for distributing legal information. While the digital era did bring down the cost of production of new legal information, the change from the analogue to the digital era was, by and large, one of translation. The information already existed: civil codes, constitutions, case law, treatises, statutes, regulations, conventions, and other legal texts were simply made available through digital technologies and on digital displays to readers who no longer had to consult physical bound volumes.

Today's stage, the computational era, promises to create new kinds of legal knowledge and information by leveraging further advances in computing power. Where the digital era merely *platformed* the same material as was available in the analogue years, computational legal tools harness more complex computing and statistical techniques to perform functions that go beyond mere information retrieval. Artificial intelligence methods such as machine learning (ML) and natural language processing (NLP) have enabled technology to perform some of the creative, intellectual work traditionally associated with lawyering, such as gleaning insights from otherwise difficult-to-parse judicial decisions and constructing new legal arguments. Perhaps most fundamentally, computational legal methods enable legal prediction, allowing lawyers to access answers to legal questions without expensive and laborious legal research.[1] The computational era and its products and services – what an emerging group of scholars have termed *computational law*[2] – provide an early indication of the sorts of innovations most likely to bring about the legal singularity.

For the legal profession, the advent of legal computation means significant short-term changes in at least two key respects. First, as lawyers continue to absorb these tools in their practice, they can offer improved legal services at higher speed, with lower costs to their clients, and with increased accuracy. Far from making lawyers redundant, these tools can function to "supercharge" lawyers' capacity, removing the tediousness associated with information retrieval and freeing up time to work on more value-added tasks (e.g., strategy). Second, and perhaps more importantly, computational legal tools bring about significant opportunities for social progress. As technology makes it easier to *know* precisely what the law is on a given legal issue without having to retain specialized professional experience, individuals will have a stronger sense of their legal rights and obligations. In the longer run, computational methods promise to profoundly alter lawyers' and judges' relationship to the law, including by introducing new modes of legal analysis through computability. For the broader public, computational legal prediction makes the law more accessible and knowable, so individuals can have an enhanced sense of their legal rights and obligations, with minimum uncertainty.

In this chapter, we outline the theory and practice of computational law. The chapter proceeds in two parts. First, we begin by demystifying artificial intelligence and describing the techniques that predominate in legal technology: machine learning and natural language processing. Second, we describe what we mean by computational law and analyse the specific ways that computational legal tools are impacting – and will continue to impact – our laws and legal institutions, by turning our law from indefinite, uncertain standards to highly query-able systems of rules.

II. Understanding Artificial Intelligence

Anyone who has ever contemplated artificial intelligence (AI) knows that it is notoriously difficult to define. Bertram Raphael, a co-creator

---

1 See, e.g., "Intelligent Diagramming & Research | Blue J," n.d., online: <https://www.bluej.com/>; Alexsei, online: <https://www.alexsei.com>.
2 Daniel Martin Katz & JB Ruhl, "Measuring, Monitoring and Managing Legal Complexity" (2015) 101:191 Iowa L Rev 191 at 243.

of the "A* search algorithm,"[3] famously derided the term AI as "a collective name for problems which we do not yet know how to solve properly by computer."[4] Though somewhat tongue-in-cheek, Raphael's contention reflected a common view that AI seems to be a catch-all term for computers performing complicated functions. In some ways, the simplest definition was among the first: John McCarthy reportedly explained AI as "machines that behave as though they were intelligent" in 1955.[5] Yet even this oft-cited definition feels unsatisfactory. After all, the most basic personal computers were able, just a few decades later, to perform complex tasks widely seen as "intelligent."

To date, there is no consensus definition of AI. In some ways, the lack of a coherent definition could very well have been a positive thing for innovation: developments as divergent as email-filtering functionality[6] and aircraft-piloting software[7] are encompassed under AI's big tent and have attracted attention and investment in large part due to popular interest in anything AI-related. But the lack of a consensus has made AI developments harder to track and their social implications harder to assess. As Latanya Sweeney explains in a review of AI scholarship, some of the leading texts have taken different views of what AI means.[8] The implications are not merely academic: Krafft et al observe that, absent definitions of which technologies fit under the AI umbrella, policymaking and regulatory implementation can suffer.[9] Regulators may be prone to implement over- or under-inclusive rules that can

---

3 James W Davis & Jeff Hachtel, "A* Search: What's in a Name?" (2020) 63:1 Communications of the ACM 36 at 36–7; see also PE Hart, NJ Nilsson & B Raphael, "A Formal Basis for the Heuristic Determination of Minimum Cost Paths" (1968) 4:2 IEEE Transactions on Systems Science and Cybernetics 100.

4 Donald Michie, "Formation and Execution Plans by Machine," in NV Findler & B Meltzer, eds, *Artificial Intelligence and Heuristic Programming* (New York: American Elsevier, 1971) at 101.

5 Wolfgang Ertel, *Introduction to Artificial Intelligence: Undergraduate Topics in Computer Science* (London: Springer, 2011) at 1 [Ertel, *Introduction to Artifiical Intelligence*].

6 See generally Emmanuel Gbenga Dada et al, "Machine Learning for Email Spam Filtering: Review, Approaches and Open Research Problems" (2019) 5:6 Heliyon 5.

7 See generally Haitham Baomar & Peter J Bentley, "Autonomous Flight Cycles and Extreme Landings of Airliners beyond the Current Limits and Capabilities Using Artificial Neural Networks" (2021) 51:9 Applied Intelligence 6349.

8 Latanya Sweeney, *That's AI? A History and Critique of the Field* (PhD Dissertation, Carnegie Mellon University, 2003) [unpublished].

9 Krafft et al, "Defining AI in Policy Versus Practice" (paper delivered at Proceedings of the AAAI/ACM Conference on AI, Ethics, and Society, New York, 2020).

Machines that **think** like humans	Machines that **think** rationally
Machines that **act** like humans	Machines that **act** rationally

Figure 3.1. Four approaches to AI

discourage continued progress or, more importantly, fail to sufficiently protect the public from AI-related risks (e.g., data privacy).

A broad look at the history of AI literature reveals some patterns. Rather than settle on a single, overarching definition, Russell and Norvig suggest that there are four AI "approaches" under which most scholarly definitions appear.[10] Figure 3.1 illustrates the four approaches.

The first approach (in the upper left quadrant of the matrix) involves machines *thinking* in a humanlike way. This approach is characterized by AI technologies that model human cognition and reasoning and approximate the steps that an intelligent individual might take to solve a problem. Newell and Simon's 1959 computer program GPS (General Problem Solver),[11] as an early example, was "more concerned with comparing the trace of its reasoning steps to traces of human subjects solving the same problems" than with necessarily solving the problems correctly.[12]

A second, related approach (in the lower left quadrant of the matrix) involves machines *acting* in a humanlike way. This approach measures the relative success or failure of a given AI tool against an individual's performance of the same cognitive task. Put differently, if the AI can perform the task in *largely the same manner* as the individual, it is intelligent. Alan Turing famously proposed what has come to be known as the "Turing Test"[13] for these sorts of machines: "A computer passes the test if a human interrogator, after posing some written questions, cannot tell whether the written responses come from a person or from

---

10 Stuart J Russell & Peter Norvig, *Artificial Intelligence: A Modern Approach* (Upper Saddle River: Pearson Education Publishers, 2016) at 1–3.

11 Herbert A Simon & Allen Newell, "Computer Simulation of Human Thinking and Problem Solving" (1962) 27:2 Monographs of the Society for Research in Child Development 137, online: <https://doi.org/10.2307/1165535>.

12 Russell & Norvig, *supra* note 10 at 3.

13 James H Moor, "An Analysis of the Turing Test" (1976) 30:4 Philosophical Studies: An International Journal for Philosophy in the Analytic Tradition 24, online: <https://www.jstor.org/stable/4319091>.

a computer."[14] Arthur Samuel's checkers-playing program on the IBM 701 was successful, for instance, because it played competitively against a human being.[15] Central to the "acting humanlike" approach is the desire to approximate human behavioural characteristics, but not necessarily optimize performance. Indeed, much like the "thinking humanlike" approach, the "acting humanlike" approach to AI does not aspire to exceed – or even necessarily improve – the limits of what humans are capable of. AI technologies that are built to think and act humanlike are generally those that are designed to interact with people on a regular basis.[16] It is no surprise, then, that nascent humanlike applications are highly concentrated in customer-facing industries, such as the chatbots that are increasingly appearing on retailers' websites.[17]

Some technology futurists anticipate legal AI that thinks *and* acts humanlike. The phenomenon of the "robot lawyer" or "robot judge," for instance, has pervaded the recent literature.[18] Some of the most critical accounts depict the robot lawyer as a dystopian figure that performs the tasks of the lawyer, but with none of the affect or normative concern.[19] Yet, in reality, modern legal technologies fall under the third AI approach (in the upper right quadrant of the matrix): machines thinking rationally. This approach assumes that the kind of manoeuvres that a human brain is capable of are representable as a set of rules and axioms. As mathematician Alfred Tarski wrote in 1936:

Complicated mental processes are entirely reducible to such simple activities as the attentive observation of statements previously accepted

14 Russell & Norvig, *supra* note 10 at 3.
15 Peggy Aldrich Kidwell, "Playing Checkers with Machines: From Ajeeb to Chinook" (2015) 50:4 Information & Culture 578, online: <https://www.jstor.org/stable/44667604>.
16 Russell & Norvig, *supra* note 10.
17 Alexandra Rese, Lena Ganster & Daniel Baier, "Chatbots in Retailers' Customer Communication: How to Measure Their Acceptance?" Journal of Retailing and Consumer Services 56 (September 2020): 102176, online: <https://doi.org/10.1016/j.jretconser.2020.102176>.
18 See, e.g., Dana Remus & Frank Levy, "Can Robots Be Lawyers?" 30 Geo J Leg Ethics 501; Andrea Roth, "Trial by Machine" (2016) 104 Geo LJ 1245; G Marchant & J Covey, "Robo-Lawyers: Your New Best Friend or Your Worst Nightmare?" (2018) 45:1 Litigation 27, online: <https://www.jstor.org/stable/27041994>.
19 See, e.g., Robert F Weber, "Will the 'Legal Singularity' Hollow Out Law's Normative Core?" (2020) 27 Mich Tech L Rev 97; Frank A Pasquale, "The Resilient Fragility of Law" in Simon Deakin & Christopher Markou, eds, *Is Law Computable? Critical Perspectives on Law and Artificial Intelligence* (Oxford: Hart Publishing, 2020).

as true, the perception of structural, purely external connections among these statements, and the execution of mechanical transformations as pre-scribed by the rules of inference.[20]

Take, as one example, a simple syllogism. Knowing that all current justices of the Supreme Court of Canada are lawyers, and that Justice Mahmud Jamal serves on the Supreme Court of Canada, an expert system designed to think rationally will logically derive that Justice Jamal is a lawyer. So long as the premises are correct, the conclusion is necessarily also correct.[21] Advances in logic have made more complex derivations possible, as logicians have developed increasingly granu-lar notations for all kinds of information in the world. These notations make it possible to describe problems to computer programs, which can then use various unfalsifiable derivation rules to arrive at conclusions. Crucially, where the "thinking humanlike" and "acting humanlike" approaches accept the limitations of human cognition and capacity, the "thinking rationally" approach aspires to ideal performance. Thus, AI technologies in this category might not reason in a manner famil-iar to humans; indeed, the processes for synthesizing information and answering questions might be unfamiliar to humans who are ill-accus-tomed to thinking in such formal steps.

The fourth and final AI approach (in the bottom right quadrant of the matrix) involves machines acting rationally, also known in the literature as the "rational-agent approach."[22] Much like the "thinking rationally" approach, the rational-agent approach aspires to ideal performance, but recognizes that rationality involves much more than making cor-rect inferences. For instance, what should an AI do in situations where there is incomplete information, thus making essential factual prem-ises uncertain? Similarly, what should an AI do in situations where an inference is not *provably* correct? Here, the rational-agent approach accommodates modes of reasoning that are not necessarily based on inferences. For instance, consider Russell and Norvig's example of

---

20 Alfred Tarski, *Introduction to Logic and to the Methodology of Deductive Science*, Dover ed (New York: Dover Publications, 1995) at 49.

21 Jan Von Plato "Kurt Gödel's First Steps in Logic: Formal Proofs in Arithmetic and Set Theory Through a System of Natural Deduction" (2018) 24:3 *Bulletin of Symbolic Logic* 319, online: <https://www.jstor.org/stable/26511367>.

22 Russell & Norvig, *supra* note 10 at 4. See also Muhammed Akif Agca, Sebastien Faye & Djamel Khadraoui, "A Survey on Trusted Distributed Artificial Intelligence" (2022) 10 *IEEE Access* 55308, online: <https://doi.org/10.1109/access.2022.3176385>.

an individual pulling her hand away from a hot stove.[23] The thinking rationally approach might prescribe thoughtful deliberation, but her ostensibly unconscious reflex to pull her hand away might be the optimal behaviour in minimizing her risk of being seriously burned. Her reflex action is, of course, rational: it accounts for certain information as productive input (e.g., her discomfort or pain in response to the stove's surface temperature). But a technology depending on formal logic might have difficulty representing an individual's instincts.

Some sceptics of AI's application to the law fail to recognize the distinctions among the four AI approaches. As noted above, most new legal technologies occupy the right side of figure 3.1's matrix. Today's AI systems are generally not aimed at creating the much-debated and derided "robot lawyer." Indeed, even the most advanced legal technologies are not being trained to approximate human behaviour just yet. Instead, these technologies are aimed at optimizing the performance of tasks that can be systematized. These tasks can sometimes involve complex judgments; in law, this can mean identifying the relative weights of different factual variables and balancing competing legal principles in making accurate and reliable predictions of what future adjudicators are likely to do in a particular legal context. In any case, the legal singularity does not depend on technologies acting humanlike. It is our contention that widespread legal prediction will dramatically reduce legal uncertainty, and that individuals and institutions will remain the law's primary interpreters and interlocutors. The vision of the legal singularity that we articulate in these pages, then, is less about there being a self-driving society, and more about there being an emergent self-driving law that individuals and institutions will sustain, support, and work to improve. Ideally, we will grapple with the legal singularity to shape it to our needs and use it to our advantage, developing the robust institutions and practices necessary to harness its advantages to promote our collective well-being.

III. Applying AI to the Law: Computational Law

With a preliminary understanding of AI established, we turn to the question of how exactly law can be computed. In this section, we discuss what is meant by computational law and how computational legal analyses work.

---

23 Russell & Norvig, *supra* note 10 at 4.

a. Should Law Be Computed?

As we explain in chapter 2, and as Oliver Wendell Holmes famously argued, to know the law means to accurately predict what future courts are likely to decide. The centrality of prediction to effective legal practice raises the question: what can lawyers do to make more accurate and insightful predictions? Today, lawyers who want to provide competent advice (i.e., predictions) are fighting an uphill battle for two reasons. First, laws are often unclear.[24] As legal scholars have observed, much of the law is presented not as clear rules (e.g., "do not drive above 100 km/h") but as standards that are highly general and imperfectly prescriptive, and can be assessed with specificity only *ex post* (e.g., drive "reasonably safely").[25] Pinpointing precisely relevant legal rights and obligations is difficult in systems where laws are formulated as open-ended, indeterminate statements.[26] This problem is especially pronounced in legal areas with substantial factual complexity. Second, the law emanates from numerous and often fractured, misaligned sources. In common law jurisdictions, the interpretive principles that guide our understanding of the law rarely come from a single case – or even a handful of cases. Rather, what constitutes the law on a given legal question emerges from an understanding of the entire corpus of case law relevant to that issue; yet lawyers rarely have the time to assess *all* cases when doing their research. In civil law systems, related problems emerge. It is often the case that underlying legal problems could be characterized in different ways, leading to the application of different legal principles; in these cases, the challenge presents as the threshold question of properly characterizing the problem. Regardless of whether one is considering the common law or the civil law, there are challenges of accommodating our messy reality with incompletely specified legal systems. As a compromise, lawyers almost always rely on some combination of intuition, experience, and research, which in

---

24 The presence of uncertainty and vagueness in the law is commonly discussed in the literature. See, e.g., Anthony D'Amato, "Legal Uncertainty" (1983) 71:1 Cal L Rev 1, online: <https://doi.org/10.2307/3480139>; see also Jeremy Waldron, "Vagueness in Law and Language: Some Philosophical Issues" (1994) 82:3 Cal L Rev 509, online: <https://doi.org/10.2307/3480971>.

25 See, e.g., Isaac Ehrlich & Richard A Posner, "An Economic Analysis of Rulemaking" (1974) 3 J Leg Stud 257. See also Anthony J Casey & Anthony Niblett, "The Death of Rules and Standards" (2017) 92 Ind LJ 1401.

26 See, e.g., John E Calfee & Richard Craswell, "Some Effects of Uncertainty on Compliance with Legal Standards" (1984) 70:5 Va L Rev 965.

common law systems often consists of reviewing a mere sampling of relevant cases[27] and in civil law systems involves various methods, including referencing treatises by learned jurists and drawing on one's professional judgment and experience.

There are at least three obvious issues with the conventional research approach. First, it is unreliable. Human intuition has proven faulty in complex professional settings. A well-known study by Grove and Meehl identified 128 other studies in various fields where algorithmic prediction outperformed human judgment.[28] The sheer volume of these findings suggests that professionals would be wise to at least question whether they indeed know better than the data, as even the best and most experienced lawyer is likely to have modest biases and blind spots that may affect their view of a case. Second, the conventional research approach is costly and time-intensive, leading to a situation in which it soon becomes economically inadvisable to continue to invest costly effort to make slow incremental improvements in one's appreciation of the merits of a case. To achieve confidence in their advice, a lawyer will often have to identify, read, and analyse a substantial volume of texts, including cases, any applicable statutes or regulations, and potentially dense secondary sources to help guide interpretation. Improvements over simple heuristics (e.g., leveraging base rates of success across wide swathes of cases) using conventional research methods will be hard won and take too much time, meaning that conventional research must accept large amounts of uncertainty. Third, this approach is insufficiently comprehensive. Even the best and most thorough researcher will occasionally miss important cases, treatise discussions, or other relevant rulings. Even if a researcher happens to identify and assemble all the relevant cases and materials, there is still no guarantee that they can synthesize the most relevant information accurately in the time reasonably available to them.

Even where researchers have – through expertise and creativity – identified the right information, and when they have the time, space, and resources, there will still be some irreducible background uncertainty. Here, it is important to distinguish legal uncertainty from case-by-case unpredictability. If a trial lawyer comments that a case is

---

27 See generally Faraz Dadgostari et al, "Modelling Law Search as Prediction" 29:3 AI & L 34.

28 William M Grove & Paul E Meehl, "Comparative Efficiency of Informal (Subjective, Impressionistic) and Formal (Mechanical, Algorithmic) Prediction Procedures: The Clinical-Statistical Controversy" 2 Psychol Pub Pol'y & L 293.

a "toss-up," for instance, they might be speaking about the fact that the applicable law is not clear. But they might also be flagging some other unknowns: a witness's demeanour, a judge's attitude, a surprising new piece of evidence, or the like – in other words, not necessarily legal uncertainty, but the kind of generalized uncertainty that exists in a highly contingent environment.[29] What we mean by legal uncertainty, then, is the *legal* part: when the content of the law is itself uncertain. Legal uncertainty is typically driven by two legal information issues. The first is as close to an immutable problem as exists in legal research: the absence of directly relevant legal information altogether. The second is a rather garden-variety sort that lawyers routinely confront, such as when words in a statute might be unclear, a court decision might be difficult to follow, or the relevant legal doctrine involves the use of what Giuseppe Dari-Mattiacci and Bruno Deffains call "vague notions" (e.g., *bona fide*, "reasonableness," etc.).[30] This type of legal uncertainty is somewhat navigable for lawyers, as some of the interpretive skills taught in law school and widely used in the profession involve reconciling competing principles, resolving ambiguities, and parsing unclear language in service of creative argument. Yet, without surveying the entire expanse of legal information, these lawyers do not meaningfully achieve certainty.

One approach to addressing these problems lies in computational law. As Atik and Jeutner explain:

Computational law concerns the expression, application and analysis of law in algorithmic form. It involves forming legal algorithms that proceed through logical processes (at the level of computer hardware, through passage between "logic gates") to create legal conclusions.[31]

The idea behind using predictive algorithms is simple. In recurring legal questions, courts use statutory or common law tests to analyse facts. Rather than look at a few cases and conjecture about how a future court is likely to treat the same issue, machine learning (ML) and natural language processing (NLP) allow us to canvass substantially larger

---

29 Scott Baker & Alex Raskolnikov, "Harmful, Harmless, and Beneficial Uncertainty in Law" 46:2 J Leg Stud 281 at 282–3.

30 Giuseppe Dari-Mattiacci & Bruno Deffains, "Uncertainty of Law and the Legal Process" (2007) 163:4 J Inst & Theor Econ 627 at 632.

31 Jeffery Atik & Valentin Jeutner, "Quantum Computing and Algorithmic Law" (2019) Loyola Law School, Los Angeles Legal Studies Research Paper No. 2019-38 at 10.

volumes of case law and other legal information. NLP allows computers to work with the meaning of text without the text having to conform to the computer's perceived needs. Put simply, computers are capable of understanding language as it is used *naturally* – in text and speech alike. This means the ability to identify meaning in facially different text renderings, and identify connections between texts where words may vary.[32] There are a variety of approaches within NLP.[33] One example of an oft-used NLP technique is part-of-speech (POS) tagging, which effectively forges structure by assigning a given word in a text with its appropriate syntactic label.[34] These labels – which can be as granular as "adjective phrase," "locative adjective phrase," "predicate adjective phrase," and the like – allow NLP not only to recognize meaning across disparate contexts but also to systematize information for better retrieval.[35] Where NLP looks for language and meaning, as Yaser S. Abu-Mostafa explains, ML "enables computers to learn from experience."[36] More specifically, ML looks for patterns that it is trained to detect. One of the most helpful features of machine learning practice is that it tends to be "agnostic" – that is, ML prefers algorithms that maximize "predictive accuracy independent of underlying theory."[37]

The primary challenge for researchers wishing to create or use computational techniques is that legal data are generally "unstructured." Unstructured data are those that do not adhere to any prescribed format

---

32 AJ Joshi, "Natural Language Processing" (1991) 253:5025 Science 1242 at 1242, online: <https://www.jstor.org/stable/2879169>.

33 Tamas E Doszkocs, "Natural Language Processing in Information Retrieval" J Am Society for Information Science (June 30, 1986), online: <https://doi.org/10.1002/(sici)1097-4571(198607)37:4>.

34 Joshi, *supra* note 32 at 1242. See also Mitchell Marcus, "New Trends in Natural Language Processing: Statistical Natural Language Processing" (1995) 92:22 Proceedings of the National Academy of Sciences of the United States of America 10052, online: <https://www.jstor.org/stable/2368613>.

35 O Arazy & C Woo, "Enhancing Information Retrieval through Statistical Natural Language Processing: A Study of Collocation Indexing." (2007) 31:3 MIS Quarterly 525, online: <https://doi.org/10.2307/25148806>; see also J Greenberg, "The Applicability of Natural Language Processing (NLP) to Archival Properties and Objectives" (1998) 61:2 American Archivist 400, online: <https://www.jstor.org/stable/40294094> and T Strzalkowski, "Natural Language Information Retrieval" (1995) 31:3 Information Processing & Management 397.

36 YS Abu-Mostafa, "Machines that Think for Themselves" (2012) 307:1 *Scientific American* 78 at 78, online: <https://www.jstor.org/stable/26016002>.

37 Benjamin Alarie, Anthony Niblett & Albert H Yoon, "How Artificial Intelligence Will Affect the Practice of Law" 68 UTLJ 106 at 116–17.

or method of organization.[38] Take, for example, judicial opinions. While opinions follow a general form – recitation of facts, discussion of relevant case law, and application of law to the facts – judges vary in the way they present this information. They vary considerably from one another in their writing style, including grammar and diction. These differences are not merely stylistic; judges use different precedent, use different terms to refer to the same substantive legal doctrines, and, perhaps most importantly, use entirely different modes of reasoning and analysis in rendering judgments. These personalized approaches to opinion writing can present obstacles to tools that seek to extract, analyse, and synthesize relevant information. Highly contextualized writing can make it difficult to identify patterns within and across opinions. Accordingly, algorithms relying on natural language processing may yield imprecise results and, predictably, more so as the complexity of the legal questions increases.

It is, of course, possible to transform such unstructured data into structured data and legal models. This process involves identifying a discrete question, the corpus of relevant documents, and the most relevant features of the information necessary to extract from the documents. This process may be time-intensive, requiring the inputs of lawyers, machine learning experts, and developers to complete each stage. The cost of applying machine learning to the resulting data – which, through these efforts, are now structured – is modest by comparison.[39]

b. On "Computational Values"

Many sceptics of legal AI take the view that computational methods are all about maximizing efficiency.[40] Of course, legal prediction in part aims to improve the efficiency of legal analysis, but such efficiency is hardly the only value served by computational law. In our view, to describe computational law merely in terms of efficiency undersells its upside. Here, we highlight three unique advantages of computational legal analysis: (1) a better accuracy-efficiency trade-off, (2) the ability to turn indeterminate standards into specified rules, and (3) personalization.

---

38 B Polnaszek, et al, "Overcoming the Challenges of Unstructured Data in Multisite, Electronic Medical Record-based Abstraction" (2016) 54:10 Medical Care e65, online: <https://www.jstor.org/stable/26418246> at e65.
39 Portions appeared in Alarie, Niblett & Yoon, *supra* at note 37 at 115–18.
40 See, e.g., Weber *supra* note 19 at 100–1.

The first benefit is that computational legal analysis remakes the traditional trade-off in legal analysis between accuracy and efficiency, or the "inherent tension between *how correct* computations are and *how long* it takes to compute them."[41] This tension can be seen in many fields, of course. Consider, for instance, the choices that go into how an image is displayed on your computer screen. For screens with poorer display quality and lower resolution, images might be displayed with fewer pixels, resulting in less accuracy in the representation of those images. Edges might be pixelated and blurred, colours might be slightly distorted, and any attempt to manipulate the perspective – for instance, by zooming in – will result in lower image quality. But even this lower-quality version is probably reasonably successful in efficiently conveying information about the image, allowing for our minds and imaginations to fill in aspects of the image that are not presented. And the lower-resolution display demands less memory and storage.[42] The stakes are somewhat higher when you consider this trade-off from the perspective of decision theory: for instance, how much time should public health policymakers take to gather more and more accurate information before restricting social interaction during a pandemic (or before relaxing restrictions after restrictions are established)? Across contexts, "gathering increasingly accurate information is a computationally expensive task that is in tension with acting efficiently."[43]

Lawyers must routinely make these sorts of trade-offs. In civilian systems, judges often act as inquisitors in certain matters, becoming actively involved in investigating the facts of a case. In these inquisitorial proceedings, judges as inquisitors are charged with getting to the bottom of things, questioning witnesses, interrogating suspects; the judge's duty is to find and weigh all the available evidence, whether it is incriminating or exculpatory for the accused. In this kind of proceeding, the inquisitorial judge reaches the decision about how to trade off accuracy and efficiency.

Likewise, adjudication systems in common law jurisdictions have developed procedural justice norms around when and how to make the accuracy-efficiency trade-off. The interest in accuracy counsels for procedures that allow litigants to establish evidence, examine witnesses,

---

41   A Feder Cooper, Karen Levy & Christopher De Sa, "Regulating Accuracy-Efficiency Trade-Offs in Distributed Machine Learning Systems" (2020), online: *SSRN* <https://papers.ssrn.com/sol3/papers.cfm?abstract_id=3650497> at 1.

42   *Ibid*.

43   *Ibid* at 2.

produce documents, and debate precedent, all with a view to providing the adjudicator with the information needed to announce a result that has a greater likelihood of being perceived as legitimate. But efficiency interests also demand procedures that necessarily limit adjudication's truth-seeking function, such as interlocutory resolutions (e.g., summary judgment) and some limitations on discovery.

These trade-offs also pervade how we understand and reason with the substantive law. Parties in common law jurisdictions who engage in legal argument make representations about what the law is without having to demonstrate whether their interpretation is indeed consistent with the entire corpus of binding case law. Courts evaluate those arguments in much the same manner. These practices are customary and are bound up in our faith that the features of the adversarial system will generate the strongest arguments on behalf of each party. However, these practices are almost certainly a product of the traditional impracticality of making more exhaustive inquiries with reliability and consistency. The promise of computational law is, in part, that the effort involved in achieving more breadth and granularity does not threaten efficiency.

Consider this example. If a corporation is not able to pay its debts and satisfy its creditors, the creditors will typically have no recourse personally against the shareholders, directors, or officers of the company. According to the statutes that establish the framework for modern business corporations, most corporations have "limited liability." The law establishes and protects the corporation's legal personality independent of its shareholders, directors, and officers. In unusual circumstances, however, the legal doctrine of "piercing the corporate veil" may apply. As students of business law will know, this veil-piercing doctrine confers courts with equitable authority to look beyond the corporate form and assign liability to those who would otherwise be third parties to legal relations between a corporation and its creditors; for example, directors or officers of the corporation.[44] This doctrine is a quintessential example of judge-made law; in common law systems, the contours of veil piercing are announced in successive judicial decisions. As a result, the boundaries of the law might change over time. Its scope might also expand or contract. Jonathan Macey and Joshua Mitts explain that, though frequently litigated, veil piercing is one of the doctrines most "shrouded in mystery," because there is little consensus

---

44 Jonathan Macey & Joshua Mitts, "Finding Order in the Morass: The Three Real Justifications for Piercing the Corporate Veil" (2014) 100:1 Cornell L Rev 99 at 100.

about when it should apply. Instead, judges and lawyers often rely on received wisdom about what triggers the doctrine's applicability. To the extent that there is any popular agreement about what matters in veil piercing, it is around a few standard justifications for when a corporate veil should be pierced, the most commonly invoked of which is undercapitalization.[45] Macey and Mitts's computational analysis, however, demonstrates that undercapitalization is not predictive of a veil-piercing outcome and is, at best, a proxy for the *real* information that tends to move courts.[46] Their study of over 9,000 cases finds that courts tend to pierce the veil where at least one of the following three objectives is in play: "(1) achieving the purpose of an existing statute or regulation; (2) preventing shareholders from obtaining credit by misrepresentation; or (3) promoting the bankruptcy values of achieving the orderly, efficient resolution of a bankrupt's estate."[47]

The insights gleaned from computational analysis of the 9,000-plus corporate veil-piercing cases are useful in at least three distinct contexts. For advocates, having a more granular understanding of what inclines courts to pierce the corporate veil allows for better-calibrated litigation strategy. For transactional attorneys, the data findings can inform entity structure and design that is *ex ante* compliant and thus better protective of clients' personal liability risk. For judges, computational analyses allow for better evaluation of the extent to which litigants' arguments are consistent with precedent. Macey and Mitts's work is a project of empirical legal scholarship, however, and the research costs associated with using traditional methods to conduct such wide-ranging studies for every discrete legal question are excessive.

This chapter has discussed how AI is shaping a new computational era with respect to legal information. This sets the stage for the emergence of the legal singularity through "complete law" and "universal legal literacy," the focus of the next chapter. We turn now to these important issues.

---

45 *Ibid* at 110–12.
46 *Ibid* at 102.
47 *Ibid* at 99.

Chapter Four

Complete Law

I. Introduction

Anyone who has ever had a lawyer among their friends or family knows the familiar frustration of asking that person a legal question and receiving the common response – often regardless of subject matter – "It depends."

The unsatisfying truth: it really *does* depend! Answers to legal questions vary based on a whole host of considerations. Can you share your Netflix password? It depends on the terms of your subscription agreement. Can directors and officers be personally liable for corporate malfeasance? Well, it depends in part on whether the corporation was set up for fraudulent purposes and whether the directors or officers authorized the alleged wrongdoing.[1] Is your pizza delivery driver properly classified as an independent contractor or an employee of the pizza shop for tax purposes? Well, if you are in the United States, that one depends on a number of contextual factors, including whether the driver uses their own car, sets their own schedule, and is free to take on outside work.[2] In Canada, it depends on different factors still.[3] The answers to these questions – and all legal questions, in fact – also depend on *where* the question is being asked, since different jurisdictions may have different rules.

---

1 See generally Jason W Neyers, "Canadian Corporate Law, Veil-Piercing, and the Private Law Model Corporation" (2000) 50:2 UTLJ 173.
2 "Topic No. 762 Independent Contractor vs. Employee: Internal Revenue Service," n.d., online: <https://www.irs.gov/taxtopics/tc762>.
3 See generally *Wiebe Door Services Ltd v Minister of National Revenue* (1986) 70 N.R. 214 (FCA).

The law is not just complex; it is *uncertain* and *incomplete*. Uncertain because the sheer number of contingent factors that need to be analysed makes it difficult to say with confidence what the law *is* on a given subject. Incomplete because many legal rules depend on *ex post* elaboration to have any specific content at all. Take our examples above. Even if you were able to corral all the necessary information to offer something more than the well-worn "it depends," there's no guarantee you've found "*the* answer."[4] Unlike physics, where correct answers remain correct answers until proven otherwise by observable physical phenomena, legal answers need to be endorsed by legal institutions. An arbitrator may be the one to decide whether you've violated the terms of your subscription agreement with Netflix. A judge might resolve the question of whether directors and officers should be held personally liable for their corporation's wrongdoing. Whether your pizza delivery driver is an independent contractor or an employee is a question not just for courts but for tax authorities, which are empowered to levy penalties for misclassification. If these legal questions ever led to disputes, lawyers would arrive with competing arguments about what the law *is* on these questions, each trying to convince a decision maker whose own view of the law will be coloured by experience, or perhaps by differing judicial philosophy or interpretive methodologies.

The stakes of this kind of legal uncertainty are high. Anthony D'Amato describes the law as "a prediction of official behavioral reaction to what [an individual] plans to do or avoid doing."[5] In other words, without a sense of what the law *is*, individuals have little sense of their real-time rights and obligations, and the law provides little in the way of direct guidance. Just as troublingly, outcomes are inconsistent; as lawyers and judges grope around for where the law *is*, so to speak, they come to divergent conclusions about its character and its applicability.

Is this degree of uncertainty inevitable? Legal uncertainty has been so widely accepted that there are virtually no meaningful reform efforts to specify the law in countries like Canada and the United States, save for sporadic attempts to codify common law doctrines and some dynamic updating of administrative regulations, which we discuss

4 Avneet Jaswal, "Bill 148 Update: New Risks for Misclassifying Independent Contractors as Employees" (23 April 2018), online: *Fasken* <https://www.fasken.com/en/knowledge/2018/04/bill-148-update-new-risks-for-misclassifying-independent-contractors-as-employees>.

5 Anthony D'Amato, "Legal Uncertainty" (1983) 71:1 Cal L Rev 1 at 1.

later in this chapter. In civil law jurisdictions, there is often a professional commitment to the idea that the civil code is complete and that one need only study it carefully for clarity to emerge. In circumstances where the civil law may admit of conceptual ambiguity, the legal community looks to its members, including the learned authors of treatises and leading jurists, for guidance and insight.

For the most part, the legal profession and law's wider epistemic community – including judges and scholars – have accepted that legal uncertainty and incompleteness are inevitable. To put this at the feet of today's lawyers would not exactly be fair, though. In fact, even Aristotle, in *Nichomachean Ethics*, all but accepted the inevitability of legal uncertainty, writing:

> Law is universal but about some things it is not possible to make a universal statement which shall be correct. In those cases, then, in which it is necessary to speak universally, but not possible to do so correctly, the law takes the usual case, though it is not ignorant of the possibility of error. And it is none the less correct; for the error is not in the law nor in the legislator but in the nature of the thing, since the matter of practical affairs is of this kind from the start. When the law speaks universally, then, and a case arises on it which is not covered by the universal statement, then it is right, where the legislator fails us and has erred by oversimplicity, to correct the omission – to say what the legislator himself would have said had he been present, and would have put into his law if he had known.[6]

Artificial intelligence – and specifically legal prediction – promises a way out of this uncertainty and incompleteness. The preceding chapter discussed how the emergent third phase of legal information – the computational era, which follows the digital era and the analogue era before it – leads to effective and accurate legal prediction. Where today's lawyers and judges work with texts and use their skills and interpretive resources to conduct legal analysis, computational tools take a different tack by treating that same text as data and performing advanced computing functions. The early evidence of computational law's promise is evident in tools like machine learning algorithms that synthesize case law and retrieve salient information, and natural language processing techniques for identifying relevant information in

---

6 Aristotle, *Nicomachean Ethics*, translated by WD Ross (Kitchener, ON: Batoche Books, 1999) at 88.

unstructured texts. These are still relatively early applications of long-standing technologies, though. Indeed, the case law–based legal prediction that undergirds the shift towards computational law involves data science techniques that have been used widely in other industries – such as financial services – for decades. From our standpoint, this is good news: if even these basic infusions of modern technologies can significantly improve legal knowledge and strike a superior accuracy-efficiency trade-off, then more sophisticated, modern applications certainly have further potential.

This chapter focuses on explaining what is meant by "complete law" and how the computational era is moving us closer to it. In chapter 7, we discuss the concept of "universal legal literacy," or what we view as the probable and most normatively desirable outcome of complete law. Taken together, complete law and universal legal literacy jointly create the conditions for the legal singularity.

We begin our discussion of complete law with the premise that the law is woefully underspecified. Computational legal tools enable the creation and evolution of law that is more robust, better differentiated, and more personalized. The companion discussion relating to universal legal literacy recognizes that legal questions – and the situations that give rise to the need for legal representation – have stakes that are too high for lawyers to monopolize both the prescription and the diagnosis. Predictive tools that are well designed and proliferate widely will give individuals and institutions – the ultimate subjects of the law – the ability to ascertain their legal rights and obligations in real time. The combination of more-exhaustive, better-specified law and universal legal literacy will result in a rapidly verifiable understanding of lawful and unlawful behaviours, and expose the menu of available legal options in any context.

II. Incomplete Law and Its Problems

a. What Is Incomplete Law?

By now, readers understand that the law is an indeterminate morass. To get more specific, the law is *underspecified*. This means that, as designed, laws are frequently not especially clear about the specific circumstances that they purport to regulate. Consider the common law. In the tort context, in determining liability for negligence, we rely on standards – *ex post* notions of what would have been "reasonably foreseeable" to a "reasonable person" in a particular setting such that a defendant might be said to have met the required "standard of care" in satisfaction of a duty of care to a plaintiff.[7] To provide practical guidance on these kinds of questions is difficult and, at best, uncertain, for a wide variety of reasons. In the context of contract law, legal incompleteness is also widely acknowledged and accepted. It is well known that contracts are virtually always incomplete: parties simply cannot foresee and address every potential future contingency. Indeed, contract scholars accept that it is inevitable that contracting parties will not be able to negotiate for the appropriate set of terms that should govern in every potential future state of the world.[8] Incompleteness abounds in public law as well. For example, US Supreme Court Justice Potter Stewart famously remarked in his concurring opinion in *Jacobellis v Ohio* about obscenity that he "knows it when he sees it."[9] Many examples could be given of the challenges of specifying in a complete way the boundaries of legal categories in private law and public law.

Consider the example of tax law, which inevitably shares in this incompleteness. Sophisticated taxpayers can exploit this incompleteness to strictly comply with the letter of the law while paying significantly lower rates of tax on their incomes. American billionaire Warren Buffett has given media interviews in which he has pointed out that he personally pays a much lower rate of tax on his income than his employees, including his secretary. Debbie Bosanek, Buffett's secretary, in 2012 paid tax in the United States at an effective rate of 35.8 per cent – more than double the rate of 17.4 per cent paid by her boss.[10] Some of the difference in the tax rates between Buffett and his secretary can be attributed to explicit and well-specified tax policy decisions – such as to impose significant levels of payroll taxes. Another key part of the difference relates to the ambiguity and incompleteness of the tax law, which allows well-advised taxpayers to make plans to steer clear of tax liability. But do we really want a tax system that does not admit of any

---

7 See, generally, *Palsgraf v Long Island Railway Co*, 248 NY 339, 162 NE 99 (1928); see also Jeremy Horder, "Can the Law Do without the Reasonable Person?," Book Review of *Rethinking the Reasonable Person: An Egalitarian Reconstruction of the Objective Standard* by Mayo Moran" (2005) 55:2 UTLJ 253; Donal Nolan, "Varying the Standard of Care in Negligence" (2013) 72:3 Cambridge L J 651.

8 Ian Ayres & Robert Gertner, "Filling Gaps in Incomplete Contracts: An Economic Theory of Default Rules" (1989) 99 Yale LJ 87 at 92–5.

9 *Jacobellis v State of Ohio*, 378 US 184 (1964) at 197 [*Jacobellis*].

10 Seniboye Tienabeso, "Warren Buffett and His Secretary on Their Tax Rates," *ABC News* (25 January 2012), online: <https://abcnews.go.com/blogs/business/2012/01/warren-buffett-and-his-secretary-talk-taxes>.

special tax-planning opportunities?[11] It has been said that a tax system breathes through its loopholes.[12]

Indeed, some of the incompleteness that we lament here can be described more accurately as features rather than bugs in our current system. The common law, for instance, develops and extends in response to social facts and prevailing societal attitudes. The common law's open-endedness also sometimes results in the law being more administratively practicable. A detailed negligence statute, as one example, has the potential to be less effective than the judicially created and reiterated legal test because statutory framers might struggle to exhaustively contemplate all the possible societal interactions that would give rise to negligent conduct, and to do so in a way that matches a judge's ability to tailor a decision in light of the facts of a particular situation. In these and other scenarios that involve regulating heterogeneous behaviour, the costs of rule making are high; lawmakers do not have the *ex ante* information to regulate effectively. Returning to our example of tax loopholes, it makes sense that lawmakers would prefer to rely upon judges to interpret and apply a highly general statute about when tax must be paid – lawmakers simply do not have the information to anticipate all the myriad complex tax transactions that tax lawyers will dream up over time to help wealthy taxpayers avoid tax. Even if all methods of tax avoidance could somehow be anticipated with near perfection, the costs of collecting that information are likely to be simply too high. But what if the costs weren't so high, and the information was indeed readily available? Furthermore, what if our legal design choices did not involve the forced, binary choice between specific, under-inclusive rules and broad standards? The advent of computational law and, specifically, the proliferation of algorithmic lawmaking make complete, differentiated law more possible.

By invoking the word "complete" in this context to describe the law, we intend to describe a legal system that exhibits three key characteristics.[13] The first characteristic of a legal system that is complete in this sense is one that is *well designed* and *optimized* to trade off appropriately

---

11 See, e.g., Tim Edgar, "Building a Better GAAR" (2008) 27 Va Tax Rev 833 at 879–84. See also Benjamin Alarie, "Trebilcock on Tax Avoidance" (2010) 60 UTLJ 623.

12 See Benjamin Alarie, "The Challenge of Tax Avoidance for Social Justice in Taxation" in HP Gaisbauer et al, eds, *Philosophical Explorations of Justice and Taxation* (New York: Springer International, 2015) at 83.

13 Portions of this discussion appear in Benjamin Alarie, "Ahead by a Century: Tim Edgar, Machine-Learning, and the Future of Anti-Avoidance" (2020) 68:2 Can Tax J 613.

among the many competing public policy goals that the legal system implicates through appropriate rules, functional standards, and reliable legal methodologies for addressing the existing gaps. We will refer to this as the "optimized design" characteristic. The second characteristic of a complete legal system is that it is *well-specified* in the sense that questions of whether and how particular rules and standards apply to any given situation can be consistently and reliably answered. This is the "deep specification" characteristic. Deep specification is present in a legal system when the characterization of events, entities, and so on within the system is consistent, aligns with the optimized public policy design of that system, and is resistant to exploitation of any kind. The third aspect of a complete legal system is that it is *administered effectively*. By effective administration, we mean that its design and specifics are capable of being consistently and reliably applied, and that only a minimum of mistakes are made in administration (i.e., the administration of the system can reliably avoid false positives and false negatives). The current systems of the law that we observe in the world fall short of meeting a standard of "completeness" that exhibits optimized design, deep specification, and effective administration. In fact, incompleteness is pervasive in the law and permeates all its areas.

b. In Search of Specificity

In a stylized model, lawmakers have an option of selecting between two types of laws – standards and rules.[14] Standards are more open-ended and depend on *ex post* adjudication to supply their content.[15] A standard might state that motorists must merge on Ontario's Highway 401 "reasonably safely" or "with great caution." The average motorist may have a sense of what this means by virtue of their past experience and understanding of the context, but anyone seeking to observe the "law" (that is, what constitutes proceeding "reasonably safely" or "with great caution") will need to consult how courts have interpreted the standard. The benefit to lawmakers is that invoking a standard in legislation incurs few costs upfront; rather than having to consider the various traffic situations, optimal speeds, collision history, pedestrian activity, or the particular density of an area, lawmakers need articulate

---

14 See generally Louis Kaplow, "Rules versus Standards: An Economic Analysis" (1992) 42:3 Duke LJ 557; see also Ezra Friedman & Abraham L Wickelgren, "A New Angle on Rules Versus Standards" (2014) 16:2 Am L & Econ Rev 499.
15 Kaplow, *supra* note 14 at 561–2.

only a discretionary objective. The canonical example of a rule – and the example that Kaplow uses in his influential early work on economic analysis of the law – is a speed limit.[16] To determine whether someone violated the speed limit requires minimal meaningful context: if the speed limit at a point on the road is fifty kilometres per hour and the vehicle is travelling at a speed less than this, a motorist can be confident that they are complying with the speed limit.

As will be familiar to many readers, rules and standards have different advantages. The primary advantage of a rule is its clarity, of course, but complex rules are quite costly to design. Specifically, lawmakers incur *ex ante* "information costs."[17] The costs of gathering information to adequately specify a rule may be difficult. For instance, laws seeking to impose environmental standards in specific industries need to take into account that industry's peculiarities; for example, regulations targeting the automotive industry may have to take into account such information as the costs of vehicle production, the emissions associated with ordinary manufacturing, and a given vehicle's life cycle. As a more specific example, consider that Transport Canada requires specific tread depth on tires for certain heavy commercial vehicles. The choice of a rule in these contexts makes sense, given that broad standards like "build safe and efficient cars" does not provide any meaningful direction and is unlikely to achieve regulators' desired outcomes. But these kinds of rules can be well calibrated only when the data are available to inform their design. Regulators in a new context where there is no data on, say, carbon emissions or motor vehicle collisions, may prefer standards that supply the necessary information *ex post*. Standards also work best in situations where the range of social activity is broad and heterogeneous. In tort law, we require that individuals exercise reasonable care to avoid negligently harming others, in part because we cannot hope to contemplate or stipulate all the situations that may give rise to a relationship in which a person owes such duties to an identifiable other.

This distinction between rules and standards sometimes appears to suggest that rules are prototypically well specified and standards are broad and contentless. In reality, the distinction between rules and

---

16 *Ibid* at 565.
17 Anthony J Casey & Anthony Niblett, "Framework for the New Personalization of Law" (2019) 86:2 U Chi L Rev 333 [Casey & Niblett, "Framework"]; see also Oren Bar Gill & Omri Ben-Shahar, "Rethinking *Nudge*: An Information-Costs Theory of Default Rules" (2021) 88:3 U Chi L Rev 531.

standards does not necessarily map neatly onto the distinction between specificity and vagueness. In this sense, both rules and standards – including those that seem well specified at first blush – can be rather incomplete. The incompleteness of rules manifests in their relatively limited scope, as well: as James W. Bowers explains, fixed rules might speak to specific factual circumstances, and tend to be useful only in those factual circumstances.[18] In other words, the costs that lawmakers incur in gathering information before regulating in an area might help to specify and differentiate the applicable rule, but, if a new set of facts emerges that exceeds the rule's narrow scope, the rule is of limited value. Perhaps more troublingly, even specific rules may be stretched to absorb new facts or to regulate in areas for which they might not have been originally contemplated. As one example, consider debates around whether cryptocurrencies are properly regulated as securities or commodities. The tax and trading rules around securities and commodities are relatively well defined, but the presence of a new financial instrument means a shoehorning exercise, where new, dynamic social facts must be forced into older categories. This places an interpretive strain on the existing law; now, suddenly, commodities-trading rules are commodities- *and* cryptocurrency-trading rules, and also, now, potentially will be the trading rules for any hypothetical future financial instrument that can be similarly analogized.

There are at least three challenges with having underspecified law. The first is that underspecified law serves an insufficient signaling function. As Casey and Niblett write of standards in particular, "citizens live in uncertainty because no one has communicated the specific content of the law to them."[19] Put a different way, without specificity there is little predictability. Cass Sunstein uses the example of Miranda rules in US criminal procedure, under which officers are instructed to advise custodial suspects of their "right to silence."[20] Sunstein explains that these rules "tell the police specifically what must be done, eliminating the guessing games that can be so destructive to *ex ante* planning."[21]

Canadian courts have recognized the risks inherent in promulgating laws that do not have sufficient *ex ante* content, but they have stopped short of impugning standards or imprecise rules, instead limiting their criticisms to laws that are vague. In *Canadian Foundation for Children,*

---

18 James W Bowers, "Incomplete Law" (2002) 62:2 La L Rev 1229.
19 Casey and Niblett, "Framework," *supra* note 17 at 334.
20 *Miranda v Arizona*, 384 US 46 (1966).
21 Cass R Sunstein, "Problems with Rules" (1995) 83:4 Cal L Rev 953 at 976.

Youth and the Law v Attorney General of Canada (*Canadian Foundation*), for instance, the Supreme Court of Canada considered s 43 of the *Criminal Code*, which provided a defence against criminal conviction for using force to "correct" children, stating that "[e]very schoolteacher, parent or person standing in the place of a parent is justified in using force by way of correction toward a pupil or child, as the case may be, who is under his care, if the force does not exceed what is reasonable under the circumstances."[22] The issue in *Canadian Foundation* – which came to be known as the "spanking case" – was whether or not the words "what is reasonable under the circumstances" were too broad.[23] The Court ultimately found that, because subsequent "judicial decisions may properly add precision to a statute," the statute it is not void for vagueness as long as it "delineates a risk zone for criminal sanction." Chief Justice McLachlin wrote:

> A vague law prevents the citizen from realizing when he or she is entering an area of risk for criminal sanction. It similarly makes it difficult for law enforcement officers or judges to determine whether a crime has been committed. This invokes the further concern of putting too much discretion in the hands of law enforcement officials, and violates the precept that individuals should be governed by the rule of law, not the rule of persons. The doctrine of vagueness is directed generally at the evil of leaving "basic policy matters to policemen, judges, and juries for resolution on an ad hoc and subjective basis, with the attendant dangers of arbitrary and discriminatory application."[24]

Yet, despite acknowledging that law must set an "intelligible standard both for the citizens it governs and the officials who must enforce it,"[25] in saying that vague laws could later be elaborated by judicial decisions, the Court was relatively less concerned with whether the teacher, parent, or guardian could make a real-time sense of what constitutes "reasonable under the circumstances." Instead, the Court did something typical of Canadian and US courts in these sorts of vagueness analyses and considered the vagueness more or less only from the

---

22 "Criminal Law and Managing Children's Behaviour," n.d., online: <https://www.justice.gc.ca/eng/rp-pr/cj-jp/fv-vf/mcb-cce/index.html>.
23 See generally *Canadian Foundation for Children, Youth and the Law v Canada (Attorney General)*, 2004 SCC 4 (CanLII).
24 *Ibid* at para. 16.
25 *Ibid*.

perspective of decision makers. The Court did not necessarily do so *self-ishly*; in fact, Chief Justice McLachlin's reasons were quite concerned with over-investing discretion in police officers, prosecutors, and judges. But the reasons quickly abandoned the pretense that the true "evil" of vagueness is that it breeds uncertainty among citizens. Indeed, the constitutional law around vagueness has developed to focus on the extent to which the characteristics of the impugned law create issues for decision makers: a law is unconstitutionally vague only where it "does not provide an adequate basis for legal debate," "does not sufficiently delineate any area of risk," "is not intelligible," and does not "offer a 'grasp to the judiciary.'"[26] Even though the requirement that a law be intelligible appears, at first blush, to be somewhat concerned with how citizens understand it, cases like *Canadian Foundation* and *R v Nova Scotia Pharmaceutical Society* demonstrate that, for the most part, courts are concerned with unintelligibility only to the extent that it undermines "legal debate."[27]

A second problem of underspecified law is that it increases *ex post* error costs. Laws that depend on after-the-fact elaboration necessarily have an expanded zone of discretion. This results in, as Casey and Niblett write, more opportunity for an adjudicator to "infect the process with noise, inconsistency, hindsight bias, or her own idiosyncratic views on what the law's objectives should be."[28] This is a substantive problem, not an issue of mere performance. Though we reserve our discussion of systematic adjudication-related biases for chapter 6 on judging, it is important to recognize at this juncture that excessive discretion confers a distinct substantive disadvantage on litigants.

A third problem of underspecified law is that it promotes unnecessary and sometimes acrimonious interaction between citizens and adjudicative bodies. This happens in two ways: by encouraging more frequent disputes, and by putting citizens in a position of dependence on legal authorities for clarification of their rights and obligations. First, an underspecified law makes disputes more likely to the extent that it promotes disagreement among litigants as to its appropriate content. As an illustration of this point, consider a hypothetical dispute between neighbourhood residents, a municipality, and a real estate developer about whether a proposed condominium project should be built adjacent to a cul-de-sac of single-family homes. Imagine that residents

---

26 *R v Nova Scotia Pharmaceutical Society*, [1992] 2 S.C.R. 606 at 639–40.
27 *Ibid.*
28 Casey & Niblett, *supra* note 17 at 334.

allege that the prospective development violated the municipality's ban on multiple-storey developments in certain sections of the town. The residents' concern is not only about stopping multiple-storey developments for their own sake, but that they will lose their scenic view and access to unimpeded sunlight. The development is underway but incomplete: it so far features a single, above-ground floor with ceilings that are about as high as two typical storeys, as well as an underground parking garage. In response to the development, the residents initiate multiple legal proceedings: one against the municipality and its chief buildings official, seeking a declaration that any permits issued are unlawful, as being inconsistent with zoning rules; another seeking an injunction against the developers for the tort of nuisance on account of the impeded sunlight.

The incomplete law is *everywhere* in this example. In the first instance, the question of what constitutes a "storey," as per the zoning law, is at issue. Here, the hypothetical property features a large single-floor facility that is nevertheless as tall as two storeys, as well as an underground parking garage that might constitute a second storey, depending on how the language of the zoning rules are construed. Moreover, whether an anticipatory nuisance suit can be filed is subject to significant legal debate. Courts have recognized anticipatory nuisance as a legitimate cause of action in an exceedingly limited set of circumstances, wherein plaintiffs are seeking injunctive relief. Additionally, whether the residents' lawsuit will succeed depends on the language of the statute. Here, the applicable zoning law appears to be quite detailed, but, in the particular context of this dispute, the key question is what constitutes a "storey." This example elucidates the challenge of analogue *ex ante* rulemaking; the zoning law itself is specific enough to include a plain language directive (do not built units with more than a single storey), but lawmakers are at the mercy of the targets of their regulation – in this case, developers – who can, at any time, introduce construction plans that are not specifically contemplated by zoning rules designed for more traditional construction projects. In any case, these substantive legal issues are reached only if threshold procedural legal issues like standing,[29] justiciability,[30] and jurisdiction[31] are appropriately resolved, which themselves import legal standards that depend on

---

29 See, e.g., Canadian Council of Churches v Canada (Minister of Employment and Immigration), 1992 CanLII 116 (SCC)
30 See, e.g., *Black v Canada (Prime Minister)*, 2001 CanLII 8537 (ONCA)
31 See, e.g., *Club Resorts v Van Breda*, (2012) SCC 17.

ex post elaboration. The residents' lawsuits are, in short, an uncertain affair from beginning to end.

This last problem of incomplete law – that it promotes more interaction between citizens and adjudicative bodies – does not manifest only as more disagreement between litigants. It also fixes the relationship between citizen and state as one of requestor and grantor. As Cass Sunstein observes, fixed rules create "rights holders," who form expectations about treatment. This is especially true where the rule that entitles the rights holder is abundantly clear. In situations where the content of the law is supplied *ex post*, clarification of the contours of the law depends on an official endorsement that, because of the procedural rules of our system, would-be rights holders must pursue themselves. Sometimes, the fixed nature of these rules permits more dignified interaction between private parties. Sunstein compares the example of a fixed, specific rule mandating retirement at age seventy with a broad standard empowering employers to terminate workers who "because of their age, are no longer able to perform their job 'adequately.'"[32] In the world of the fixed rule, employers can hypothetically spare a declining worker from the indignity of a competence assessment by promoting a uniform legal policy.

c. Degradation of Legal Certainty

Our discussion of legal uncertainty and incomplete law has focused largely on the *initial* uncertainty and incompleteness of the law – that is, uncertainty that exists when a law is passed, a doctrine is announced, or a regulation promulgated. This is a significant problem, because incomplete law: (1) serves an insufficient signalling function; (2) increases *ex post* error costs; and (3) promotes more interaction between citizens and adjudicative bodies, much of which can be costly and disadvantageous.

But these problems are compounded by the fact that legal certainty further degrades over time. Anthony D'Amato identified two ways in which such degradation can happen. First, "rules may become more uncertain 'on the books.'"[33] To D'Amato, this means that a law, as written, may end up deviating from its expected meaning because of the successive interpretation by adjudicators. Sometimes this can arise

---

32 Cass Sunstein, *Legal Reasoning and Political Conflict* (Oxford: Oxford University Press, 1998), at 115.
33 D'Amato, "Legal Uncertainty," *supra* note 5 at 4.

from a misreading of legislative intention, but often it results from courts carving a law to find exceptions – which may be necessary – or identifying further meanings that are consistent with the law's spirit. It is best to think of this form of degradation more descriptively than normatively; courts are where the rubber meets the road, and sometimes otherwise untested laws become altered, even slightly, to be more practicable in real-world situations. D'Amato also argued that, as prospective litigants gain information about how a given law is being interpreted, they may seek to influence the legislative process through lobbying and other forms of advocacy to have the law changed in a specific way.[34] Lawmaking in democratic societies, if not a truly open process, is at least a contested arena where those with privileged access can affect outcomes. And because these privileged, motivated parties will seize onto some dimensions of the law more than others, lobbying and advocacy can lead to some internal inconsistencies and misalignments when construing the law.

In addition to law becoming less certain "on the books," it also becomes less certain over time because the actors that the law targets will adjust social behaviour to limit the law's application to their circumstances. In one sense, this is hardly an issue: if a law targeting industrial polluters results in lower industry-wide emissions, one could argue that law is effective. D'Amato is instead concerned with the type of behaviour modification that leads prospective litigants to exploit the law's ambiguities or cleverly seek to reclassify their behaviour in a way that places them outside of the law's reach.[35] Imagine a law seeking to encourage automobile manufacturers to reduce emissions by requiring them to build a certain number of low-emission vehicles. California's Air Resources Board (CARB) introduced such a regulation in 2012, which required the state's largest automobile manufacturers to build a "zero-emissions vehicle."[36] Not doing so would mean that those automakers – which included giants like Honda, General Motors, Ford, and Toyota – would no longer be able to sell *any* cars in California. The companies responded by building cars that were designed and built to meet the law's minimum dictates, but were never actually sold in California, or were sold in such limited quantities as to make them

---

34 *Ibid* at 4–6.
35 *Ibid*.
36 Jim Motavalli, "Do California's Zero Emission by 2035 Rules Go Far Enough?" *Autoweek* (25 August 2022), online: <https://www.autoweek.com/news/industry -news/a40993559/california-zero-emission-by-2035-rules-passed/>.

basically unavailable to consumers.[37] These vehicles, which came to be called "compliance cars,"[38] ensured that the companies could continue to operate in California. In the broadest sense, the companies' behaviour is lawful, but it is specifically calibrated to defeat the regulation's public policy objective. This response creates a burden on regulators to thereafter interpret the law either more narrowly or more expansively, or perhaps to update it to account for and respond to these evasive manoeuvres.

D'Amato's account underestimates the extent to which law degrades over time. Writing in 1983, D'Amato could not necessarily have anticipated the explosion of legal information that we accounted for in our earlier description of the shift from analogue to digital to computational eras. The proliferation of legal data in the form of voluminous case law, statutes, regulations, and interpretive material is exceedingly difficult for even the most capable lawyer or judge to corral and make sense of at a high level without discriminating by sampling or paying disproportionate attention to only certain data. That is, of course, unless you *compute* it. Indeed, there is a peculiar counter-tendency: more information means less clarity for individuals, but considerably more clarity for machine learning algorithms, which might prefer yet more information.

III. How Computation Encourages Completeness

The incompleteness of the law is understandable, given the current state of our overall legal development and technology. Since our techniques and methods for improving the law remain slow and crude, we can have only limited confidence in our ability to craft improvements, given the limits to our knowledge and understanding. Many interdependencies in the legal system work like a Rubik's cube – any change to one aspect will affect many others.[39] This complexity, path-dependency, and interdependence make introducing change difficult to do well, so we tend to prefer the gradual and incremental over the bold and potentially better and more effective. The relatively static nature of the current statutory, regulatory, and administrative approach to the different

---

37 Vlad Zecevic, "The Days of the Electric Compliance Car Are Almost Over" *JET Charge* (22 December 2021), online: <https://jetcharge.com.au/compliance-cars-electric-doomed/>.
38 Sami Hajj-Assaad, "What Is a Compliance Car?" *AutoGuide* (28 March 2014), online: <https://www.autoguide.com/auto-news/2014/03/compliance-car.html>.
39 JB Ruhl & Dan M Katz, "Measuring, Monitoring, and Managing Legal Complexity" (2015) 101 Iowa L Rev 191 at 208.

areas of law means that law cannot specifically and proactively address every potential future contingency in an optimal way. Since the incompleteness of the law is a product of our current level of development along numerous dimensions (including legal, social, political, and technological), we take this in 2023 to be a pervasive feature of just about every area of law.

Critics might initially balk at this description and point to examples of complex and highly differentiated statutes – Canada's *Bankruptcy and Insolvency Act*, for example – where the law as written contemplates myriad situations and gives its subjects somewhat specific directives about what constitutes lawful or unlawful behaviour.[40] The difficult task here is to imagine something *more* specific and differentiated. Indeed, we are somewhat agnostic about the form that rules take so long as they are effective at regulating in their target area and, most importantly, so long as they do not create or exacerbate inequalities. To the extent that we make normative pronouncements here, it is about the benefits of more complete, specified law. We treat the content of those complete and specified laws as being beyond the scope of this general discussion.

Figure 4.1 illustrates what rules are possible when considering the trade-offs that rulemaking demands. The higher that a law appears on the y-axis, the more information its design requires. The more rightward a law appears on the x-axis, the more specific it is. Importantly, this model does not suggest an ordinal ranking of normative desirability; standards are lowest in the diagram because they are the least specific and require the least information, not because they are the least valuable.

Figure 4.1 shows four kinds of rules that lawmakers can select from in an era of advanced computation. *Standards* require the least amount of information and are the least specific. *Rules* require more information but are also potentially more specific. With the ability to compute, however, rule designers have the choice of selecting two more advanced types of legal rules: *dynamic rules* and "*microdirectives*," a term we borrow from Casey and Niblett.[41]

Dynamic rules have the minimum specificity of rules, but capture some of the flexibility of standards. The way this is achieved is by what we term "responsive tailoring." Imagine that lawmakers wanted to improve road safety. A rule would expressly prohibit an action (do not drive above 80km/h) or prescribe an action (drive no less than

---

40 *Bankruptcy and Insolvency Act*, RSC 1985, c B-3.
41 Casey & Niblett, *supra* note 17 at 338.

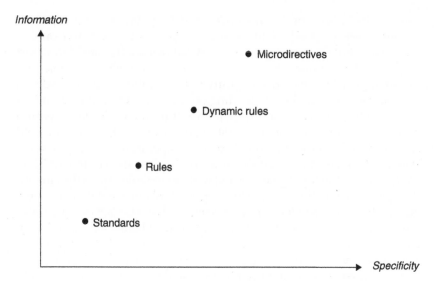

Figure 4.1. Specificity of rulemaking and information requirements

40 km/h on highways). Standards would articulate a broad objective and use contextual analyses to determine whether the behaviour was lawful or unlawful (drive reasonably safely). A dynamic rule would have, at a minimum, the specificity of the rule (do not drive above 80 km/h) but, in pursuing the same objective as the standard (reasonably safe driving), would permit modulation. Here, predictive algorithms could aid in responsive tailoring. For instance, based on traffic data, including predictions of future accidents, a dynamic rule might adjust the speed limit for inclement weather, weekends, or periods when the predicted traffic density is considerably less or greater than the typical flow. Dynamic rules recognize that there is a better way than a static, one-size-fits-all rule to achieve a regulatory objective.

The stylized example of the speed limit understates dynamic rule-making's virtues. Consider how dynamic rulemaking might assist with bringing clarity to the law's most indeterminate standards. Take negligence, for instance. Readers familiar with the tort law will know that indeterminate standards abound in negligence – adjudicators depend on concepts of duty, proximity, reasonable care, reasonable foreseeability, among others. How courts approach these concepts is clear only if one is familiar with the expanse of relevant case law or, at a minimum, the leading appellate court decisions. Indeed, even causation is unfixed; rather than treat causation as cause-in-fact or as empirically verifiable, courts – including the Supreme Court of Canada – have preferred a "common sense" (read: highly imprecise) inquiry to a scientific one.

Focusing now on standards of care, recall that courts considering tort disputes will examine whether a defendant acted with reasonable care in situations where they owed a duty to foreseeable plaintiffs, and will even adjust the standard, depending on the context that the defendant is in. Imagine hiring a contractor to install plumbing in your Toronto home. The contractor installs plumbing that is meant to withstand cold winters, but, because of record freezing temperatures, the pipes burst. Will you succeed in a negligence action against the contractor? Not likely. The contractor probably acted with reasonable care in the circumstances by winter proofing. This hypothetical, interpolated from the famous English case *Blyth v Birmingham Water Works Co*,[42] demonstrates how vital context is to the determination of whether one acted with reasonable care. The appropriate standard of care will also depend on some of the vital characteristics of the alleged tortfeasor; children, for instance, are subject to a more relaxed standard of care, whereas individuals with special skills and knowledge will be expected to behave with a heightened standard of care when operating in their domain. A surgeon, therefore, might be required to act reasonably carefully when walking down the street, but is subject to a considerably more exacting standard when performing surgery. The incompleteness is self-evident here; all anyone knows is that they must act reasonably carefully in most situations, but ascertaining what the triggering event is for a change in the applicable standard of care is an *ex post* endeavour. Predictive algorithms informed by real-world risk and safety data, however, enable us to get more granular about the applicable standards of care. If the question of what constitutes reasonable care depends primarily upon what is reasonable in the circumstances, then tools that give prospective tortfeasors a real-time sense of situational risk will not only encourage more robust risk-mitigating precautions, but also give courts data-informed baselines against which to assess defendant behaviour.

US administrative law provides an analogue model for this. As Wagner et al explain, Congress has made efforts to ensure that agencies are promulgating rules that remain effective over time, including "formal requirements imposed by statute or executive order that agencies review their regulations and modify them as appropriate."[43] The

---

42 *Blyth v Birmingham Water Works Co* (1856), 11 Ex Ch 781, 156 ER 1047.
43 Wendy Wagner, William West, Thomas McGarity & Lisa Peters, "Dynamic Rulemaking" Western Political Science Association Working Paper, 20 February 2016, at 5, online: <http://www.wpsanet.org/papers/docs/Dynamic%20Rulemaking.docx>.

purpose of these congressional requirements is to ensure that regulations remain responsively tailored to emergent conditions, such as new technology. Predictive algorithms can contribute by providing the necessary foresight to inform dynamic rulemaking and by automating the process.

The fourth kind of rule – the *second* type of rule enabled by computation – is the microdirective. Casey and Niblett describe microdirectives as follows:

> In a world of rules and standards, a legislature hoping to optimize safety and travel time could enact a rule (a sixty miles-per-hour speed limit) or a standard ("drive reasonably"). With microdirectives, however, the law looks quite different. The legislature merely states its goal. Machines then design the law as a vast catalog of context-specific rules to optimize that goal. From this catalog, a specific microdirective is selected and communicated to a particular driver (perhaps on a dashboard display) as a precise speed for the specific conditions she faces. For example, a microdirective might provide a speed limit of 51.2 miles per hour for a particular driver with twelve years of experience on a rainy Tuesday at 3:27 p.m. The legislation remains constant, but the microdirective updates as quickly as conditions change.[44]

Thus, where dynamic rules take specific contexts into account to articulate the optimal legal rule, microdirectives are even more granular still – they are *personalized*. If the goal of speed limits is promoting road safety, then a superior approach would be one that better maximizes safety and minimizes harm. Think of something as simple as personalized speed limits that account for a driver's experience as well as road conditions and other contextual factors.

Figure 4.2 illustrates how the four levels of law discussed above can be divided between analogue and computational law. Computational law – represented by the area above the dotted line – intervenes in legal rulemaking to enable the two more-specific types of laws: dynamic rules, which respond to context, and microdirectives, which both respond to context and personalize based on synthesizing yet more information.

---

44 Anthony J Casey & Anthony Niblett, "The Death of Rules and Standards" (2017) 92:4 Ind L J 1401 at 1404.

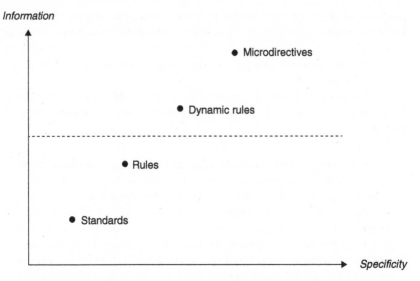

Figure 4.2. Computational law for directives and microdirectives

IV. Complete, as in No Gaps – *Not* Complete, as in Done

Some readers will understandably balk at our claim that the law can ever be meaningfully "complete." An important terminological clarification: we do not invoke the term "complete" here as a synonym for "finished," as in an artistic masterpiece or a chess game played through to checkmate. Even in a complete legal system, individuals and communities can be expected to advocate for legal changes and to advance competing views about just outcomes. That, in and of itself, does not threaten the notion of complete law.

Our notion of a complete law refers more to a practical completeness – that of adequate coverage. Thus, our notion of complete law would, for example, reject uncritical acceptance of US Supreme Court Justice Potter Stewart's characterization of obscenity as something that he knows when he sees,[45] and instead demands that the boundaries of legal obscenity be articulated, such that those bound by the laws have a sense of what kinds of behaviours they can lawfully engage in.

---

45 *Jacobellis, supra* note 9.

Chapter Five

Defending the Legal Singularity from Its Critics

I. Introduction

There is a growing literature that criticizes the project of computational law and the legal singularity. These criticisms generally fall into one of two related types. The first type argues that computational law is a reductionist project. These scholars view the entire enterprise of legal prediction as faulty because it does not capture the uniqueness and multidimensionality inherent to legal reasoning. Scholars in this camp, which would include Frank Pasquale[1] as well as Simon Deakin and Christopher Markou,[2] have also argued that data science's learning processes and the techniques of legal reasoning differ practically and epistemically to the point of being irreconcilable. These criticisms tend to portray the legal singularity as a theory that does not sufficiently attend to the law's social context. Sceptics such as Jennifer Cobbe have argued that advocates for computational methods in the law are hyper-focused on improving how the law functions and pay little attention to how the law is produced and the "structures of power, knowledge, and capital" that functional improvements might further entrench.[3] A second, related type of criticism views the eventual legal singularity as a threat to the rule of law. Scholars such as Robert F. Weber have argued

---

1 See generally Frank Pasquale, "The Resilient Fragility of the Law" in Simon Deakin & Christopher Markou, eds, *Is Law Computable? Critical Perspectives on Law and Artificial Intelligence* (Oxford: Hart Publishing, 2020) v [Pasquale, "Resilient Fragility"].

2 Simon Deakin & Christopher Markou, "From Rule to Legal Singularity" in Deakin & Markou, *supra* note 1, 1 at 5–7 [Deakin & Markou, "Rule"].

3 Jennifer Cobbe, "Legal Singularity and the Reflexivity of Law" in Deakin & Markou, *supra* note 1, 107 at 124.

that legal prediction is a fundamental threat to law's "normative core," and thus undermines certain pillars of liberal democratic order.[4]

In this chapter, we respond to these leading criticisms of computational law and the legal singularity. Alongside our review of the major critiques, we observe that sceptics of the legal singularity make some routine errors. For the purposes of this discussion, we engage arguments that discuss the concept of the "legal singularity" or "computational law" directly. There are, of course, much broader criticisms concerning the disparate racial, gender, and class impacts of legal prediction; we address those later in our penultimate chapter on the ethics of predictive analytics and algorithmic decision-making.

Before beginning, it is worth making two cautionary points for our readers. The first is to acknowledge up front the awkwardness inherent in defending the legal singularity – which has yet to come about – from critics who cast doubt on the feasibility of its eventual emergence *at the same time* as we are defending it from critics who acknowledge that it very well could come about but imagine many ways it could be harmful. In this book, we are certainly predicting that a legal singularity will likely come to pass, but our work is to track and analyse the forces that are likely to bring it about and to conjecture about some of the likely implications. It is not possible for us to accurately forecast its precise contours. The distinction is meaningful. Critics of the legal singularity tend to charge its enthusiasts with a more specific vision than we can possibly hope to offer in these pages. A second cautionary point: some critics take issue with the legal singularity as a *theory*, and some take issue with it as a prospective *event*. By contrast, Jennifer Cobbe – who doubts the likelihood of a legal singularity altogether[5] – takes the view that "better law," as advocated by legal singularity enthusiasts, is not normatively desirable, given that the nature of law is to reflect social realities that themselves might not be desirable (e.g., hierarchies and power asymmetries).[6] We respond to the various forms of critique together here.

II. Is Computational Law Reductionist?

Scholars arguing that data science techniques are too limited to capture the complexity of legal reasoning represent computational law's

---

4 See generally Robert F Weber, "Will the 'Legal Singularity' Hollow Out Law's Normative Core?" (2020) 27 Mich Tech L Rev 97.

5 Cobbe, *supra* note 3 at 108.

6 *Ibid* at 132–3.

fiercest – and earliest – critics. Scholarship in this area is typically focused either on the extent to which judges' work cannot be replicated through computational techniques, or on how machine learning is a poor fit for the kind of reasoning and argumentation that lawyers engage in. We address these below.

a. Pasquale, Hildebrandt, and Law's Unquantifiable Essence

A rather substantial literature argues that efforts to replicate judicial reasoning necessarily depend on overly formalistic models of judging. According to this view, advocates of computational law short-change important aspects of judging, such as the role judges play in appealing to public reason and evaluating social values. An early version of this critique was offered in 1998 by Giovanni Sartor and Karl Branting, who advocated caution in developing technologies that modelled judicial behaviour.[7] Sartor and Branting argued that the sophistication inherent in judicial reasoning is due to the combination of "legal expertise" and "cognitive and emotional competence."[8] Efforts to use algorithms beyond the "straightforward application of clear-cut rules to uncontroversial facts," then, are fraught:[9] how are algorithms to resolve new cases not contemplated by historical data, or effectively resolve issues where the facts and legal rules are themselves contested? According to Sartor and Branting, "No simple rule-chaining or pattern-matching algorithm can accurately model judicial decision-making because the judiciary has the task of producing reasonable and acceptable solutions in exactly those cases in which the facts, the rules, or how they fit together are controversial."[10]

Frank Pasquale offers an updated version of this view, arguing that AI is ill-suited for the kinds of complex, normative judgments inherent in legal reasoning. Pasquale occasionally concedes that computational law provides some meaningful insights. For instance, he explains that, if one adopts the view of a "tough-minded pragmatist," laws can be computed to the extent that they can help lawyers to predict whether "some police force, administrator, or judge will stop, penalise, or reward an action."[11] But to Pasquale, this is tantamount to a "narrow

---

7 Giovanni Sartor & Karl Branting, "Introduction: Judicial Applications of Artificial Intelligence" in Giovanni Sartor & Karl Branting, eds, *Judicial Applications of Artificial Intelligence* (Norwell, MA: Kluwer Academic Publishers, 1998) 1.

8 *Ibid* at 5–6.

9 *Ibid* at 6.

10 *Ibid*.

11 Pasquale, "Resilient Fragility," *supra* note 1 at vi.

game of foretelling the future."[12] He makes the point that, no matter how much computational legal methods might operationalize the law, legal decision-making is chock-full of disagreements about what ought to occur and how important legal principles ought to be weighed. To use Pasquale's example, consider *stare decisis*. In a given dispute, there might be disagreement about the importance of the applicable precedent and about "which interpretive methodology would best ensure its determinacy and generality." Adjudicating these sorts of controversies, Pasquale suggests, would be beyond the rational input-to-output mechanisms of computation.[13] Pasquale also predicts that AI will have a hard time grappling with the "essence" of proceedings – that is, the meaning that cannot be easily gleaned from the mere words of an opinion.[14] This is a rather common argument in the literature about AI and the law.[15]

Pasquale's view here is motivated by the belief that law and legal process have distinct public value that is threatened by computerization, and that these values are at least partially expressed in subtext and manner and not in the words that might be used as productive inputs for algorithms. He writes:

> But of course there is much more to law and legal process, particularly as social values evolve and the composition of the courts and the bar changes. AI is a long way from explaining *why* a case should be decided a certain way, and how broadly or narrowly an opinion ought to be written. Nor have technology firms proven themselves particularly adept at recognizing the many values at stake in such questions. Given that law is a human institution primarily concerned with human activities, it is quite possible that AI will never attain such forms of reason and evaluation. These skills and competences require normative judgment, and can only be legitimate when completed by a person who can subjectively understand what she or he is imposing on others when decisions are made.[16]

As an initial matter, Pasquale's critique of computational law depends on a remote and oftentimes esoteric conception of what law is and ought

---

12 *Ibid.*
13 *Ibid* at vii–viii.
14 *Ibid* at vi.
15 See, e.g., Deakin & Markou, "Rule," *supra* note 2 at 5–6. See also Mireille Hildebrandt, "Code-driven Law: Freezing the Future and Scaling the Past" in Deakin & Markou, *supra* note 1, 67 at 78.
16 Pasquale, "Resilient Fragility," *supra* note 1 at vii.

to be. To Pasquale, judicial opinions are more than their text, and litigation is about more than its outcomes. That is true, of course, but only in some senses. Judges, as human beings, may decide to resolve disputes according to principles (or biases, or predilections, or tastes for discrimination) that they are not necessarily compelled to disclose in their written reasons.[17] Moreover, judicial reasoning often involves interpretive manoeuvres that are not automatically accessible to untrained readers. But Pasquale's account goes much further in suggesting that there is an unquantifiable "essence" about judging that is worth preserving, and that lawyers are uniquely capable of deciphering it. In an article called "The Substance of Poetic Procedure" from the journal *Law and Literature*, Pasquale fleshes out this view more forcefully, rejecting any conception of lawyers as mere technical experts, in favour of an aspirational view of lawyers as decipherers of a social reality that is more contingent and layered than algorithms can ever properly discern.[18]

Here, we do not wish to rehash a century of debate about whether the law has content independent of its instrumental uses. We do not have more to say than Holmes, Hart, Dworkin, or Fuller on these matters. But Pasquale does not merely describe the law as complex and intractable – he defends it as such. Where some critics of computational law nevertheless concede a need for more simplicity in legal process,[19] Pasquale apparently believes that law's complexity is tied to its inherent value, writing that efforts to simplify "can dull us to the value of the complexity and intractability of the real."[20]

We observe at least three issues with this account. First, Pasquale contemplates a sharp distinction between law as experienced by its professional interlocutors (judges and lawyers) and law as experienced by its subjects (judges, lawyers, and everyone else). Law, to Pasquale, is a rich, value-laden, and tangled web. Untangling it is necessarily an elite pursuit, like explicating poetry.[21] The problem with this story is that it seemingly casts judges and lawyers as masters of the legal universe and

17 See, e.g., Jerome Frank, "Are Judges Human? Part One: The Effect on Legal Thinking of the Assumption That Judges Behave Like Human Beings" 80 U Pa L Rev 17 at 36–8. See also Bruce Ackerman, *The Failure of the Founding Fathers* (Cambridge, MA: Harvard University Press, 2005) at 8–10.

18 See generally Frank Pasquale, "The Substance of Poetic Procedure" (2020) 32:1 Law & Literature 1 [Pasquale, "Substance"]. See also Frank Pasquale, "A Rule of Persons, Not Machines: The Limits of Legal Automation" 87 Geo Wash L Rev 1 at 29–30 [Pasquale, "Rule"].

19 See, e.g., Weber, *supra* note 4 at 101. See also Jennifer Cobbe, *supra* note 3 at 109.

20 Pasquale, "Resilient Fragility," *supra* note 1 at xv.

21 See generally Pasquale, "Substance," *supra* note 18.

their litigants and clients – and by extension the public – as, at best, bit-players, or pawns. If this is true, our account begins with the view that this represents an inequitable distribution of epistemic and interpretive power. Though his broader work suggests an attentiveness to inequality, Pasquale's critiques of computational law here appear uninterested in a discussion of the burdens and resulting unfairness that the complex, difficult-to-parse laws impose on individuals and communities. He is not alone. Some other descriptive accounts of law's complexity likewise fail to grapple with the consequences of this complexity persisting. Markou and Deakin, for instance, describe legal reasoning as an "exercise in experimentation,"[22] without reference to or apparent concern for those who can scarcely afford for their life, liberty, or property to be experimented with.

Nor does Pasquale acknowledge how the very legal complexity that he defends is itself contributing to prohibitively expensive legal services. As Gillian Hadfield explains, the complexity involved in legal reasoning has direct effects on the cost of legal services by requiring that lawyers spend significant time and effort on legal analysis.[23] It also has indirect effects, as complicated law renders clients unable to properly gauge the quality of legal services, thereby making "price and quantity in the market predominantly the result of beliefs and wealth, rather than cost."[24] That Pasquale sidesteps this issue is especially confounding, given his acknowledgment that "[o]ur legal system exacerbates inequality because of uneven access to resources for advocacy."[25]

Central to Pasquale's defence of the specialness of law is a distinction between lawyers as members of a shared vocation and lawyers as service providers. Pasquale charges Richard and Daniel Susskind with

---

22 Christopher Markou & Simon Deakin, "Ex Machina Lex: The Limits of Legal Computability" (2019) in Deakin & Markou, *supra* note 1 at 63.

23 Gillian K Hadfield, "The Price of Law: How the Market for Lawyers Distorts the Justice System" (2000) 98:4 Mich L Rev 953 at 965.

24 *Ibid* at 995.

25 Frank Pasquale, "Automating the Professions: Utopian Pipe Dream or Dystopian Nightmare?" *Los Angeles Review of Books* (15 March 2016) [Pasquale, "Automating"], online: *LARB* <https://lareviewofbooks.org/article/automating-the-professions -utopian-pipe-dream-or-dystopian-nightmare> at para 12. In fairness, Pasquale is not indifferent to the disparities produced by the legal system. He simply believes that law's value is, at least sometimes, bound up in its indeterminacy. To Pasquale, that indeterminacy is not all bad; in the extreme, indeterminacy might look like incoherence, but, for most cases, some degree of indeterminacy means flexibility and adaptability, which can make for more responsive law. See generally Pasquale, "Resilient Fragility," *supra* note 1 at xv.

failing to understand this distinction in his review of their popular book, *The Future of the Professions*.[26] We would agree with Pasquale that the distinction exists, but we take issue with the implicit claim that it should exist in the way that it currently does. Take, for instance, Pasquale's contrasting how lawyers "work *with* clients" to how others work "*for* bosses or shareholders."[27] Here, Pasquale elevates lawyers to a co-equal role with those they represent. By contrast, our notion of the legal singularity anticipates an eroding distinction between law as experienced by lawyers and law as experienced by the public. If the law becomes knowable and at all times predictable to its subjects, the public can become the masters of – at a minimum – the garden-variety disputes that they are most likely to encounter. The public's mastery could be achieved by leveraging technology to combat the indeterminacy that Pasquale not only concedes is endemic to the law but also celebrates.[28]

In addition to his fixation with the specialness of the legal profession, a second major problem with Pasquale's critique is that he takes for granted the extent to which the important legal process values he seeks to protect are already painfully obscured by modern adjudication practices. If the claim is that technologies cannot pick up on judges' subtle value judgments and delicate normative discretion, then it raises the question of why this information is so hard to pick up on in the first place. We contend that the answer is because little about judicial practices has been properly systematized. Take, for instance, Pasquale's contention that "AI is a long way from explaining ... how broadly or narrowly an opinion ought to be written."[29] This is less a claim about AI's shortcomings than it is about the fact that judges appear to be relatively unconstrained in determining the narrowness of rulings. Currently, it is not just AI that might have difficulty determining how and when a ruling should be narrow: it is also the judges themselves![30] Perhaps more importantly, it is also lawyers and clients. If nothing else, Pasquale's criticism counsels for more standardization of judicial practices, not against fruitful applications of computational law.

---

26 Richard Susskind & Daniel Susskind, *The Future of the Professions* (Oxford: Oxford University Press, 2015).
27 Pasquale, "Automating," *supra* note 25 [emphasis in original].
28 Pasquale, "Rule" *supra* note 18 at 45–8.
29 Pasquale, "Resilient Fragility," *supra* note 1 at vii.
30 See, e.g., Antonin Scalia, "A Rule of Law Is a Law of Rules" (1989) 56 U Chi L Rev 1175.

Indeed, a common feature of the computational-law-is-reductionist camp is the relative ease with which they let current adjudication practices off the hook. As one example, consider Mireille Hildebrandt's concern that the transition to computational law may "render decisions based on its output inscrutable and thereby incontestable."[31] To Hildebrandt, contestability is an essential feature of complete legal systems. Contestability is, of course, possible only where outputs are legible, but Hildebrandt's contention is that, in many cases, computed decisions will be understandable only to individuals with specialized skills in complex machine learning applications.[32] For Hildebrandt, even expert validation of AI software is insufficient; she measures the relative opacity of a computational legal method by how well its chief stakeholders can understand its processes.[33] This line of criticism takes the rather unambitious view that innovations in legal methods ought to be capped by what today's lawyers and judges are capable of understanding. This view is not merely pessimistic; it is at odds with the history of adoption of increasingly complex technologies by professionals, lawyers included. Moreover, upskilling is especially possible in the legal profession, where the requirements include a professional degree and a licence (which itself requires standardized exam success and continuing education). Legal education reforms can take us at least part of the way towards knowledge that responds more effectively to our inevitable technological contexts.

Even assuming, for the sake of argument, that Hildebrandt is correct that computational methods will make algorithmically assisted judicial decisions out of reach for the average lawyer, we ask: why not extend the critique further and lament how inaccessible modern judicial decisions are to the public? Consider Hildebrandt's statement about AI-informed legal software: "Most of us lack the skills to make sense of it; we may in fact be forced to depend on claims made by those who stand to gain from its adoption and on the reputation of those offering this type of data driven legal service."[34] Remove the words "data driven" from the passage above, and Hildebrandt could just as easily be talking about the dependent relationship that laypeople have with lawyers and judges. The promise of legal prediction is the elimination of legal uncertainty and a real-time sense of one's legal rights and obligations

---

31 Mireille Hildebrandt, "Law as Computation in the Era of Artificial Legal Intelligence: Speaking Law to the Power of Statistics" (2018) 68:S1 UTLJ 12 at 28.
32 *Ibid* at 29.
33 *Ibid*.
34 *Ibid*.

and the consequences that flow from specific factual precedents. Much like the public, lawyers and judges stand to benefit from the specification of laws from open-ended standards to a dense thicket of rules that, though highly complex, will be organized in query-able systems and thus knowable *ex ante*. That this system might demand more technical skill from judges and lawyers in the short term is largely beside the point.

Returning now to Pasquale. In addition to over-emphasizing the specialness of lawyers and under-attending to the problems of modern adjudication, a third issue is that Pasquale's critique is fundamentally unimaginative. He insists on a totalizing image of legal prediction that – for some reason – involves no public deliberation about the content of the law, no legislative process, no policymaking, and no civil or criminal procedure. Put another way, despite being intensely protective of legal process against the threat of automation,[35] Pasquale fails to imagine that legal process can play *any* role at all in preventing the harms that he foresees. Pasquale is not alone here: Markou and Deakin contend that machine learning might not be more accurate than human decision-making in classifying workers because "there is no technically optimal solution to the question of how many employees or independent contractors there are in a given industry or economy."[36] Here, Markou and Deakin do not contemplate the possibility of *ex ante* public policy processes. If the issue is that society has not agreed on the proper distribution between independent contractors and employees, then the solution should be to forge consensus. Computational legal methods can do some of the work in exposing misclassification, in surfacing enforcement issues with respect to certain classification factors, and in forecasting how different worker profiles will tend to be classified by future courts. The task of deciding what we *want*, though, remains a deeply human endeavour.

At bottom, computational legal methods are aimed at resolving ambiguity and uncertainty in substantive legal questions and forecasting substantive legal outcomes. This is fundamentally a claim about substance and not procedure. The ability to predict legal outcomes (and turn open-ended standards into highly specified rules) is about clarifying the content of the law and achieving substantive completeness. Put differently, it is about making the law knowable *ex ante* rather than

---

35 See, e.g., Pasquale, "Resilient Fragility," *supra* note 1 at xv, where he cautions against even the aspiration to develop automation as "dangerous."

36 Markou & Deakin, *supra* note 22 at 63.

merely discoverable *ex post*. But our account of the legal singularity does not, for instance, mandate that legal systems abandon the principle of providing written reasons to litigants. Nor does it demand that we preclude contestation by jettisoning rights to counsel or appeal. If critics are willing to imagine it, there is considerable space for procedural buffers against the abuses that can be imagined.

b. Ideology, Social Context, and the Legal Singularity

One of Pasquale's go-to manoeuvres is to associate computational law enthusiasts with ideologies that he finds personally repugnant. At various times, supporters of legal automation are neoliberals or practitioners of "vulgar law & economics."[37] In one particularly exciting rhetorical flourish, Pasquale describes legal technology enthusiasts as prioritizing "computational puzzles over social problems, matching and sorting over judgment and persuasion."[38] Elsewhere, he laments the prospect of what he calls "total algorithmatization," a term that consciously invokes Marx's concept of total subsumption.[39] The effect of the reference, of course, is to accuse computational lawyers of relentlessly pursuing productivity and capital at the expense of all else.

These sorts of critiques are not responsive to anything written by scholars in the emergent field of computational legal studies. At the risk of speculating, we would suggest that they appear instead to be motivated by a generalized antipathy towards automation. As a result, Pasquale is prone to invoking wildly divergent examples of automation gone wrong as cautionary tales for the legal profession. The few items that Pasquale marshals as examples of specific legal issues that ought not to be resolved computationally are flawed. Take his discussion of how the law classifies workers as either independent contractors or employees. To Pasquale, this is an example of where computational lawyers engage in "escapism": rather than dealing with the social and political issues that underlie the worker classification, he contends, computational lawyers take the easy route and try to commit the complex legal question to computers.[40] Markou and Deakin take a similar view, observing that applying machine learning techniques to the

---

37 See, e.g., Pasquale, "Substance," *supra* note 18 at 2.
38 Pasquale, "Resilient Fragility," *supra* note 1 at xiv.
39 Pasquale, "Substance," *supra* note 18 at 3n17.
40 Pasquale, "Resilient Fragility," *supra* note 1 at xiv.

worker-classification question is likely to obscure the political judgments that go into the distinction.[41]

These accounts are contradicted by some of the computational legal research on precisely the same worker-classification question. Recent work by Charlotte Alexander and Mohammad Javad Feizollahi used machine learning to examine a decade of employee *mis*classification decisions in US federal courts, finding that definitional issues in the common law test and inconsistent application of certain factors lead to fairly predictable misclassification.[42] Charlotte Alexander's empirical work also demonstrates that the stakes are high: the same dataset used in the Alexander and Feizollahi study revealed that women and people of colour are much more likely to be misclassified as independent contractors, the consequence of which is that these individuals are unable to seek relief under federal antidiscrimination statutes unless they seek reclassification via (prohibitively expensive) lawsuits.[43] To put it starkly, an unreasonably high number of employers currently get away with infringing on workers' rights – both purposely and inadvertently – through misclassification, in part because of the imprecise legal standard.

Even in this narrow example, the modes of legal reasoning that Pasquale, Deakin, and Markou champion as essential for social justice purposes have tended to produce outcomes that make the prospect of securing justice even more remote for workers. Computational legal methods reveal this to be the case, but also suggest corrective courses of action. For instance, while legislatures can work to fix the definitional issues that Alexander and Fiezollahi have identified, judges can use the predictive analytics to adhere more closely to legal precedent. Or, where they wish to make discretionary interventions, judges can use the data to assess the ultimate impact on individuals and labour relations. While this is happening, would-be litigants can use prediction tools to assess their likelihood of success on the merits, and employers can use the same tools to structure work arrangements that do not run afoul of federal law. None of these outcomes suggests the ambivalence

---

41 Markou & Deakin, *supra* note 22.

42 See generally Charlotte S Alexander & Mohammad Javad Feizollahi, "Decisional Shortcuts and Selection Effects: An Empirical Study of Ten Years of US District Courts' Employee Misclassification Decisions" (2019) [unpublished] archived online: *Department of Labor* <https://www.dol.gov/sites/dolgov/files/OASP/evaluation/pdf/LRE_Alexander-DecisionalShortcutsandSelectionEffects_December2020.pdf>.

43 Charlotte S Alexander, "Misclassification and Antidiscrimination: An Empirical Analysis" (2017) 101:3 Minn L Rev 907 at 910.

about individual rights, collective rights, or social justice that Pasquale and others associate with computational law.

So, why the dim view of computational lawyers? Deakin and Markou contend that "the legal singularity is implicitly a proposal for eliminating juridical reasoning as a basis for dispute resolution and normative decision-making."[44] To them, AI research rests too heavily on symbolic and mathematical logic, which necessarily abstracts from the context in which law and its institutions develop. Deakin and Markou write:

> But if mathematical logic cannot capture the "situation-specific understanding" of legal reasoning and the complexity of the social world it exists in – at least to any extent congruent with how natural language categories cognise social referents and character of meaning – the hypothetical totalization of "AI judges" implied by the legal singularity would instantiate a particular view of law: one in which legal judgments are essentially deterministic or probabilistic outputs, produced on the basis of static or unambiguous legal rules, in a societal vacuum. This would deny, or see as irrelevant, competing conceptions of the law, in particular the idea that law is a social institution, involving socially constructed activities, relationships, and norms not easily translated into numerical functions.[45]

In our view, this critique comes from a fundamental misunderstanding of what computational law sets out to do. Computational legal methods harness computing power to synthesize larger volumes of legal information more quickly and with more granularity than is possible within analogue systems. But computational law makes use of the same building blocks as traditional legal reasoning, namely established rules of law and established facts. When systems of adjudication are operating according to their stated purpose, litigants should expect that courts will apply well-publicized legal rules to proven facts and provide a reasoned and transparent rationale for judgment. Assuming courts are not purposefully departing from this general process, this information can indeed be used as productive inputs for legal prediction. Consider how courts are bound to the principles of *stare decisis* and how judges are, by professional custom, expected to express their judgments in a manner consistent with the principles of legal reasoning. Lawyers today depend upon a consistent judicial process to meaningfully advise clients about everything from litigation strategy to settlement and to

---

44 Deakin & Markou, "Rule," *supra* note 2 at 5.
45 *Ibid* at 6.

future behaviour. Where judges deviate from these broad outlines, lawyers are not necessarily well-positioned to provide sound advice, or at least are worse off than if the legal process remained dependable.

In chapter 2, we discussed a continuum that classifies different types of legal information according to degrees of predictiveness (see figure 2.1). Primary statements of law (like the words of a statute and a judge's opinion) are certainly the most predictive of the outcome, but algorithmic design is also informed by material such as treatises (secondary statements of law), legal interpretive sources (such as scholarship and commentary), as well as non-legal interpretive sources like information from cognate disciplines or scientific and social-scientific facts.

The Canadian employment law doctrine of "reasonable notice" provides a good example of how algorithmic prediction can process information that illuminates broader social context. Employers in Canada have a common law duty to provide employees that are terminated without cause with a reasonable notice period, or payment in lieu of that reasonable notice.[46] "Reasonableness," is, of course, a fuzzy standard. In the leading case that announced the relevant factors, *Bardal*, the court even went as far as to say that "[t]here can be no catalogue laid down as to what is reasonable in particular cases."[47] As a result, these disputes are rather messy case-by-case determinations that nevertheless depend reliably upon certain variables: Anthony Niblett's empirical work shows that courts are swayed primarily by a former employee's length of service.[48] But other relevant factors can include, for instance, whether similar employment is available in the former employee's geographical area.[49] A machine learning algorithm aimed at predicting how much notice a former employee is entitled to can take stock of how all prior courts treated the primary statements of law (e.g., the *Bardal* factors) and will absorb all relevant facts about the circumstances of the employment, but it can also synthesize – as one example – job market data so as to contextualize the difficulty level of the former employee's future job search, demographic data, and so on. The designer of a reasonable notice predictor, then, can choose to consider all the salient social context information. Deakin, Markou, Pasquale, and Cobbe do not trust these designers to make the right choices, and so

---

46 Reaffirmed in the 2008 decision *Keays v Honda Canada Inc*, 2008 SCC 39 at para 28.
47 *Bardal v Globe & Mail Ltd*, 1960 CarswellOnt 144 at para 21, 24 DLR (2d) 140.
48 Anthony Niblett, "Algorithms as Legal Decisions: Gender Gaps and Canadian Employment Law in the 21st Century" (2020) [unpublished], online: *SSRN* <https://papers.ssrn.com/sol3/papers.cfm?abstract_id=3702495> at 10.
49 *Ibid*.

they overstate the incompatibilities between computational legal methods and traditional legal reasoning.

c. The Limits of Techno-Critique

At this juncture, it is worth acknowledging that some of the scepticism of computational law has been helped along by some unfortunately flawed examples of machine learning's application to the law. One example is a study by Aletras et al, which Pasquale and Glyn Cashwell rightly criticize for its methodological shortcomings.[50] In their takedown, Pasquale and Cashwell observe that using case law as "data" ignores the human context of a judge *actually writing the facts that inform algorithms*. Put differently, using a judge's own words as inputs for prediction fails to acknowledge the extent to which judges are not neutral descriptors of underlying case facts, and understates the extent to which judges may editorialize to legitimize their chosen outcomes.[51]

Pasquale and Cashwell's criticisms of Aletras et al's study are well taken. But their critiques quite clearly extend beyond the narrow study,[52] and thus merit a response. Here, we do not take the view that predictive algorithms based on prior case law data are perfect. However, Pasquale and Cashwell's claim that a "truly predictive system would use filings of the parties, or data outside the filings, in existence before the judgment itself"[53] demands interrogation. We agree that predictions based on competing court filings would be helpful in determining what sorts of arguments are most persuasive before tribunals. But competing court filings, even if equally biased on both sides, do not necessarily themselves have to provide true accounts of case facts. The various recitations of facts in parties' filings will tend to be drafted in a manner aimed at vindicating a litigant's theory of the case. This happens stylistically through litigants' choices to emphasize or de-emphasize certain facts, but also substantively in litigants' decisions to include and omit elements from the factual record. Judicial fact descriptions, though imperfect, are at least subject to the buffers of legal process: judges are called on to be impartial and independent, and judges' fact-finding responsibilities

---

50 See generally Frank Pasquale & Glyn Cashwell, "Prediction, Persuasion, and the Jurisprudence of Behaviorism" (2017) University of Maryland Legal Studies Research Paper No. 2017-34, online: *SSRN* <https://papers.ssrn.com/sol3/papers.cfm?abstract_id=3067737>.
51 *Ibid* at 5–7.
52 *Ibid* at 12–13.
53 *Ibid* at 5.

demand that they account for evidentiary considerations such as reliability and credibility. Moreover, judges render decisions at the end of a legal process where the facts themselves are examined and contested, whereas parties' court filings describe facts before they are subjected to *any* scrutiny.

Even with this said, Pasquale and Cashwell's criticisms fail to give computational technologies their proper credit. Even if one concedes that Pasquale and Cashwell are right that predicting with historical case data is not *true* prediction, such algorithms still resolve an important ambiguity: how judges decide cases after certain facts are established. Resolving this ambiguity alone creates considerable opportunity for lawyers to strategize towards desired outcomes. Yet Pasquale and Cashwell seem generally unconcerned with the client-service advantages of even imperfect algorithmic prediction.[54] To make this point more clearly, imagine a human rights lawyer trying to persuade a trial judge that their client's disabilities were not properly accommodated in the workplace. Imagine the lawyer had access to what Pasquale and Cashwell imagine as a "truly predictive system"[55] – namely, an algorithm trained on the parties' court filings. What task, exactly, would the algorithm perform? As a matter of timing, the parties already would have constructed their arguments and made their submissions. Arguably, the point at which predictive technology could be helpful to promote access to justice has passed. It could be argued that, for the lawyers involved, knowing how to formulate their filings to maximize the expected potential of a result in favour of their clients would be a valuable thing to predict. The challenge in this context is that the optimal filing for each side would depend on the filing of the other. And it is likely that the most successful filings might do violence to the truth or the lawyers' professional obligations and duties, or both.

Taken together, these criticisms of computational law as reductionist fail to recognize the emergent field as giving rising to an ongoing process of improvement to the law and legal institutions. In our view, current systems barely scratch the surface of legal technology's potential. Critiques that are hyper-focused on today's capabilities, then, risk becoming outdated by the next technological improvement. The first wave of scholars who cautioned against the application of computing techniques to law, for instance, all clearly contemplated computing models that were far

---

54 *Ibid* at 12, where the authors "question whether the results of such projects are useful to the legal system."
55 *Ibid* at 5.

more rigid than the kind of detailed modelling possible with modern machine learning and big data. Many of today's machine learning techniques are now capable of the evaluation and reasoning skills that early critics thought unlikely or impossible.

III. Does the Legal Singularity Threaten the Rule of Law?

In addition to criticisms of computational law as reductionist, some scholars have argued that the legal singularity poses a distinct threat to the rule of law. These two types of criticisms overlap. Some in the computational-law-is-reductionist camp, such as Hildebrandt, Markou, and Deakin, are motivated chiefly by a concern that law's normative aspirations are being shortchanged by what is in their view a new kind of dogmatic formalism. We consider some of the leading criticisms below.

Perhaps the strongest "computational-law-is-reductionist" critique comes from Robert F. Weber in the aptly titled "Will the Legal Singularity Hollow Out Law's Normative Core?" In that article, Weber argues that, despite its efficiency advantages, legal prediction will "[dissolve] the normative content of the two core pillars of the rule of law: the predictability principle" and the "universality principle."[56]

As Weber summarizes, the predictability principle holds that members of liberal political societies should be able to "predict how the law will apply to them."[57] This predictability takes two distinct forms. The first is what Weber calls the "weak-form" predictability principle, which is the essential functionalist view that predictability is good because it allows for social planning and coordination. The second type, or "strong-form" predictability, views predictability as good because it "operates as a check on the exercise of arbitrary governmental power."[58] In other words, governments are less likely to exercise authority in arbitrary ways if said arbitrariness is likely to be viewed as a deviation from normal – i.e., predictable – legal rules. In Weber's view, proponents of legal prediction are guilty of placing weak-form, functionalist predictability above all else, thereby threatening the law's normative commitment to non-arbitrariness. Put differently, as technologists operationalize the law to better facilitate social planning, they undermine the rule of law's link to its broader social and political purpose.[59]

---

56 Weber, *supra* note 4 at 97.
57 *Ibid* at 102.
58 *Ibid.*
59 *Ibid* at 97.

Weber's strong-form predictability has its origins in Lockean political theory. Locke famously argued in his *Two Treatises of Government* that, since governments derive their legitimacy from public consent, they must necessarily be constrained by "established standing laws, promulgated and known to the people, and not by extemporary decrees."[60] In this sense, Locke considered law that is publicized and known to the public to be a bulwark against abuse. Put differently, if the laws are established and if the consenting public is aware of them, then that public can withdraw consent wherever those laws are breached or ignored altogether.

Weber's otherwise thoughtful critique here makes a significant error. In warning that the legal singularity might undermine the necessary predictability of modern legal systems, Weber fails to acknowledge – or at least underemphasizes – that this predictability is more of an abstract notion than a reality. The kind of predictability that Weber prizes as essential to the rule of law is, in short, elusive. Much of his argument hinges on legal systems needing to be "roughly predictable" to inculcate a sense of the rule of law and protect individuals from illegal overreach.[61] Yet Weber neither makes the affirmative case for the current system as being at all predictable nor acknowledges the threat that the current state of widespread legal uncertainty poses to the rule of law. In fact, a substantial empirical literature exists, dating back as early as the 1960s, to demonstrate that the public has little – or, at least, *poor* – knowledge of the law.[62] More recently, empirical studies have demonstrated the following: that employees were not substantially aware of their rights under their employment agreements,[63] and that fewer than half of observed citizens were aware of the criminal law right

---

60 *Ibid* at 132, quoting John Locke, *Two Treatises of Government*, ed by Peter Laslett (Cambridge: Cambridge University Press, 1988) at 358–9.

61 *Ibid* at 131.

62 See, e.g., Charles F Cortese, "A Study in Knowledge and Attitudes towards the Law" (1966) 2 Rocky Mountain Social Science J 192.

63 Pauline T Kim, "An Empirical Challenge to Employment at Will" (1998) 23:2 New Zealand J Employment Relations 91; Pauline T Kim, "Norms, Learning and Law: Exploring the Influences of Workers' Legal Knowledge" (1999) 2 U Ill L Rev 447; and Pascoe Pleasence, Nigel J Balmer & Catrina Denvir, "Wrong about Rights: Public Knowledge of Key Areas of Consumer, Housing and Employment Law in England and Wales" (2017) 80:5 Mod L Rev 836, all cited in Benjamin Van Rooij, "Do People Know The Law? Empirical Evidence about Legal Knowledge and Its Importance for Compliance" (2020) University of California Irvine School of Law Research Paper No 2020–2.

against self-incrimination or the presumption of innocence.[64] Opinion polls administered to laypeople have also demonstrated that the public views certain laws – tax codes, for instance – as too complex.[65] Like Pasquale, Weber makes the mistake of thinking that predictability to elite professional intermediaries (e.g., lawyers) is a sufficient stand-in for the predictability of law for its subjects.

Studies have demonstrated that even *engaged* citizens do not generally have reliable knowledge of the law. A 1992 study by Reifman, Gusick, and Ellsworth, as one example, found that the average respondent *who had actually served on criminal or civil juries* was unable to correctly answer half of the tested questions about the duties and rules for jurors.[66] There are similar studies finding that public knowledge of family, criminal, and employment law is poor,[67] despite the high salience of these substantive areas to the lives of the studies' participants. As explored in the treatment of legal information in chapter 2, legal uncertainty is a problem that plagues even lawyers, a group for whom substantive knowledge of the law is a matter of professional responsibility. The reality that lawyers need specialized skills and training to conduct effective legal research and provide sound advice makes it clear that accurate legal information is practically inaccessible to laypersons.

Even aside from the empirical evidence suggesting that people do not generally know the law, there is ample reason to believe that the law is becoming less and less knowable. As Guido Calabresi famously wrote, the American legal system – as just one example – underwent a process of "statutorification," whereby more and more legal doctrines that would have previously been the principal domain of courts were being announced by legislatures in difficult-to-parse statutory schemes.[68]

---

64 Van Rooij, *supra* note 63 at 9, citing Stan L Albrecht & Miles Green, "Cognitive Barriers to Equal Justice before the Law" (1977) 14:2 J Research in Crime and Delinquency 206.

65 See, e.g., Pew Research, "Federal Tax System in Need of Overhaul" (19 March 2015), online: *Pew Research Center* <https://www.pewresearch.org/politics/2015/03/19/federal-tax-system-seen-in-need-of-overhaul/>. The report notes that 44 per cent of respondents are bothered "a lot" by the complexity of the federal tax system.

66 Van Rooij, *supra* note 63 at 9–10, discussing Alan Reifman, Spencer M Gusick & Phoebe C Ellsworth, "Real Jurors' Understanding of the Law in Real Cases" (1992) 16:5 Law & Human Behavior 539.

67 Van Rooij, *supra* note 63 at 7–12.

68 Richard Neely, "Obsolete Statutes, Structural Due Process, and the Power of the Courts to Demand a Second Legislative Look," Book Review of *A Common Law for the Age of Statutes* by Guido Calabresi (1982) 131:1 U Pa L Rev 271 at 272, online: <https://doi.org/10.2307/3311834>.

Scholars have long written about the law's resulting complexity. In fact, the complexity of modern law is so well known that it is taken for granted in other fields; for instance, in his seminal 1995 book on complexity theory, *At Home in the Universe*, developmental biologist Stuart Kauffman used the common law as an example of a system giving rise to complex adaptive behaviour.[69]

Weber's account of the importance of the predictability principle also fails to pay sufficient attention to the extent to which the building blocks of legal predictability – precedential court decisions – no longer provide clarity or certainty in twenty-first-century legal practice (if they ever did). Much like the proliferation of complex statutory networks, the corpus of case law that constitutes the common law is itself swelling.[70] The increased number of precedents means two things. First, searches are increasingly showing that there is case law standing for an ever-growing list of purported legal principles. Clever lawyers, particularly those with access to digital research databases, now have an easier time finding case law in support of virtually *any* legal argument they wish to make.[71] Of course, this is supposed to be, and sometimes is, constrained by the various rules around *stare decisis*, including the preference for binding jurisdictional precedent.[72] A second consequence of an increased volume of precedent is that legal rules have ever-expanding universes of applicability. Creative litigants can succeed in expanding the scope of legal rules.[73] Also, as social contexts change, laws that were contemplated for specific purposes become adapted for and used in others. This is especially true where new technologies and financial instruments are developing at a rate faster than the ability of legislators and judges to craft responsive law, leading to what Joan Heminway has referred to as organically evolving legal patchworks.[74]

---

69 JB Ruhl & Daniel Martin Katz, "Measuring, Monitoring, and Managing Legal Complexity" 101 Iowa L Rev 191 at 205, citing Stuart Kauffman, *At Home in the Universe: The Search for Laws of Self-Organization and Complexity* (New York: Oxford University Press, 1995) at 169.

70 William B Eldridge & Sally F Dennis, "The Computer as a Tool for Legal Research" (1963) 28:1 Law and Contemp Probs 78 at 78.

71 *Ibid* at 220.

72 *Ibid*.

73 Ronald J Allen, "Complexity, the Generation of Legal Knowledge, and the Future of Litigation" (2013) 60 UCLA L Rev 1384 at 1408.

74 See generally Joan Heminway, "The Legal Regulation of US Crowdfunding: An Organically Evolving Patchwork" (2017) University of Tennessee Legal Studies Research Paper No. 335, online: *SSRN* <https://papers.ssrn.com/sol3/papers.cfm?abstract_id=3061552>.

Of course, we are not contending that Weber would deny that the law is complex and that relevant legal information is hard to find and synthesize adequately. Rather, we argue that Weber makes an error that is common to many critics of the legal singularity: his work fails to reckon with contemporary legal systems' current characteristic deficiencies. Much as Hildebrandt and Pasquale take computational law to task without acknowledging the legal process failures that make legal computation desirable (and, we would argue, normatively necessary), Weber condemns the legal singularity as bound to erode predictability without meaningfully considering the extent to which the legal profession's own doctrines, cultures, and institutions might have long eroded the Lockean predictability that he is apparently nostalgic for. In our view, there is a lack of meaningful predictability in the law on three related levels. First, primary statements of law, be they in judicial opinions or statutes, can be impenetrable, highly complex, and dangerously underspecified. Second, the kinds of legal information that would make meaningful prediction possible is practically inaccessible to laypeople and frequently inaccessible to lawyers due to resource constraints or missing information. Third, judicial discretion and the manipulability of broad legal standards make it difficult, absent computational methods, to predict with sufficient granularity what is likely to happen in a particular context or court case.

Turning now to the universality principle, which he explains as "the rule of law depend[ing] in part on law's general applicability to all legal subjects,"[75] Weber argues that the desire to highly specify the law undermines the political community that the law forges. As an initial matter, that Weber is so strident about the virtues of universality is surprising. He explains that "[a]n implicit bedrock of the universality principle is that the differences among legal subjects are outweighed by what we – or, better still, 'we' who are, as Blackstone puts it, the 'community in general' – have in common." He calls this "a logic of political connectedness" and contrasts it with how the "epistemology of data science implies a logic of total differentiation, with each data point, including data concerning legal subjects, being unique."[76]

The law's "general applicability to its subjects" might well be an aspiration, but it is one that is contradicted by the experience of the law's subjects in ways that Weber is barely attentive to. Decades of critical legal theory have challenged the notion of universality in legal doctrine.

---

75 Weber, *supra* note 4 at 103.
76 *Ibid.*

Angela Harris's seminal article "Race and Essentialism in Feminist Legal Theory" memorably opens by criticizing the "universal voice" in the Preamble of the United States Constitution, explaining that expressions of political community inherent in statements like "we the people" depend on the silence of disparate groups.[77] Yet Weber calls for a level of abstraction in legal rights and obligations that rather anachronistically assumes common interests.

Weber also understates the extent to which day-to-day law already aspires to specificity and differentiation. Casey and Niblett explain that, the law of negligence, as one example, is designed to account for any relevant factors bearing on an individual's conduct, such that courts can decide about how "a reasonable person would have acted in the *same situation*."[78] Think, also, of standards of care. Courts routinely require that individuals with specialized skills and knowledge exercise more care than laypeople, or, conversely, allow for individuals with diminished capacity to satisfy a lower standard of care. A doctor treating an injured person is held to a higher standard by law than a layperson who might clumsily offer assistance.[79] The point here is that the two individuals in this example already operate under what is effectively different law. Granted, the so-called objective standard is still the rule rather than the exception, but, at a minimum, there is allowance for *some* meaningful particularization. Likewise, under some tax systems in the Anglo-American legal world, liability for certain errors or eligibility for penalty relief depends in part on a consideration of the taxpayer's education and skills.[80] Indeed, anywhere that a legal rule involves consideration of factors such as reasonableness, intent, good or bad faith, or an individual's skill or knowledge, there is potential for considerable personalization.[81] Perhaps Weber takes the view that law is not personalized unless it specifically targets individuals by name, identity, or class.

---

77 See generally Angela P Harris, "Race and Essentialism in Feminist Legal Theory" (1990) 42:3 Stan L Rev 581.
78 Anthony J Casey & Anthony Niblett, "A Framework for the New Personalization of Law" (2019) 86 U Chi L Rev 333 at 335.
79 Omri Ben-Shahar & Ariel Porat, "Personalizing Negligence Law" (2015) 91:3 NYL Rev 627 at 629–30.
80 See, e.g., *Meixner v The Queen*, 2005 TCC 283 at para 66 (court agrees with respondent's counsel that "a person with the Appellant's level of education and experience would have had at least a basic idea that property transactions could have such consequence").
81 See generally Ben-Shahar & Porat, *supra* note 79.

Here, it is worth reciting the advantages of personalization that Weber dismisses as a "new data epistemology [that] ... requires an atomistic pulverization of groups in general, including the citizenry, the polity ..."[82] Personalization has clear benefits beyond the efficiency gains that, as Weber acknowledges,[83] come with enhanced legal prediction. The primary benefit is that personalization allows for clear objectives. As Casey and Niblett explain, lawmakers can get away with enacting a legal rule without specifying its purpose, whereas algorithms need to be directed about "what to do with the data."[84] The algorithmic design process necessitates specific objectives. Better yet, the algorithmic design process demands that the objectives be stated *ex ante*. As an illustrative example, imagine town lawmakers enacting legislation to regulate noise. In our current context, the rulemaking process is rather straightforward: lawmakers receive input from various stakeholders and promulgate a rule after some deliberation and democratic consent. As part of the rulemaking exercise, legislators must, of course, balance competing interests. In the case of noise regulation, lawmakers are aware that some noise is necessary to facilitate socialization, transportation, and economic activity, among other things. Lawmakers are also aware that some societal actors are greater noise-producers than others – a concert hall, for instance, might be, on average, considerably louder than a local library. Lawmakers also know that the absolute volume is not the only factor that goes into determining whether noise is offensive or not. The concert hall, for example, might be much louder than the local manufacturing plant, but the sound of music might be more acceptable than the clanking of metal and the humming of machinery. In the pre-personalization world, lawmakers would try to identify a noise limit that reduced unnecessary noise without stifling too many of the listed productive activities. But how exactly would they do so? At best, lawmakers would make crude *ex ante* judgments about optimal noise levels. Even if informed by studies about noise mitigation, the law would be limited unless it took account of individual actors' noise pollution and set standards accordingly. Worse yet, the public might have only a vague sense of what interests were considered in the rulemaking process.

In a world where big data dramatically reduce information costs,[85] lawmakers can have access to real-time information about

---

82 Weber, *supra* note 4 at 157–8.
83 *Ibid* at 101.
84 Casey & Niblett, *supra* note 78 at 339.
85 *Ibid* at 340.

noise-producers, which can then be used to inform an algorithm that identifies the optimal – or highest acceptable – noise output for each actor (e.g., concert hall, factory, school, etc.). To instruct an algorithm that can effectuate their preferred public policies, lawmakers might have to specify their objectives. An algorithm that is programmed to pursue an objective of "no noise" might suggest promulgating a rule that allows for – say – 40 decibels of noise (a level of volume consistent with whispering) from 6:00 p.m. to 6:00 a.m. To avoid that kind of result, lawmakers would have to be deliberate about which factors they want the algorithm to consider and precisely how these factors should be weighed.[86] The public would also benefit here by gaining a clear sense of the competing interests that underlie the rules they are subject to. Contrary to Weber's claims, the benefits of more legal certainty go far beyond functional predictability and, indeed, implicates the rule of law; individuals would be made aware of the extent to which certain state actions would impose constraints, the severity of those constraints relative to others in the community, and the data-informed rationale for imposing those constraints.[87]

To the extent that Weber's notion of universality is really a stand-in for a certain brand of legal equality, he still fails to meet his burden of explaining precisely how that equality is compromised by the differentiation and personalization that legal prediction makes possible. Weber prefers what he terms "abstract equality" to "particularistic inequality"[88] but makes no allowance for the possibility of *particularistic equality*. This equality can be achieved in two related ways. First, much like the noise pollution example above, legislation can be drafted *ex ante* with a view to its likely disparate impact. Second, more particularization means more efficient allocation of law's burdens. Imagine, for instance, tax laws that are sensitive to the inequities that have been revealed by recent scholarship. As one example, consider Dorothy A. Brown's findings that the substantive requirements of certain federal tax laws trigger a disproportionate number of audits of low-income taxpayers, even where there is no evidence of wrongdoing.[89] The combination of computational methods and taxpayer data would lay bare this inequality and permit lawmakers to intervene. At that point, there are a multitude of choices: administrative rules that contemplate differential

---

86 *Ibid.*
87 *Ibid* at 344.
88 Weber, *supra* note 4 at 158.
89 See generally Dorothy A. Brown, "Race and Class Matters in Tax Policy" (2007) 107 Colum L Rev 790.

audit triggers depending on income, new substantive law statutes, procedural rules that enable more robust forms of relief, and so on.

Above all, in inviting readers to think of the legal singularity as a system on autopilot, Weber dramatically understates the role that people and politics will continue to have in shaping normative outcomes. Predictive analytics, as he concedes, "*might* reveal divergences between law's claim to universality and its actual operative distinctions."[90] As one example, leveraging big data to predict employment claims might reveal patterns and practices of discrimination that have been exceedingly difficult to establish in courts. Yet, for some reason, Weber imagines that these newly exposed inequalities will exist in plain sight without any effort to correct them. Even if lawmakers do not have an appetite to correct inequalities on their own volition, they are not suddenly impervious to political pressure, organized social movements, or legitimate stakeholder influence. It is not clear why Weber believes a legal singularity necessarily means a closed system of domination. Much like other critics of the legal singularity, Weber also understates (or simply does not imagine) the likely role of legal process in ameliorating the harms he is certain will come about. Suppose, for example, an aggrieved citizen challenges a burdensome tax provision that applies *only to her*. Adjudicating the constitutionality or applicability of that personalized law can be an individualized determination, and courts may be less inclined to preserve an inequitable provision because of the broader impact of striking it down. Weber's criticisms of the legal singularity are well taken, but not sufficiently imaginative.

Finally, even if Weber is right that the legal singularity will undermine the law's normative content such that the rule of law is threatened, he dramatically understates the role of other social and political institutions as bulwarks for the rule of law. Weber takes cover behind Joseph Raz's "narrow formulation"[91] of the rule of law as "specifying that the rule of law's importance as an antidote to arbitrary government was primarily attributable to the values of predictability and universality."[92] But Weber draws Raz's conception too narrowly. Raz's "The Rule of Law and Its Virtues" famously enumerated "principles which can be derived from the basic idea of the rule of law": prospectivity and clarity of laws, stability, judicial independence, openly accessible courts, and

---

90 Weber, *supra* note 4 at 154.
91 *Ibid* at 126n115.
92 *Ibid* at 164.

so on.[93] Weber's account largely ignores these, and does not consider the impact the legal singularity might have in bolstering these rule-of-law values. In some ways, the narrow focus on predictability and universality lead Weber to second-best discussions of principles that are themselves fundamental to the rule of law. The result is an unnecessarily narrow critique of the legal singularity that makes contested claims about predictability and universality, but does not adequately consider the other important principles that sustain the rule of law.

---

93 Joseph Raz, "The Rule of Law and Its Virtues" in *The Authority of Law: Essays on Law and Morality* (New York: Oxford University Press, 1979) 210 at 214–19.

Chapter Six

Implications for the Judiciary

I. Introduction

Thus far in this book, we have discussed what the legal singularity is, described the role of legal information and the proliferation of computational law and legal prediction, and defended the legal singularity against critics who believe it to be either a remote possibility or normatively undesirable. The remainder of this book moves beyond tracking these emerging phenomena and toward describing the legal singularity's future promise. We begin in this chapter with what laypeople and professionals alike might think of as the law's "home": the courts.

It goes without saying that courts are central to our conception of the law, both as clarifiers of legal rules and doctrine and as enforcers. The vitality of judiciaries was perhaps best summed up by Alexander Hamilton in Federalist No. 22, where he wrote – famously under the pseudonym Publius – that "Laws are a dead letter without courts to expound and define their true meaning and operation."[1] In this chapter, we will discuss the problems with the judicial system today, including inconsistency, bias, and a lack of both transparency and expertise, and that it simply takes too long to reach an adjudicated outcome. The computational era is bringing changes to this system. Judges will be better able to decide matters of fact, expert and non-expert. They will be better equipped to make predictions about the consequences of their decisions, improving the quality of the policy decision-making function they inevitably serve. Adopting computational methods into the judiciary will create various challenges, like concerns about fairness and

---

1 Alexander Hamilton, "The Federalist Papers: No. 22" (1787), online: *Yale Law School, Avalon Project* <https://avalon.law.yale.edu/18th_century/fed22.asp>.

propriety in decision-making, but the methods themselves will help to resolve some of those concerns. The result is that judges will be able to do legal research faster. There will be more certainty in how most cases will be decided on both the facts and the law, leading to more settlements. There will be better explanations for decisions, especially discretionary ones. Judges will know the repercussions of their decisions and thus be better able to decide those flip-of-a-coin cases that prediction machines cannot necessarily resolve satisfactorily.

In the end, judges will have a harder job: factual and legal uncertainty will decrease to the point that the cases going to court will be complex and challenging, but judges will have a lot of help in making those decisions – from computational tools, counsel, and each other. What's more, in making those policy choices, computational methods will help. Computational tools will assist judges in finding the normative values that appeal to them and to others in order to help make tough calls. People may have concerns about this coming world, but when the full impact of technology begins to be felt throughout the law, we are going to be able to benefit from better judicial decision-making for everyone involved.

II. The Pitfalls of the Modern Judiciary

a. Biases and Human Weaknesses

To launch our discussion, consider the following situation. A mother is prosecuted for the murder of her child. The prosecution's case involves all sorts of harrowing facts: the mother waited roughly one month to report her two-year-old daughter missing after being the last person seen with the child and, in that month, lived her life normally, even going so far as to get a tattoo that said *bella vita* ("beautiful life" in Italian).[2] The prosecution also released documents showing that the mother wrote in a journal entry: "I completely trust my own judgment[.] I know that I made the right decision. I just hope that the end justifies the means."[3] The facts get even more harrowing. The child's skeletal remains – found

---

2 Camille Mann, "Casey Anthony Trial Update: Anthony Got 'Bella Vita' Tattoo While Caylee Was Missing," *CBS News* (15 June 2011), online: <https://www.cbsnews.com /news/casey-anthony-trial-update-anthony-got-bella-vita-tattoo-while-caylee-was -missing/>.

3 Steve Helling, "Defense: Caylee's Mother's Diary Was Written in 2003," *People* (19 February 2009), online: <https://people.com/crime/defense-caylees-mothers-diary -was-written-in-2003/>.

almost six months after the mother was accused – showed that she had been bound with duct tape.[4] A crime scene investigator told jurors that he smelled "human decomposition" coming from the trunk of the mother's car.[5]

Readers who regularly consume American television news may recognize these facts as being about the trial of Casey Anthony, a young mother accused of killing her daughter, Caylee, and her highly publicized trial in Orlando, Florida. To the dismay of many close observers, the jury announced a not guilty verdict.[6] According to *People* magazine in an interview with one of the jurors, some of the jury's thinking was affected by the different attitudes of the prosecutor and defence attorney:

> [The juror] described lead prosecutor Jeff Ashton as "ambitious" and "arrogant." He said that one of the other prosecutors was "mechanical and cold." But the juror had a different take on lead defense attorney Jose Baez. "He was the only one in the room who seemed like he cared," the juror said. "We talked about that in the jury room."[7]

Of course, the juror's explanation here does not comport with public attitudes about criminal trials; if the sustained outrage about famously acquitted persons such as O.J. Simpson and Casey Anthony is any indication, the public generally expects that the legal process will vindicate their sense of right and wrong. Yet studies have shown that juries are susceptible to poor reasoning and factual errors, due to cognitive biases and, indeed, emotions like disgust and anger. As Guthrie, Rachlinski, and Wistrich summarize: "Researchers have found, for example, that juries believe that litigants should have predicted events that no one could have predicted, allow irrelevant or inadmissible information to influence liability determinations, defer to arbitrary numerical

4 Emily Friedman, "Caylee's Mouth and Nose Were Covered with Tape," *ABC News* (19 July 2009), online: <https://abcnews.go.com/US/story?id=7884395>.

5 Camille Mann, "Casey Anthony Car Smelled of Human Decomposition, Days Witness at Trial," *CBS News* (27 May 2011), online: <https://www.cbsnews.com/news/casey-anthony-car-smelled-of-human-decomposition-says-witness-at-trial/>.

6 US Weekly Staff, "Casey Anthony Found Not Gulty of Murder," *US Weekly* (5 July 2011), online: <https://www.usmagazine.com/celebrity-news/news/casey-anthony-found-not-guilty-of-murder-201157/>.

7 Steve Helling, "How Casey Anthony Was Acquitted: The Jurors Explain Their Controversial Verdict," *People* (5 July 2018), online: <https://people.com/crime/how-casey-anthony-was-acquitted-jurors-explain-verdict/>.

estimates, and rely on incoherent methods to calculate damages."[8] Christopher R. Drahozal calls these "cognitive illusions."[9] Even judges, with special skills and perhaps a well-steeled scepticism, are not immune: experimental research shows that, compared to jurors, "judges are less affected by some cognitive illusions, but similarly affected by others."[10] Some studies reveal how ostensibly insignificant circumstances can affect judicial decision-making. Tania Sourdin explains:

> [A]djudicative decision-making can be influenced by a range of factors that can influence substantive justice. These include a range of impacts on the decision-maker that include: when and what a person has eaten; the time of day; how many other decisions a person has made that day (decision fatigue); personal values; unconscious assumptions; reliance on intuition; the attractiveness of the individuals involved; emotion.[11]

Multiple research studies have shown that judges are constrained by cognitive biases, and that such biases influence their decision-making. The fact that judges make decisions under uncertain, time-pressured conditions encourages their reliance on cognitive shortcuts. According to the results of an experiment by Guthrie, Rachlinski, and Wistrich, "Whether they were aware of it or not, the judges' judgments in hindsight were influenced by knowledge that they could not have had in foresight."[12] Moreover, there is research illustrating how formal, algorithmic methods of prediction outperform humans in predicting outcomes across several settings.[13]

Furthermore, judges are susceptible to erroneous legal reasoning. While bound by precedent, they can overlook precedents that were controlling or persuasive, including their own decisions. They also generally have a choice of which precedents to rely on in making their decisions, and, in some cases, judges appear to choose those cases in accordance with their own ideological stances. Personal political views and values also play a significant role in judicial decision-making;

---

8 Chris Guthrie, Jeffrey J Rachlinski & Andrew J Wistrich, "Inside the Judicial Mind" (2001) 88 Cornell L Rev 776 at 780–1.

9 Christopher R. Drahozal, "A Behavioral Analysis of Private Judging" (2004) 67:1/2 Law & Contemp Probs 105 at 106.

10 Ibid.

11 Tania Sourdin, "A Broader View of Justice" in Michael Legg, ed, The Future of Dispute Resolution (Australia: LexisNexis Butterworths, 2012).

12 Guthrie, Rachlinski & Wistrich, supra note 8 at 803.

13 William M Grove et al, "Critical versus Mechanical Prediction: A Meta-Analysis" (2000) 12 Psychological Assessment 1.

Anthony Niblett has shown that California judges dealing with uncon-scionability cases, as one example, generally cite the same precedent, but arrive at decisions that correlate with their political preferences.[14]

Another obstacle to impartial and accurate judicial reasoning is lim-ited information. Although they are educated and guided by the parties in each case, such as expert witnesses, judges are often generalists who are not themselves experts in the matters (both factual and legal) that they adjudicate. However, even if all judges were experts in the fields within which they most commonly adjudicate, they would still be ham-pered by incomplete information. Although modern technology allows for greater quantity and quality of evidence than ever before, there are always missing puzzle pieces – not every conversation is recorded, not every street is equipped with surveillance cameras, and not every indi-vidual's move is traceable through mobile phone data. Establishing the factual details of any given event is a challenging task, particularly when adversarial parties armed with teams of expert witnesses attempt to disprove one another's accounts. Consequently, judges tasked with fact-finding are left to navigate a hazy labyrinth of evidence, expert opinions, and their own biases.

The inevitable lack of certainty in judicial findings is reflected in the legal burdens of proof: preponderance of the evidence in most civil actions (when the fact finder must be "persuaded by the evidence that the claim is more probably true than not true"),[15] proof beyond a reason-able doubt in criminal actions ("proof that leaves you firmly convinced that the defendant is guilty").[16] Proof of *certainty* is a burden noticeably absent in this list, precisely because to demand it would be to demand an impossibility.

Although inevitable, the lack of certainty in judicial fact-finding leads to troubling implications. One such implication is that the court's fac-tual findings constitute, at best, a legally endorsed story about what happened in a case rather than what *actually* happened. The general public, however, usually perceives this endorsed story as the unques-tionable truth. This is a problem, because courts usually make factual findings not only regarding the events of a specific case but also about

---

14 Anthony Niblett, "Tracking Inconsistent Judicial Behavior" (2013) 34 Intl Rev L & Econ 9.

15 Andreas Glöckner & Christoph Engel, "Can We Trust Intuitive Jurors? Standards of Proof and the Probative Value of Evidence in Coherence-Based Reasoning" (2013) 10:2 J Empirical Leg Stud 230.

16 Lawrence M Solan, "Refocusing the Burden of Proof in Criminal Cases: Some Doubt About Reasonable Doubt" (1999) 78 Tex L Rev 105 at n48.

certain mechanisms of the world as well. For example, the court may find that Mr. Smith was home at six o'clock (finding about an event) and that women and men process psychological trauma differently (finding about a mechanism of the world). Even more worryingly, judges themselves often perceive this story as the unquestionable truth. A vast reduction in the uncertainty inherent in current judicial fact-finding would thus be tremendously beneficial to both litigants and the greater public. We believe that such elimination will be approximated with the emergence of artificial intelligence tools in the courtroom.

b. Courthouse Overcrowding and Delayed Justice

When Amine Nayel watched his son Fouad leave their home on Father's Day, he could not imagine that this would be the last time he would see him alive. Fouad was lured to a hunting camp and shot twice. Adam Picard was arrested and charged with Fouad's murder, but was set free when his lawyer successfully argued that Picard's right to trial within a reasonable time had been violated. What did Amine feel watching the man accused of murdering his son walk away?[17]

This Canadian case was one of many in which stays of criminal proceedings have been granted due to delays in trial proceedings. When a case is stayed, there is no trial and no judicial decision. Victims are left without answers, perpetrators walk out free, and those falsely accused are denied a chance to clear their name. There are other problems caused by delays: the quality and reliability of evidence decreases, the connection between the offence and its resolution is weakened, and the public's faith in the justice system is compromised. Sometimes, delays in legal proceedings can be helpful, often in ways that are underappreciated. The extra time may reduce pressure on the parties, allowing them to consider their options in a calm and deliberate manner. It also enables judges and lawyers to focus on avoiding making rushed mistakes that harm the parties and drain the resources of the legal system. However, as the Picard example above illustrates, delays can also have negative consequences. And among the causes of delayed justice are the various human and procedural constraints involved in judicial decision-making. Judicial oversight and error result in inconsistent rulings and

---

17 Sean Fine, "Trial Limits Leave Dead Man's Parents on Long Road to Justice," *Globe and Mail* (11 June 2017), online: <https://www.theglobeandmail.com/news/national/murder-charge-dismissal-leaves-fouad-nayels-parents-waiting-for-justice/article35281939/>.

poor case-management, which contribute to overcrowded courthouses and lengthy trials.

c. The Implications of Court Design

Structural frameworks and court design affect judicial decision-making in several ways. As one of us wrote alongside Andrew Green in the book *Commitment and Cooperation on High Courts: A Cross-Country Examination of Institutional Constraints on Judges*, differences in court design – how judges are appointed, whether they sit in panels, how many cases the court hears – influence how judges decide. In a discussion about the judiciary, the importance of court design must not be underestimated:

> The design of a court, and the level of commitment and cooperation it engenders, is central to a just legal system. It creates the basis for the rule of law – most obviously by influencing the extent to which outcomes are determined by personal preferences of judges – but in other ways such as through framing the influence of democratic principles. It fosters access to justice such as through rules about standing and appeals to high courts. It guides the development, consistency, and coherence of the common law through, for example, affecting the availability and strength of precedent.[18]

Differences in design affect the judiciary in two fundamental dimensions: commitment to their personal and political views, and cooperation with other judges. Thus, altering the way that court systems are designed will alter judicial decision-making. For example, in the United States, the process of electing judges has significant effects on judicial decision-making, both before and after the elections. In 2015, the Brennan Center for Justice analysed empirical studies on the topic and found that "the pressures of upcoming re-election and retention election campaigns make judges more punitive toward defendants in criminal cases."[19] We predict that court design will undergo radical transformations in both the near and distant future.

---

18 Benjamin Alarie & Andrew James Green, *Commitment and Cooperation on High Courts: A Cross-Country Examination of Institutional Constraints on Judges* (Oxford: Oxford University Press, 2017) at xiv.

19 Kate Berry, *How Judicial Elections Impact Criminal Cases* (New York: Brennan Center for Justice, 2015) at 1.

III. Computational Solutions in the Courtroom

a. Human Experts

Before we begin exploring the ways in which advanced computational methods will transform the courts and the judiciary, it is important to note that humans will always have a role in the legal process. Despite the promising opportunities presented by technology, which we will discuss in detail in the following sections, leaving the determination of justice solely up to statistics and mathematics is irresponsible at best. As American mathematician Cathy O'Neil argues in her book *Weapons of Math Destruction*, the unregulated and unsupervised use of algorithms and big data can have a negative societal impact, leading to discrimination and amplifying existing inequality.[20] Moreover, removing humans from the process may well raise due process concerns, as people have the right to have their case heard by a human judge.

In the following sections, we will discuss the ways in which computational prediction will lead to better decision-making. However, it must be remembered that prediction is just one element of any decision-making process. As Agrawal, Gans, and Goldfarb discuss, machine learning (ML) decision systems enable, at a minimum, prediction, but also judgment, action, and outcome, and leverage three types of data: input, training, and feedback.[21] While computational methods will certainly advance prediction and data processing, other elements, such as judgment and outcome evaluation, may well be better suited for human minds.

Whether the human judge or legal expert is better positioned as the manager and supervisor of legal algorithms or an equal contributor and teammate in the decision-making process, or perhaps both, is left to be seen. This answer will depend on a variety of factors, such as the advancement of the algorithms *and* the humans, who may one day be equipped with AI-powered brain enhancements. The day may come when humans will seamlessly blend with technology, blurring the line between humans and machines. The point, however, is that humans – whether in their current form, or a future augmented one – will have a

---

20 See generally Cathy O'Neil, *Weapons of Math Destruction* (New York: Crown Books, 2017).

21 Ajay Agrawal, Joshua Gans & Avi Goldfarb, *Prediction Machines: The Simple Economics of Artificial Intelligence* (Cambridge, MA: Harvard Business Review Press, 2018).

role and a place in the process, and it is important to keep this in mind as we consider the opportunities presented by future technologies.

b. Legal Research

Participants in adjudication buy into the convenient myth that judges can leverage complete knowledge of the settled law. Sometimes this reflects an unfounded faith in judges themselves as expert-level legal thinkers, but, just as often, it is based on the belief that judges will at least become aware of all of the relevant legal information through party briefing or other elements of the adversarial process. With the advent of computational legal research tools, this aspiration will be close to the truth. Right now, judges frequently rely on the arguments presented by clerks and the parties' lawyers. The problem with such reliance is that clerks and lawyers do not have complete knowledge of the settled law either, which is compounded by the fact that there is variability in the quality of legal representation (with many litigants having no representation at all). In chapter 2, we described how barriers to accessing information might further compromise the known universe of case law in any given decision-making context. Consequently, judges often need to conduct legal research themselves in an effort to "equalize" the playing field in the courtroom.

With the emergence of computational law tools, such as legal predictive technology, all parties involved will increasingly have equal access to all of the relevant law. As a result, the legal characterization of the dispute will no longer be entirely in the hands of the litigants' lawyers. Parties will no longer have the opportunity to present false or incomplete law on the matter, whether intentionally or inadvertently. Judges, or their law clerks, will be able to conduct independent and considerably more efficient legal research, thereby lowering the risk of missing relevant cases and making other research-related errors.

Judges will also be able to use AI-powered tools to check their judgments for legal errors, such as missing statute references or relying on cases that have since been reversed. Software will analyse the judgment through natural language processing and pick up on relevant legal subject matter. So, for example, in a judgment dealing with conveyancing in Ontario, the software will recognize the need to reference the *Statute of Frauds*.[22] This will be an improvement over the current system, in which research is constrained by having to enter the right combination, and

---

22 *Statute of Frauds*, RSO 1990, c S19.

sometimes even the right order, of words. Thus, computational tools will help judges avoid errors and the extra expenses that they cause.

Judges could use similar technology to proactively read pleadings. Rather than preparing for hearings by reading pleadings and conducting digital legal research, judges could upload the pleadings into an AI-based platform and receive a preliminary report of the relevant issues, statutes, and cases. This will help judges prepare for hearings faster and better, as they will be able to use their time crafting pointed questions for the lawyers and perhaps engaging in thorough analysis of specific issues that go beyond mere case law or statutory requirements. Another advantage of having preliminary reports is that they would help judges screen for vexatious litigants, as the software could keep a database of all pleadings and flag litigants who show a pattern of abusing the system. The same technology could be applied to motions and applications as well.

c. Document Drafting

Like lawyers, judges do a fair amount of routine drafting of documents, generally orders, and rulings. AI-based legal drafting software will streamline this process as well. Several businesses are already offering such software for lawyers. It is likely that judges will come to rely on it as well (or a version of it designed specifically for the judiciary). Instead of starting with a precedent order and working from there, for example, the judge will simply instruct the software that an injunction is needed and answer a few questions. The order will be customizable, as the judge will have the opportunity to add or remove parts of the produced document. As a result, the amount of time that judges spend on drafting will be greatly reduced. Lest this be regarded as fanciful, one of us recently co-authored the first law review article with an AI – GPT-3.[23]

d. Expert Evidence

Expert witnesses play an important role in legal proceedings that require their expertise for the interpretation of evidence, such as forensic evidence in criminal trials. Judges and juries need the help of experts to explain to them what blood spatter patterns, gunshot residue, and tire

---

23 See Benjamin Alarie, Arthur Cockfield & GPT-3, "Will Machines Replace Us? Machine -Authored Texts and the Future of Scholarship" (2021) 3:2 Law, Technology & Humans 5, online: <https://doi.org/10.5204/lthj.2089>.

marks say about the actions of the alleged perpetrator and the victim. Each side brings their own expert witnesses to explain the evidence in a way that most favours their narrative. Although expert testimony is useful, it raises several problems. The first is rather straightforward: expert witnesses can, either intentionally or inadvertently, provide inaccurate and/or misleading testimony. Such testimony has resulted in wrongful convictions, such as in the Canadian case *R v Mullins-Johnson* in which William Mullins-Johnson was convicted of first-degree murder based on inaccurate medical expert findings. Mullins-Johnson spent eleven years in prison before the conviction was quashed, and he was subsequently awarded $4.25 million in compensation.[24]

A second problem is that judges and juries may simply misinterpret the testimony, even if it is accurate. As discussed earlier, judges are susceptible to numerous types of cognitive bias. Consider, for example, the way that the representativeness heuristic affects judges' assessment of expert evidence. People rely on this heuristic when making categorical judgments (i.e., identifying whether something or someone belongs to a category): the more the item or person in question appears to be representative of a certain category, the higher the likelihood that the item or person will be perceived as a product of that category. So, for instance, people will judge evidence of the accused acting nervous and uneasy as evidence of guilt. Although useful in some situations, the representativeness heuristic can lead to troublesome reasoning fallacies such as the "inverse fallacy," the tendency to treat the probability of a hypothesis given the evidence the same as the probability of the evidence given the hypothesis. Guthrie, Rachlinski, and Wistrich explain how this fallacy affects the way that judges and juries interpret expert evidence:

> Suppose, for example, that a forensic expert testifies in a criminal case that a DNA sample from the defendant matches the DNA sample found at a crime scene. Further suppose that this expert indicates that the probability that a randomly selected sample would match the sample from the crime scene is one in a million. Committing the inverse fallacy here means believing that the likelihood that the defendant is innocent is also one in a million. This inference, however, would be incorrect because the probability that the defendant is innocent also depends on the size of the population from which the suspect's DNA was drawn and the reliability of the DNA test. If the defendant were randomly selected from a population of

---

24 *R v Mullins-Johnson*, 2007 ONCA 720.

four million suspects, for example, one would expect that there are three other people who are just as likely to have committed the crime as the defendant.[25]

Judges are tasked not only with understanding expert evidence but also ensuring that it is relevant and reliable. However, this responsibility is particularly challenging, as the judge is unlikely to have expertise in the subject matter. In other words, judges are left having to decide matters in which they lack the relevant expertise. Computational methods will mitigate these problems. Research tools powered by machine learning will assist judges in assessing expert witnesses. By searching through scientific journal databases and synthesizing information, these tools will identify what is and what is not generally accepted by experts on a given subject. There are promising developments in this field already, such as the AI-powered search tool Meta. According to its co-founder Sam Molyneux, Meta used artificial intelligence "to analyse new scientific knowledge as it's published – along with the majority of what has been written, throughout modern history."[26] Similar tools could be tailored for use by the judiciary, taking into account the unique needs of judges as researchers and decision makers. For example, a feature could reveal how similar expert evidence has been treated by judges in the past.

Computational methods will also help judges decide between expert opinions in an efficient and informed way. This is a little less radical than it sounds. Historically, "assessors" have been called to Commonwealth admiralty courts to advise judges when they decide factual questions about sailing matters on which average judges lack necessary expertise. Given that the judiciary has been comfortable relying on the experience and expertise of such human "assessors," there is no good reason why analogous computational assessment should cause alarm.[27] By processing and analysing vast amounts of data, ML tools can bring judges closer to having a well-rounded understanding of expert witness testimony and evidence interpretation. These tools will be especially useful in situations where the subject matter lacks

25 Guthrie, Rachlinski & Wistrich, *supra* note 8 at 807.
26 Liat Clark, "Why the Chan Zuckerberg Initiative Is Buying AI Search Tool Meta," *Wired* (24 January 2017), online: <https://www.wired.co.uk/article/chan-zuckerberg -initiative-buys-ai-scientific-search-tool-meta>.
27 See, e.g., Anthony Dickey, "The Province and Function of Assessors in English Courts" (1970) 33 Mod L Rev 5.

scientific consensus, which can be particularly challenging for non-expert juries and judges to comprehend and apply to the case at hand.

Another important benefit to bringing computation into the domain of expert evidence is the mitigation of cognitive biases and logical fallacies. Instead of relying on heuristics to aid them in making difficult decisions on subject matter that they do not fully understand, judges will be able to employ computational research and modelling tools to develop a more objective understanding of the issues at hand. Imagine, for example, software that would model the probability of the DNA evidence belonging to someone other than the defendant in an accurate and accessible way. Even such relatively simple visualization of probability data in the context of forensic evidence interpretation will lead to more accurate and impartial decision-making. Ultimately, the introduction of computational methods into the realm of expert evidence will allow for admissible evidence to be identified and interpreted on a rigorous and principled basis rather than on judicial intuition, leading to a more efficient and just process overall.

e. Changes to Fact-Finding Procedures

Every day, juries and judges across the world are tasked with deciding matters of fact. Was the defendant inside the victim's apartment at the time of the murder? Did the defendant's failure to put up a warning sign cause the plaintiff's head injury? Such matters are decided at the trial level, where, as we discussed, expert witnesses often play an important role in explaining the evidence. The ultimate findings of fact, however, rest with the judges (and the juries, in some cases). This is troublesome for a few reasons. As we explained earlier, juries and judges are susceptible to multiple cognitive biases. Furthermore, most such findings are made in the context of general uncertainty about a multitude of other relevant facts. Much fact finding therefore involves probabilistic reasoning, which is itself subject to biases and fallacious heuristics.

Beyond improving judges' assessment and interpretation of expert evidence, computational methods will likely assist them in fact finding more generally. Computational tools will be particularly useful in mitigating the damaging presence of uncertainty in the fact-finding process. There are, broadly speaking, two general types of uncertainty: uncertainty about the events of the past, and uncertainty about the events of the future. ML-powered modelling and predictive technology will help to decrease and, in some cases, eliminate both types of uncertainty. Consider, for example, the challenges that juries and judges face when assessing footage from surveillance cameras – a common type of

evidence, which can contain valuable information. Often, the low quality of the footage makes it difficult for humans to identify that information. When University of Illinois scholar Yingying Zhang disappeared
in June 2017, investigators had surveillance video showing Zhang getting into an inconspicuous vehicle. To their frustration, the footage was
too blurry for them to read the licence plate, and identifying the driver
was exceedingly difficult. It was not until one of them noticed that the
car had a minor defect – a dent on the hubcap of one of the front tires –
that the team was able to track down the suspect.[28] How many similar
breakthroughs would be possible if investigators, juries, and judges
had access to AI-powered tools that could scan video and audio footage for such identifiers within seconds? How much trial time would
be saved if digital evidence could be analysed through data-driven
predictive technologies? We believe that the answer to both questions
is "a great deal."

Employing computational methods in fact finding will have an effect
similar to introducing computation to expert-evidence assessment:
judges and juries will no longer have to rely on heuristics as a crutch
to overcome the inevitable challenges of probabilistic, and sometimes
purely speculative, reasoning. Instead, they will have an opportunity
to engage with data-driven, impartially produced reconstructions of
past events and realistic models of future events. Our aim here is not
to argue that such tools are necessarily superior to human reasoning.
As we mentioned before, there are advantages to some hallmarks of
human thought: heuristics, empathy, and human connection, among
others, are all useful in some respects. Rather, we believe that computational methods will serve as tremendously useful aids to human decision-makers by filling in the gaps in human knowledge and reasoning
and by flagging and mitigating their limitations.

f. Discovery

An element of the civil process that we have discussed a few times in this
book is discovery. Discovery is something that happens before the trial
where the parties must give each other relevant documents and other
evidence. There are several reasons for discovery. The process enables

---

28 Chuck Goudie & Barb Markoff, "Exclusive: Campus Cops Say Car Hubcap Key to
Solving Murder of University of Illinois Scholar Yingying Zhang" *ABC Eyewitness
News* (19 September 2019), online: <https://abc7chicago.com/brendt-christensen
-u-of-i-scholar-murder-university-illinois-killed/5553642/>.

the parties to assess the strengths and weaknesses of one another's case, thereby informing them whether it is best to settle (perhaps one side realizes that their case is too weak to pursue the trial). It also helps the parties narrow the legal issues that will be raised during the trial. Given the number and complexity of the documents that are submitted, going through them takes a lot of time. Advances in communication and digital technologies have made the discovery process even more laborious. Imagine, for example, how many pages of evidence a single email inbox or computer hard drive would produce. Due to the adversarial nature of litigation, it is in the interest of each side to get as much of the other side's information as possible while withholding their own information. The role of the judge in this process is supervisory: the parties can complain to the judge for a finding that something is being unfairly withheld, or that a question should not have been asked or answered. Such complaints can extend the discovery process, run up costs, and consume the judge's already limited time.

Computational methods will be valuable in mitigating these problems. For example, ML software can be used to scan and analyse hundreds of documents and make predictions on the basis of statutory input and previous judicial rulings (i.e., how judges dealt with similar documents in the past). The parties may choose to agree not to contest the software's results, or they may ask a judge to supervise it and make the ultimate finding. In any case, the availability of such tools will lessen the time that judges and parties spend on the discovery process. Furthermore, the cost of discovery will decrease, as lawyers will be able to avoid charging clients for hours of manual analysis and evaluation of potential evidence.

g. Predictive Technology

It is possible for AI-based tools to predict how a judge would decide a fact-intensive binary question on the basis of decided cases. Thus, judges can use these tools in the preliminary stages of their analysis in order to quickly develop a grasp of the relevant case law and the main legal issues driving the case. If the prediction heavily weighs in one direction (e.g., the result is that there is a 90 per cent likelihood that the plaintiff will lose), and the judge believes that it is accurate, the judge may advise the parties to consider settlement or may dismiss the case altogether. As predictive technology becomes more advanced, different types of data can be used as input for the predictions. For example, social science data or even signifiers of prevalent societal attitudes (derived from Twitter feeds, influential opinion pieces from established magazines, and so on) may be included alongside statutory require-ments and legal precedent. Such advances may lead to the acceptance of legal-prediction software not merely as a descriptive tool (i.e., as something that tells the judge what the law on a given issue is), but a prescriptive one as well (i.e., as something that tells the judge what the law on a given issue *should be*, in light of prevailing social norms). This will be particularly important in difficult cases where the solely case law–based computation shows that both parties have roughly equal likelihood of winning. Such cases will present the courts with the opportunity to explicitly address the policy reasons guiding the law at any given moment, and to have an open and transparent conversation about whether these reasons are flawed or outdated.

h. Case Management

Not every matter that comes before a judge during a lawsuit truly requires the judge's attention. Some jurisdictions have tried to deal with the overwhelming number of applications and motions by having other officials, like masters or prothonotaries, hear such matters. The disadvantage of this solution is that it consumes more public resources and does not solve the problem of volume.

What could be done instead is delegating these matters to be first processed by AI-powered tools. If a party disagrees with the result, they can have a right to appeal to a judge, with a costs order against them if the appeal is used frivolously. At the very least, such tools could efficiently classify disputes into distinct categories, with some taking priority over others. Judges could then attend to the cases that require their attention most first, and then proceed to the others as time per-mits. This approach would be a better division of judicial labour and resources than assigning a handful of cases varying in complexity and importance to one judge to manage completely on their own. Here, it is important to note that case management is a skill that some judges lack. Indeed, a report by the Canadian Standing Senate Committee on Legal and Constitutional Affairs identified the lack of robust case manage-ment as "one of the most significant factors contributing to delays" in court proceedings.[29] Introducing computational methods to help judges

---

29 Standing Senate Committee on Legal and Constitutional Affairs, *Delaying Justice Is Denying Justice: An Urgent Need to Address Lengthy Court Delays in Canada (Final Report)* (June 2017) at 2, online: <https://sencanada.ca/content/sen/committee/421 /LCJC/reports/Court_Delays_Final_Report_e.pdf>.

manage cases efficiently will resolve this problem, allowing them to focus their time and energy on judging and helping claimants.

i. Fair Settlements

For many litigants today, going to trial is akin to gambling: they have a chance of winning, a chance of losing, and no way to predict exactly what is going to happen. They may lose because their case is weaker or because the judge makes a mistake. As we have seen, this will to change in the future as the computational era progresses: litigants, lawyers, and judges will have predictive legal technologies to aid them in anticipating the outcomes of cases and avoiding errors. As noted at the beginning of this chapter, the fact-finding process will also improve dramatically. Thus, those who know they are guilty or in the wrong will have no incentive to pursue lengthy lawsuits proclaiming their innocence.

What we will witness as a result is that fewer cases will go to trial, and more disputes will end in settlements. With both parties having a good understanding of their case and evidence, and a prediction of the outcome, there will be no point in pursuing the lengthy and expensive ordeal that is the trial (even if it will be much faster and less expensive than it is today). Beyond leading to a greater number of settlements, computational methods will also change the settlement process itself, leading to more fair and optimal settlements.

What is an optimal settlement? Here, it is helpful to consider several economic models of adjudication and settlement. In 1984, George Priest and Benjamin Klein published their seminal paper "The Selection of Disputes for Litigation," in which they advanced the following model:

> According to our model, the determinants of settlement and litigation are solely economic, including the expected costs to parties of favorable or adverse decisions, the information that parties possess about the likelihood of success at trial, and the direct costs of litigation and settlement. The most important assumption of the model is that potential litigants form rational estimates of the likely decision, whether it is based on applicable legal precedent or judicial or jury bias.[30]

Drawing on this model, we can see how the rate of settlements would be predicted to increase with the introduction of computational methods.

---

30 George Priest & Benjamin Klein, "The Selection of Disputes for Litigation" (1984) 13:1 J Leg Stud 1.

Predictive technologies in particular will transform the factors that Priest and Klein identify as the determinants of settlement and litigation. Consider, for example, the information that parties possess about the likelihood of success at trial. As we discussed earlier, AI-based prediction tools will provide parties (and their counsel) with significant amounts of information about the outcome of the trial. Not only will each party have a good idea of their likelihood of success, they will also have an understanding of what motivates this likelihood. Furthermore, computation will produce predictions that are rational, grounded in an objective evaluation of the relevant case law and the facts at hand.

Computational methods will improve both the fairness and efficiency of settlement as well. Even if litigants do aim to achieve a fair settlement, they face numerous challenges: incomplete information, unpredictable results, and cognitive biases, among others. As we explained earlier, computational tools will remove these obstacles by providing accurate, complete, and objective guidance to the parties and their advisors. On its own, the concept of "fairness" may be subjective, and the parties may suspect one another of dishonesty. Having an unbiased, third-party assessment of the settlement proposals would promote trust between the parties, and would improve the likelihood of achieving an objectively fair outcome through settlement.

IV. The Paradox of Judging in the Computational Era

One of the noteworthy consequences of introducing computational methods to judicial decision-making is that judges will find themselves having to acknowledge the decisions and predictions made by their AI-powered aids. As the technology advances and begins to incorporate not only legal input but social science data as well, judges may find themselves having to explain disagreements between their own considered judgments with the predictions made by legal-prediction tools. In other words, judges will be less able to simply ignore or dismiss the determinations and predictions made by these computational tools without suffering the potential loss of perceived legitimacy of their decisions.

Due to computational advances, judges will also be expected to determine cases using deeper reasoning and second-order thinking. Just as lawyers will consider higher-level consequences in their advice to add value for their clients when the law becomes more accessible and knowable through predictive technology, judges will consider higher-level consequences of their judgments in order to add value for the public at large (and, more to the point for many judges, to insulate their decisions from public criticism or being turned over on appeal to a higher court). Today, few judges have the luxury of thinking of the law as an end in itself. In the future, aided by the power of legal AI-based tools, judges will spend more time thinking about what the law should be, rather than what the law is and how it applies to a particular case. Using predictive modelling and data analysis technologies will allow judges to see the short- and long-term consequences of their decisions, and will lead to better policy decisions.

The result of this evolution of judicial reasoning will be a paradox of judging: as more cases will be settled due to increased legal and factual certainty, only the most normatively difficult cases will go to trial. These will be the cases where the law is on the side of both parties, and the determining factors are normative policy considerations. In other words, although it may seem that computational methods will make the work of judging easier, it will in some ways make it much more challenging. Although human judgment will continue to determine the most difficult policy cases, AI-powered legal tools will increasingly help along the way. To make the optimal decision, a judge needs to be able to predict as many of the consequences of that decision as possible with as much certainty as possible. Computational methods can produce predictions of what will happen if a course of action is adopted. For instance, if a judge must decide whether a planning decision to deny the building of a grocery store in a subdivision is reasonable, an AI-powered tool might flag the *benefits* of locally available fresh food to the youth in the community, and the *negative* consequences of creating a high-traffic business in the middle of a neighbourhood. By modelling the different possibilities, judges will be able to compare apples to apples and make an informed normative judgment between the competing values at stake.

a. Beyond Physical Courtrooms and Human Judges

I. NEURAL LACES

Earlier we discussed the need to ensure that humans remain involved in the judicial process. One way to achieve that is through the implementation of AI-powered devices to enhance cognition, perhaps through a direct physical interface between the device and a person's brain or nervous system. Although it seems radical, such devices are already in development. Neuralink, a technology start-up, is in the process of developing brain-machine interfaces. While interest in this area is still new, early successes are being claimed in the area of brain disease research.[31] Recently, research has demonstrated some "potential benefit" of brain-computer interfaces for individuals suffering from amyotrophic lateral sclerosis (ALS) who have impaired muscular function.[32] It may take some time before such technology advances to the point where judges can use AI-powered devices, but these developments suggest that it is possible.

II. ONLINE COURTS AND DISPUTE RESOLUTION

Imagine discovering that you have a legal problem. You sit down at your desk and open an online court website on your laptop. After allowing the site to access your location and send notifications to your mobile phone, you click on the "new dispute" tab. The system asks you to complete a quick survey, which takes you no more than five minutes. Next, you see an "assessment complete" message, which explains that, based on the information you provided, your problem would best be addressed outside of court. The system gives you an option to open a document outlining the reasoning behind the assessment, which you must view before you can formally contest the assessment. You choose to proceed, and find yourself automatically redirected to a list of the top-rated local alternative dispute-resolution service providers for your specific issue. The first on the list has great reviews, and specializes in your problem, so you sign up for a consultation. With your consent, the results of your survey and your identification data are forwarded to the service provider. The next morning, you attend a consultation through a video conference. Your problem is resolved without further involvement from you by the end of the week.

Although this scenario may be difficult to imagine today, computational methods will make it, or some version of it, a reality in the future. Legal software technologies powered by machine learning and natural language processing will transform the way people interact with the legal system. The word "courtroom" will no longer evoke only images of large sleek rooms with wooden desks, chairs, and podiums. The birth of the internet and advanced communication technologies has led to the gradual migration of many court procedures and services to an online, virtual format. The emergence of computational tools will accelerate this migration and cause a fundamental restructuring and

---

31 Kyle Wiggers, "Neuralink Demonstrates Its Next-Generation Brain-Machine Interface," *Venture Beat* (28 August 2020), online: <https://venturebeat.com/2020/08/28/neuralink-demonstrates-its-next-generation-brain-machine-interface/>.
32 Dennis J McFarland, "Brain-Computer Interfaces for Amyotrophic Lateral Sclerosis" (2021) 61 Muscle Nerve 6.

transformation of the processes involved. "Online courts" will mean much more than having traditional hearings over a video link.

In his 2019 book *Online Courts and the Future of Justice*, Richard Susskind discusses at length the possibilities and advantages of the next generation of online courts. He distinguishes between two aspects of online courts: online judging, which refers to the determination of cases by judges in a process that does not involve the parties gathering together in a brick-and-mortar courtroom; and extended courts, which is the idea that technology allows legal service providers to provide additional support with wider remit than the traditional court, such as systems that advise on non-judicial settlement. Susskind proposes a three-tier model for online courts: (1) *assessment* (helping users categorize and classify their problems with a view to prevent disputes from arising); (2) *facilitation* (providing services to help contain disputes, preventing escalation, and encouraging non-judicial settlement); and (3) *determination* (judicial decisions).[33] Computational methods will likely power most, if not all, of the new services and technologies involved in the realization of these three tiers. As we have already discussed, judges will use AI-based predictive tools to aid them in decision-making during case management and determination. Similarly, such tools will assist claimants and legal aid providers through the processes of dispute assessment and facilitation. In the next section, we explore how computational methods can optimize one of the most important components of dispute facilitation: alternative dispute resolution.

III. ALTERNATIVE DISPUTE RESOLUTION

Technologically powered alternative dispute resolution (ADR) is not a thing of the future. Consider, for example, Cybersettle, a New York–based company that resolves insurance disputes.[34] It confidentially takes offers to settle and a range of acceptable offers from both sides. If it finds common ground, it generally splits the difference and binds the parties. If there is no common ground, it invites new offers. The magic is that, by getting rid of the back-and-forth involving third parties and bluffing in negotiation, parties can settle their disputes to their mutual satisfaction much quicker and without one party feeling like it got squeezed by the other. This technology could be adopted by court systems in the same way that mandatory mediation has been adopted.

---

33 Richard Susskind, *Online Courts and the Future of Justice* (Oxford: Oxford University Press, 2019).
34 "Overview" *Cybersettle*, online: <http://www.cybersettle.com/>.

It could also, in principle, be extended in its capacity to resolve multi-dimensional non-damages disputes, like what a fair use of property might be by an alleged tortfeasor in a nuisance case.

Another example of online-based ADR is British Columbia's Civil Resolution Tribunal. It works similarly to the regular court process, with serving of documents, encouragement of settlement, and, if necessary, adjudication by a tribunal member, but it is entirely online. In a sense, right now it is only a digital version of the traditional court system, but the potential created by its infrastructure is limitless when combined with computational methods. There are four stages at which such methods can help. The first is the pleadings stage. The second is the mediation/settlement stage, where something like Cybersettle or an AI-powered version thereof could be used. The third is the legal research stage, where the parties (or a human judge) could use accessible legal computational technology to prepare their case for trial. The fourth is the adjudication stage, where an AI-based software could be used to make preliminary findings akin to those made by today's tribunal members. It would need natural language capability and might at first be limited to cases decided on written submissions without pictures, but later it could expand to deal with all forms of media. Computational methods would accelerate the process dramatically and also increase the quality of the decisions.

V. Possible Roadblocks to Adoption

The forecasts and proposals we make above may raise concerns. Here, we will address the objections and obstacles that may arise as computational methods enter the courtroom. An overarching point underlies our responses here: in criticizing computational solutions, we must not downplay the deficiencies of the current system. We must also be realistic in our expectations, and refrain from comparing the implementation and effects of potential changes to some idealistic and non-existent version of the system. As Richard Susskind opines on the criticism of online courts,

> Most critics of online courts are romantic transcendentalists rather than pragmatic comparativists. When confronted with the idea of online courts, they swiftly isolate the shortcomings both of online judging and of extended courts and seek to show how they fall short of some idealized, perfect model of the court system ... In response, comparativists must remind the critics that the proposed new system, *overall*, takes us to a better place.[35]

---

35 Susskind, *supra* note 33.

People are generally resistant to change. However, judicial institutions perhaps have special reasons to be opposed to the changes we described earlier. First and foremost, a judicial institution is one that is maintained by the habit of looking to accepted past authority for answers. Institutional constraints surrounding this reliance on past authority make the judiciary slow to adapt to innovative change. As we have already discussed, court design (how judges are appointed, whether they sit in panels, how many cases they hear, the rules and norms of particular courts, etc.) also constrains or shapes the choices made by judges. As legal technology evolves and enters the courtroom, we must not expect judges to be its avid supporters. Incorporating computational methods into the judiciary, and doing so well, will require some educational and perhaps legislative efforts. Educating judges and enacting legislation that mandates and regulates the use of computational methods will serve to bring them legitimacy and ensure that they are used to the benefit of the society.

VI. Looking Ahead: The Evolution of the Judiciary

Although it is difficult to predict with accuracy what the judiciary will look like in the next century, we can certainly speculate. Artificial intelligence systems will radically reduce the cost of gathering and processing legal information and will allow for far greater sharing, testing, and verifying of legal perspectives than is conceivable today. The judges of the future will be able to rely on the enormous advantages of low-cost, practically limitless, and widely distributed computing power. This power will allow for distributed decision-making: the next century will witness a shift from a conception of the judiciary as an individual judge or a small group of judges to a collaborative network populated by humans, humans with AI, and pure AI systems. Not only will this shift establish a more dynamic and democratic legal system (as the increased numbers of decision makers will better represent the general population's interests), but it will also empower the judiciary with vast amounts of data and information, as well as practical objectivity. Thus, the judges of the distant future will approach achieving what the ancient Egyptian viziers could only imagine: the omniscience and impartiality afforded to the divine.

As computational power increases, so too will the accuracy of judicial decisions. Today, courts often reach inaccurate decisions – for example, in negligence cases, they misidentify the perpetrator of the act, whether the act was in fact committed, whether the act was the case of harm, and so on. Such inaccuracies lead to errors, whereby the courts falsely sanction the innocent or mistakenly exonerate the guilty. Thus, the importance of accurate decision-making is intuitive. Kaplow and Shavell identify other significant benefits of accuracy through an economic inquiry: greater accuracy in determining liability enhances deterrence, allows for more precise control of behaviour, reduces the imposition of socially costly sanctions, and improves the selection of filed cases. The computational law of the future will reduce the costs of acquiring data and knowledge: specially trained algorithms will be able to reconstruct past events as well as accurately model future hypotheticals. These tasks can perhaps be completed in seconds, saving precious resources. As a result, judges will make fewer and fewer inaccurate decisions, which will gradually materialize the benefits identified by Kaplow and Shavell.[36]

Greater computational power will also allow judges to partake in sharing, testing, and verifying perspectives. In combination with other technology, artificial intelligence will transform the judicial decision-making process. Once the judiciary is not as limited by resource constraints, judicial panels will have room for vastly greater numbers of decision makers. Thus we can imagine, for example, a Supreme Court with the equivalent of one hundred, five hundred, or perhaps even a million or more algorithmic or human judges. Stretching our imagination even farther, we may picture a system in which each individual is able to vote by algorithmic proxy on matters that are before the Supreme Court, with the aid of a machine-learning algorithm that computes that individual's unique goals and values, and advises on the basis of those values. The system will suggest one vote or another on the legal policy question as issue, or perhaps it will even recommend that the individual abstain from voting due to some external circumstances. The point of these speculative ideas is to show in theory just how much potential computational law has for improving the judiciary and the rest of the legal system in ways that are difficult for us to imagine. These improvements may take less or perhaps more than a century, but we speculate that they may one day materialize.

---

36 See generally Louis Kaplow & Steven Shavell, "Accuracy in the Determination of Liability" (1994) 37:1 J Law & Econ 1.

Chapter Seven

Towards Universal Legal Literacy

I. Introduction

Thus far, we have outlined the concept of the legal singularity and underscored its importance to our collective future and situated it as part of a historical trend towards increased computation of legal information. We have explained how computational legal methods bring us closer to legal certainty, and have defended the legal singularity against theoretical and practical criticisms. We have also explored how the legal singularity might affect the future of courts and judges. Naturally, keen readers might be asking themselves: well, what does this all mean for lawyers? Put even more cynically: is there anything left for us lawyers to do, post–legal singularity?

First, some reassurance: the road to the legal singularity is paved with abundant opportunities for lawyers to continue to play a vital social role. Lawyers using computational legal tools will be able to engage in much more advanced application of core lawyering skills such as legal analysis and advocacy. In the meantime, however, the legal profession *must* come to terms with the inevitable need to adapt to and embrace new methods, as well as the need to remove barriers to technological adoption, lest the traditional profession finds itself bypassed by more flexible organizations and institutions. Some of the barriers to the adoption of technology in the legal profession are structural, such as restrictive professional licensure regimes, unresponsive regulators, and outmoded models of legal service delivery that threaten access to justice. But some of these barriers are attitudinal: lawyers are often conservative and resistant to innovation, and, as we discussed earlier, some scholarly members of law's epistemic community react with hostility to the idea of incorporating legal prediction into legal practice.

Yet despite these barriers, computational legal technologies continue to take root throughout the profession. As this process continues, and as technologically literate law graduates become lawyers, enter practice, and take up positions in the professional community, the recalcitrance will diminish – at least among the next generation.

Therefore, the time to imagine how the legal profession might look – and what it might accomplish in improving the lives of the broader public – is now. We advance a bold position: the only true resolution to the access-to-justice issue is what we call *universal legal literacy*. Universal legal literacy contemplates a future wherein *all* individuals with legal needs can, with relative ease and comfort, understand their legal rights and obligations. It is substantially more likely to be brought about through widely available and artificially intelligent legal prediction than under the status quo.

This chapter proceeds in three parts. In the first section, we discuss what we call the legal profession's problem state, focusing on the lack of affordability and on excessive legal complexity. In the second section, we describe universal legal literacy and propose technological and regulatory interventions that can best support its development. In the third section, we imagine what lawyering – and the market for legal services – might look like on the path to the legal singularity.

II. The Legal Profession's Problem State

Much scholarly effort has explored how to explain why lawyers and legal services are so unattainable to so many who need them. Here, we focus on two problems that we contend are leading causes of inaccessible legal services. First, unaffordability: legal services are too expensive for many, and can cause substantial financial strain to even those who can stretch to afford them. Second, complexity: law is difficult to understand, technical, occasionally ambiguous, and too contingent for laypeople to perform their own legal tasks. Even when individuals do engage lawyers to help, the information gulf is so wide that few are able to evaluate whether the services they receive are of acceptable quality, and fewer still can intervene. The information asymmetry that exists between lawyers and clients, then, often contributes to poor service and high prices.

a. Problem I: The Market for Legal Services

I. THE UNAFFORDABILITY PROBLEM
Ask a layperson for one word to describe lawyers, and you would not have to wait long before you hear "expensive." This common intuition

is borne out empirically: decades of studies have shown that "corporations, organizations and governments" receive most of the legal services, not individuals.[1] Where these services are available for individuals, they are often prohibitively expensive. A recent study shows that the average hourly rate for a lawyer in the United States is $262 per hour.[2] In states such as California, New York, and Delaware – where corporate legal services are especially common – average hourly rates for lawyers exceed US$330.[3] In Washington, DC, lawyers command US$380 per hour on average.[4] In Canada, the story is largely the same: on average, lawyers with just one year of experience cost CA$332 per hour, with that figure rising to CA$446 in Ontario.[5]

The unaffordability problem manifests differently depending on the context, of course. Some individuals with means may retain lawyers only when they face significant legal trouble – criminal charges, for instance – or in situations where losing the dispute would create disastrous personal and financial consequences (as in family law and tax law matters). Still, even in these high-stakes disputes, some will choose to represent themselves. In her study of legal representation in family law, Julie Macfarlane found that 64 per cent of family law litigants in Canada are self-represented.[6] Of this number, some 43 per cent earn above the median Canadian income.[7] Perhaps most revealingly, 53 per cent of these started the proceedings with a lawyer but could not afford the "ballooning fees."[8] Most of these individuals would never obtain *ex ante* legal advice to avoid these disputes in the first place, as the price is simply too high.

The poor do not even get to make this choice. The American Bar Association estimates that, in some US jurisdictions, more than 80 per cent

---

1 Gillian Hadfield, "The Price of Law: How the Market for Lawyers Distorts the Justice System" (2000) 98 Mich L Rev 4 900 at 902 [Hadfield, "Price"]; see also Gillian Hadfield, "Lawyers, Make Room for Nonlawyers" *CNN* (25 November 2012), online: <https://edition.cnn.com/2012/11/23/opinion/hadfield-legal-profession/index.html?hpt=hp_bn7>.

2 Clio, *2020 Legal Trends Report* (Themis Solutions, 2020) at 80, online: <https://www.clio.com/wp-content/uploads/2020/08/2020-Legal-Trends-Report.pdf>.

3 *Ibid.*

4 *Ibid.*

5 "Fees Rising before Downturn" *Canadian Lawyer Magazine* (11 May 2020) 15, online: <https://cdn-res.keymedia.com/cms/files/ca/120/0299_637245655342367595.pdf>.

6 Julie Macfarlane, *The National Self-Represented Litigants Project: Identifying and Meeting the Needs of Self-Represented Litigants (Final Report)* (May 2013) at 33, online: <https://representingyourselfcanada.com/wp-content/uploads/2016/09/srlreportfinal.pdf>.

7 *Ibid* at 27–9.

8 Daniel Fish, "Are There Too Many Lawyers?" *Precedent JD* (6 September 2017), online: <https://precedentjd.com/news/are-there-too-many-lawyers/>.

"of litigants are unrepresented in matters involving basic life needs, such as evictions, mortgage foreclosures, child custody disputes, child support proceedings and debt collection cases." Most of the remaining perhaps 20 per cent obtain civil representation through the web of federal and state-funded legal service providers, which have stringent eligibility requirements.[9] As hard as these legal service providers work, they also have notoriously high caseloads and limited resources to contend with the myriad challenges that indigent clients face.[10] The well-resourced lawyers available via the private market tend to charge hourly rates that are out of reach for most individuals. In some jurisdictions, the unaffordability problem is compounded by the absence of local lawyers to meet immediate needs. As Baxter and Yoon discover in their study of Ontario, access to justice is also a geographic problem: some areas have so few available lawyers that they are effectively "advice deserts," and often the lawyers are distributed across large distances, which makes them effectively unavailable.[11] Unsurprisingly, this spatial access-to-justice problem significantly affects populations that already suffer from inadequate public and private services, such as Indigenous populations or the rural poor.

What makes the unaffordability problem so frustrating for observers is that it is not actually caused by a lack of lawyers. In fact, at the very same time that most people cannot afford legal services, both the *number* of lawyers and the *per capita proportion* of lawyers are increasing in Canada and the United States.[12] The sheer number of lawyers has outpaced the number of available lawyer positions, leading numerous

---

9 Commission on the Future of Legal Services, *Report on the Future of Legal Services in the United States* (2016) at 12, online: <chrome-extension://efaidnbmnnnibpca jpcglclefindmkaj/https://www.americanbar.org/content/dam/aba/images /abanews/2016FLSReport_FNL_WEB.pdf>.

10 Hadfield, "Price," *supra* note 1 at 960, noting that legal aid societies account for less than 1 per cent of total revenues to legal services, and that only 1 per cent of lawyers work either as legal aid lawyers or public defenders.

11 Jamie Baxter & Albert Yoon, "No Lawyer for a Hundred Miles? Mapping the New Geography of Access to Justice in Canada" (2015) 52:1 Osgoode Hall LJ 9 at 11.

12 Lawyer numbers from Federation of Law Societies of Canada, "Statistics," online: <https://flsc.ca/resources/statistics>. Population data found at MacroTrends, "Canada Population 1950–2021," online: <https://www.macrotrends.net/countries/ CAN/canada/population>; Cara N. Carson with Jeeyoon Park, *The Lawyer Statistical Report: The U.S. Legal Profession in 2005* (Chicago: American Bar Foundation, 2012) at 2, online: <https://iptlc.usc.edu/wp-content/uploads/2019/10/2005-Lawyer-Statistical-Report-_FINAL.pdf>. Population data found at "US Population by Year", online: *Multpl* <https://www.multpl.com/united-states-population/table/ by-year>.

commentators to refer to a "jobs crisis" in the profession.[13] Any keen observer might wonder: how is there such a need for lawyers, but at the same time an oversupply?

The answer lies in a close examination of the legal market and its various distortions. One significant distortion identified by Gillian Hadfield is that the legal market is effectively a competitive bidding process between well-resourced organizations on one end and relatively poorly resourced individuals on the other.[14] Both enter the legal services market as consumers, yet organizations have disproportionate buying power that compels many legal service providers to pursue their business. The result is that legal services are often tailored to, designed for, and marketed to large corporations. Hadfield sums this up as a "disproportionate allocation to the corporate sphere."[15]

II. CONSEQUENCES OF UNAFFORDABILITY

In a word, the state of affordable access to lawyers in Canada and the United States is *abysmal*. Most people do not have any meaningful hope of affording legal services. Legal services are disproportionately focused on serving moneyed interests. But in addition to the obvious consequence of unmet legal needs, there are at least two further implications of the unaffordability problem. First, and perhaps most significant, is the impact unaffordability has on the rule of law. As we discussed in response to the criticisms of computational law and the legal singularity by Pasquale, Hildebrandt, and Weber, the rule of law depends on laws being knowable and predictable. Knowability demands that lawyers serve as information intermediaries; the public, having no specialized legal training, requires learned interlocutors to keep them apprised of their rights and obligations. In a market where the lucrative upside is concentrated in corporate services, however, lawyers are less incentivized to disseminate such information, and are certainly incentivized to charge for it. Where lawyers do provide information as a public service, it usually comes from the network of underfunded legal service organizations that are financially vulnerable. Of course, some lawyers provide information altruistically and on a *pro*

---

13 See, e.g., Jules Lobel & Matthew Chapman, "Bridging the Gap between Unmet Legal Needs and an Oversupply of Lawyers: Creating Neighborhood Law Offices – The Philadelphia Experiment" (2015) 22:1 Va J Soc Pol'y & L 71. See also Daniel Fish, "Are There Too Many Lawyers?" *Precedent JD* (6 September 2017), online: <https://precedentjd.com/news/are-there-too-many-lawyers>.
14 Hadfield, "Price," *supra* note 1 at 998–9.
15 *Ibid* at 957.

bono basis; this is laudable, but hardly dependable and certainly not adequate as a solution.

A second consequence relates to the ever-expanding role of lawyers in public and private life, a phenomenon that legal scholars call "juridification," or what Kerry Rittich describes as the "growing eminence of law and rights."[16] One manifestation of juridification is the growth in the sheer volume of laws makes it such that more and more areas of public and private life implicate a statute or regulation. In a study of the United States and Germany from 1994 to 2008, Katz et al found "impressive expansion in the size and complexity of laws over the past two and a half decades."[17] In an even shorter period – 1997 to 2006 – Ashworth and Zedner found some 3,000 new criminal laws in England and Wales.[18]

Some of this occurred in the context of a wider movement towards what Guido Calabresi and others, including Ellen Ash Peters, have called "statutorification."[19] Calabresi and Peters understood that common law systems shifted in the latter half of the twentieth century from a reliance on *ad hoc* adjudication to statutes and regulations as the law's primary source.[20] But one understudied dimension of statutorification is the extent to which non-legal rules were being revised to be more law-like, so to speak. Take, for instance, professional responsibility codes governing the legal profession. The early iterations of the American Bar Association's *Model Rules* were highly general and designed much more as "aspirational principles for good deportment" rather than as substantive rules for how lawyers ought to govern themselves in specific contexts.[21] By the time the modern iteration of the *Model Rules* was promulgated in 1983, it bore little resemblance to its predecessor documents: it was full of quasi-criminal, black-letter rules that contemplated specific sanctions.[22] This trend to more law-like

---

16 Kerry Rittich, "B. Reasons's Lure: The Enchantment of Subordination: Enchantments of Reason/Coercions of Law" (2003) 57 U Miami L Rev 727 at 727.

17 Daniel Martin Katz et al, "Complex Societies and the Growth of the Law" (2020) 10 Scientific Reports at 1, online: *Nature* <https://www.nature.com/articles/s41598-020-73623-x.pdf>.

18 Andrew Ashworth & Lucia Zedner, "Defending the Criminal Law: Reflections on the Changing Character of Crime, Procedure, and Sanctions" (2008) 2 Crim L & Philosophy 21 at 32.

19 Ellen Ash Peters, "Common Law Judging in a Statutory World: An Address" (1982) 43 U Pitt L Rev 995 at 998.

20 *Ibid* at 1008.

21 Vincent Johnson, "The Virtues and Limits of Codes in Legal Ethics" (2000) 14 Notre Dame JL Ethics & Pub Pol'y 25 at 27.

22 *Ibid* at 44.

rulemaking is observable everywhere from corporate employee policies to organizational by-laws. The takeaway here is that legal services are largely unaffordable at the very moment when lawyers' influence approaches its zenith, suggesting that more and more people may be left behind in an increasingly legalistic world.

III. RESPONSES TO THE UNAFFORDABILITY PROBLEM
BY THE LEGAL PROFESSION

What does this all have to do with the affordability problem? Quite simply: there are more laws, laws are more complicated, there are more lawyers, and lawyers are more important. Not being able to afford a lawyer, then, means being structurally precluded from participating in an ever-growing slice of public and private life.

The legal profession is often expected to fix – or at least comment on – its own unaffordability problem. The problem with this, of course, is that the profession is self-regulated, and lawyers have an effective monopoly on the provision of legal services. Some scholars have suggested that lawyers have a collective interest in maintaining the rather lucrative status quo.[23] For a long time, this claim had doctrinal cover in the United States; until the 1975 US Supreme Court case of *Goldfarb v Virginia State Bar*, the American legal profession enjoyed a judge-made exemption from antitrust laws, and so state bars were able to impose minimum fee schedules, actions that would violate the price-fixing provisions of the *Sherman Act* in most other industries.[24] Canadian courts have condoned similarly anti-competitive behaviour. In the 1982 *Jabour* case, the Supreme Court of Canada upheld the Law Society of British Columbia's right to regulate – i.e., largely prohibit – certain lawyer advertising.[25] The appellant, Donald Jabour, advertised in a newspaper "legal services at prices middle income families can afford."[26] The Law Society took steps to discipline Jabour for "conduct unbecoming a member."[27] The Supreme Court of Canada held that the *Combines Investigations Act* – the predecessor to the *Competition Act* – was not violated, effectively putting conduct properly regulated by law societies

---

23 See, e.g., Gillian Hadfield, "Legal Barriers to Innovation: The Growing Economic Cost of Professional Control over Corporate Legal Markets" (2008) 60:6 Stan L Rev 1689 at 1690–4.

24 *Goldfarb v Virginia State Bar*, 421 US 773 (1975).

25 *Canada (Attorney General) v Law Society (British Columbia)*, [1982] CarswellBC133, [1982] 2 SCR 307 [*Jabour*].

26 *Ibid* at para 19.

27 *Ibid* at para 20.

outside the scope of Canadian competition laws.[28] Commenters have since pointed to other legal ethics rules – for instance, those prohibiting non-lawyer ownership of law firms – as responsible for a certain degree of anti-competitiveness.[29]

Whether or not lawyers self-consciously undermine the affordability of legal services, one thing is certain: lawyers have not been sufficiently effective in resolving access-to-justice issues. The available solutions have tended to be partial or stopgap measures. To lawyers' credit, it would be unfair to say that the legal profession has turned a blind eye to the affordability problem; in fact, few topics have captured the attention of the professional community as much as access to justice. The American Bar Association and the Canadian Bar Association both have Access to Justice committees, which disseminate resources and issue reports. In Canada, former or current members of the Supreme Court have been rather active on the issue of access to justice. In 2016, Thomas A. Cromwell (with the lawyer Siena Antsis) wrote of the access-to-justice gap in the *Queen's Law Journal*.[30] In 2020, Justice Rosalie Abella took to the pages of the *Globe and Mail* to describe civil dispute resolution as failing to "deliver justice to ordinary people with ordinary disputes and ordinary bank accounts."[31] In 2021, former Chief Justice Beverley McLachlin described the COVID-19 pandemic as an "opportunity to build a better justice system,"[32] a full ten years after she had described increasing access as "an issue dear to my heart."[33]

The problem is not a lack of attention. Rather, it is diagnoses that do not properly account for the structural market failure in legal services, and prescriptions that largely absolve the status quo. Unsurprisingly, the policy responses to these access-to-justice issues have let lawyers

---

28 *Ibid* at para 95.

29 See, e.g., Ken Chasse, "Alternative Business Structures' 'Charity Step' to Ending the General Practitioner" (2017), online: *SSRN* <https://papers.ssrn.com/sol3/papers.cfm?abstract_id=3020489>.

30 Siena Antsis and Thomas A Cromwell, "The Legal Services Gap: Access to Justice as a Regulatory Issue" (2016) 42:1 Queen's LJ 1.

31 Rosalie Silberman Abella, "Our Civil Justice System Needs to Be Brought into the 21st Century," *Globe and Mail* (24 April 2020), online: <https://www.theglobeandmail.com/opinion/article-our-civil-justice-system-needs-to-be-brought-into-the-21st-century>.

32 Beverley McLachlin, "Access to Justice: When Life Gives You Lemons," *Lawyer's Daily* (19 May 2021), online: <https://www.law360.ca/articles/26825/access-to-justice-when-life-gives-you-lemons-beverley-mclachlin>.

33 Beverley McLachlin, Keynote Address delivered at Access to Civil Justice for Middle Income Canadians Colloquium, 2011.

largely off the hook, instead focusing on, for instance, underfunding of legal service organizations. While these funding increases are sorely needed, such proposals fall short of addressing the underlying problems contributing to affordability.

Take one prominent Canadian example. In 2013, the Action Committee on Access to Justice in Civil and Family Matters released a detailed report that took a broad view of access-to-justice problems in Canada and considered not just the affordability of legal services, but also issues like overly complex court processes. The committee, chaired by former Chief Justice McLachlin, announced a "Nine Point Access to Justice Roadmap."[34] One of the goals was to make "essential legal services available to everyone"[35] by 2018. The committee's report counseled specific improvements such as alternative billing practices, occasional outsourcing of legal services, and more delegated authority to paralegals, as just a few examples.[36] Throughout, the document described access to justice issues as "gaps,"[37] the same language preferred by regulators and access-to-justice advocates alike. The implication: the fundamentals of legal services provision are strong but need to extend wider. Indeed, few of the specific recommendations addressed how deeply implicated lawyers are in the unaffordability problem. As Ken Chasse observes, the recommendations were akin to trying to "remedy a cold" by "blowing your nose to simplify the act of breathing."[38] The report, like most access-to-justice efforts, stopped dramatically short of proposing meaningful structural changes.

b. Problem II: Excessive Legal Complexity

The unaffordability problem pervading the market for legal services is intimately related to a second problem that is a major theme of this book: legal complexity. Earlier, we discussed the substantive complexity of the law and some of the ways that computational technologies

---

34 Action Committee on Access to Justice in Civil and Family Matters, *Access to Civil and Family Justice: A Roadmap for Change* (Ottawa: Action Committee on Access to Justice in Civil and Family Matters, 2013), online: <https://www.cfcj-fcjc.org/sites/default/files/docs/2013/AC_Report_English_Final.pdf>.
35 *Ibid* at 14.
36 *Ibid.*
37 *Ibid*, e.g., at iii, 2, 24.
38 Ken Chasse (14 July 2014), comment on Malcolm Mercer, "You Can't Have It Both Ways" *Slaw* (4 July 2014), online: <https://www.slaw.ca/2014/07/04/you-cant-have-it-both-ways-2>.

might help to accommodate and mitigate this complexity. In this section, we focus on the extent to which the legal profession itself has been a purveyor of some of the complexity that makes the law inaccessible to many who need it most.

First, consider the relationship between complexity and unaffordability. In a 1992 essay called "The Market for Lawyers," the labour economist Sherwin Rosen asked: "why is it that law and medicine are our most highly paid professions?"[39] Zeroing in on law, Rosen announced what later became the conventional view: lawyers, like many professionals, are compensated in the marketplace for the expenses they incur to become lawyers. The implication is that, so long as law remains a complex endeavour that is costly to train for, legal services providers will always have ways to justify high prices.

Yet it would be a mistake to think of the legal profession as a straightforward "cost-equals-price" market story. This conventional view is complicated by the fact that lawyers offer what the economics literature calls a *credence good*.[40] Lawyers participate in market transactions as well-informed experts who sell their services to less well-informed, non-expert consumers. As Hadfield explains, "Buyers of credence goods are unable to assess how much of the good or service they need; nor can they assess whether or not the service was performed or how well."[41]

As an illustration, consider another example of a credence-good market transaction: taking a computer for repairs. Imagine yourself as the owner of a laptop with a somewhat unreliable spacebar key. After trying to fiddle with it yourself, you realize it must be a mechanical problem and take it to a nearby shop for repairs. There, the repairwoman tells you that keyboard problems are ordinarily related to malfunctioning "switches" – the mechanism beneath the keys that registers each typing stroke. You leave the computer with her and, after a brief time, return to the store to collect it. You learn that, in addition to fixing the affected switch, the repairwoman replaced every other switch on the keyboard as well as the wiring in the keyboard's matrix, which she explains to you as the circuit board that controls all typing functions. You test the computer out and, satisfied that it is working, pay the $200 repair fee. The repair fee strikes you as high, but you are grateful that

39 Sherwin Rosen, "The Market for Lawyers" (1992) 35:2 JL & Econ 215 at 216.
40 Uwe Dulleck & Rudolf Kerschbamer, "On Doctors, Mechanics, and Computer Specialists: The Economics of Credence Goods" (2006) 44 J Econ Literature 5.
41 Hadfield, "Price," *supra* note 1 at 968–72.

your laptop is in order, and you further tell yourself that the work that the repairwoman described sounded complicated and so the steep fee is reasonable.

The laptop owner in this example suffers from three information disadvantages. First, she depends on the repairwoman to diagnose the problems with the laptop's keyboard. Whether or not the laptop owner has a hunch about the problem being localized to the spacebar key might help, but the repairwoman's superior knowledge about the switch mechanisms and the circuit board means that her explanation will be more compelling, in any event. Second, the laptop owner depends on the repairwoman to perform the solution. This second disadvantage is particularly troubling in situations where the skilled professional charges according to the time or complexity involved in a task. Third, even after the repairs are completed, the laptop owner has virtually no way to determine *ex post* whether the repairs were necessary. To further illustrate this third information disadvantage, imagine that all the repairs other than the switch replacement for the spacebar key were, in fact, unnecessary. In that situation, the improperly repaired laptop would operate *exactly as the properly repaired one would*, because the problem that was localized to the spacebar key would have been fixed in either scenario. The result is a consumer with virtually no way to gauge the necessity of the services she received.[42] Perhaps most concerningly, each of these three information disadvantages can exist even in a situation where the repairwoman acted in good faith and to the best of her abilities.

This predicament is familiar to anyone who has tried to have a car repaired, only for the mechanic to identify that the problem is with a component you did not even know existed. How much you know about cars will likely dictate the extent to which you contest the bill – or even the extent to which you ask for clarification. The very same problem exists in transactions for legal services. Consumers of legal services depend on their professional interlocutors for both diagnosis and solution, as well as the professional's representation regarding the efficacy of their proposed course of action.[43] Clients with some level of legal sophistication – for instance, the general counsel of a corporation that retains an external law firm – may be well positioned to interrogate the need for

---

42 Rudolf Kerschbamer, Daniel Neururer & Matthias Sutter, "Insurance Coverage of Customers Induces Dishonesty of Sellers in Markets for Credence Goods" (2016) 113:27 Proceedings of the National Academy of Sciences of the United States of America 7454 at 7454.

43 Hadfield, "Price," *supra* note 1 at 969.

certain services. For the most part, however, information disadvantages pervade most lawyer-client relationships.

Importantly, the issue with credence goods is not merely that the experts that provide them have market power. Two additional problems exist. First, there is considerable opportunity for fraud and abuse (e.g., charging for services that were not meaningfully rendered). Second, providers of credence goods have little incentive to provide "goods or services that fit the needs of the customers," since, because of information disadvantages, customers are not well positioned to advocate for their own needs.[44]

Lawyers who are conscientious with respect to their clients' information disadvantages might compensate by providing a more robust explanation of the law, but such efforts are both discretionary and hardly enough to bridge a knowledge gap that is widened by years of specialized training. In some credence-good markets, policymakers may choose to mitigate the issue by establishing labelling practices or professional designations.[45] An American taxpayer seeking professional help in filing their tax returns, for instance, might obtain some comfort knowing that their chosen tax preparer is an "Enrolled Agent" with the Internal Revenue Service, a designation that includes an examination, continuous professional education, and a "suitability check." But these labels work to mitigate the credence-good problem only where they serve to meaningfully differentiate services. Occupational licensing in the legal profession is certainly not an effective signal of quality when choosing among lawyers; it is a basic requirement for all lawyers.

Consumers of legal services end up navigating the marketplace by using a collection of imperfect proxies for quality. One such proxy could be the lawyer's experience or education level. Though this might be useful information when selecting a lawyer, it does not necessarily indicate their quality. In any case, clients are still tasked with evaluating the lawyer's performance on an ongoing basis throughout the relationship. The laptop owner in our previous hypothetical might have found a repairwoman with an excellent reputation, but nevertheless had insufficient information to determine whether the repairs she received were necessary or reasonably priced. A second, more troubling, proxy for the quality of legal services is, ironically, price. There is a popular view that

---

44 *Ibid* at 968–72.
45 See, e.g., Brian Roe & Ian Sheldon, "Credence Good Labelling: The Efficiency and Distributional Implications of Several Policy Approaches" (2007) 89:4 American J of Agricultural Economics 1020.

more expensive lawyers are better, a view which is not well supported empirically.[46]

Even still, this understates the credence-good problem in the market for legal services. As we discussed earlier, legal complexity is not mere difficulty, but difficulty *in addition to* ambiguity and uncertainty. The law is substantively hard to grasp (thus justifying the involved training), it is often indeterminate, and the legal process it is effectuated through (i.e., adjudication by human beings trying to make sense of the same difficulty and indeterminacy) produces outcomes that are highly variable. Consider once more the example of the laptop repairwoman; in that hypothetical, the repairwoman's expertise is based on her understanding of the laptop's underlying engineering, which is premised on reliable knowledge of computer systems and their mechanics. In legal practice, little is as certain as the operability of a keyboard switch or a laptop's circuit system. Instead, clients seek counsel from experts who themselves make inferences and judgments that are, in the best circumstances, informed predictions about processes that they do not control.[47] Moreover, lawyers make such predictions in contexts of incomplete – and occasionally inaccessible – information.

One consequence of this form of legal complexity is that it is nearly impossible to compare and ascertain the quality of lawyers' performance. Hadfield writes:

> Did the plaintiff win because of the lawyering or in spite of it? What particular lawyering decisions did, and did not, contribute to the outcome? Legal malpractice standards reflect this: lawyers will be held legally accountable for failing to file documents within statutory time limits or for mishandling funds, but their judgments will not be "second-guessed." Lawyers' judgments are insulated from review in a way that doctors' judgments, for example, are not. Relatedly, providers of legal services will generally provide no assurances about either outcome (except indirectly through contingency fees) or the amount of time that a matter will take; that the market for legal services is so overwhelmingly characterized by the absence of flat rates is evidence of this.[48]

---

46 Hadfield, "Price," *supra* note 1 at 971.
47 *Ibid* at 971–2.
48 *Ibid* at 970.

Here, Hadfield observes how difficult it is to meaningfully examine lawyer quality; more recently, researchers such as Daniel Linna have also observed that the legal profession barely attempts to measure performance, or "at least not in a way that other industries would recognize."[49] As a consequence, prices in the credence-good market for legal services tend to bear little relationship to lawyer quality.

To date, there are no empirical studies establishing what proportion of legal services are unnecessary, in part because of the lack of meaningful standards for what constitutes "necessary" legal work. But the economics literature suggests that services with credence characteristics often feature "undertreatment" and "overtreatment."[50] Undertreatment occurs when a consumer receives low-quality services for the price. This would occur in legal services where a lawyer drafts a defective contract, for instance. Overtreatment occurs whenever "additional benefits to the consumer are smaller than the additional costs,"[51] such as a wholesale replacement of a laptop's keyboard matrix when only a single switch demanded fixing. Overtreatment is everywhere, in both low- and high-stakes contexts. Wolinsky found that most automobile repairs are unnecessary,[52] while Gruber, Kim, and Mayzlin found that "the relative frequency of Caesarian deliveries compared to normal child births reacts to the fee differentials of health insurance programs for both types of treatment."[53] In the extreme, overtreatment is fraudulent. But consider how easy overtreatment is in the context of the lawyer-client relationship. Given the complexity inherent in the substantive law, a lawyer may bill for confirmatory legal research (e.g., to double-check that their understanding of the law is correct). This legal research could take hours and hours, depending on the lawyer's access to legal information, their skill as a researcher, and the relative clarity of the law at issue. Absent legal sophistication, a client will have little ability to determine whether the confirmatory research was necessary.

---

49 Daniel Linna, *Research Handbook on Big Data Law*, ed by Roland Vogl (Cheltenham, UK: Edward Elgar Publishing, 2021) at 404.

50 Kerschbamer, Neururer & Sutter, *supra* note 42 at 7454.

51 *Ibid* at 7454.

52 Asher Wolinsky, "Competition in Markets for Credence Goods" (1995) 151:1 J of Institutional & Theoretical Economics (JITE) Zeitschrift Für Die Gesamte Staatswissenschaft 117.

53 Uwe Dulleck, Rudolf Kerschbamer & Matthias Sutter, "The Economics of Credence Goods: On the Role of Liability, Verifiability, Reputation and Competition" (2009) Institute of Labor Economics Working Paper No. 4030 at 4, citing J Gruber, J Kim & D Mayzlin, "Physician Fees and Procedure Intensity: The Case of Cesarean Delivery" (1999) 18:4 J of Health Economics 473.

The nature of legal research is such that even the lawyer may not even know for certain if confirmatory work is necessary.

III. The Solution: Universal Legal Literacy

By now, the access-to-justice problem is understood and acknowledged in all corners of the legal profession. Lawyers are abundant, but their efforts are allocated such that corporate clients are better served than individuals with acute legal needs. The market for lawyers' services is so imperfect that it does not follow the traditional rules of supply and demand, nor are its prices based on truly competitive dynamics. Solutions are ineffective, in part because they aim at addressing the unaffordability problem alone. As we discussed above, these sorts of solutions underestimate the role of legal complexity as the driver of law's incoherent and insufficiently competitive marketplace.

Put more starkly: law, as it is currently conceived, is the problem. Access-to-justice initiatives that focus on closing "gaps," then, are insufficient, as they presume that the fundamental nature of the lawyer-client relationship is strong and simply needs to be extended to all. As the credence-good problem demonstrates, more representation alone does not solve the disadvantageous position that consumers of legal services find themselves in. So long as an information disadvantage exists, clients will not be able to adequately gauge lawyer quality, influence prices, or discourage overtreatment or undertreatment of legal problems. Here, we take a bold view and suggest that access to justice can be meaningfully achieved only with universal legal literacy.

a. Imagining Universal Legal Literacy

Universal legal literacy recognizes that legal questions – and the situations that give rise to the acute need for legal representation – are too important for lawyers to be in the position of monopolizing both the diagnosis and the prescription. In other credence-good transactions, such as in doctor-patient relationships, the gulf between professional and layperson knowledge is essentially unavoidable: doctors can do their best to explain illness and treatment, but the human body is, as a matter of fact, complex. In law, there is no such immutable reason for individuals to struggle to understand their legal rights and obligations. Universal legal literacy means that individuals will have, at a minimum, the wherewithal to evaluate their own legal needs such that lawyer-client relationships are not so imbalanced.

First, a note on terminology. Universal legal literacy is exactly as it sounds – an aspiration for *all* individuals to understand the substantive laws that govern them. The concept is not new. Scholars have used the specific term "legal literacy" since at least the early 1980s. James Boyd White described legal literacy in 1983 as "the degree of competence in legal discourse required for meaningful and active life in our increasingly legalistic and litigious culture."[54] In White's rendering, individuals do not need to know how to handle their own legal affairs directly, but would at least know when to engage "specialists," and would have the capacity to "advance ... [their] own interests" in more personal affairs that implicate laws, such as landlord versus tenant disputes, interactions with the police, or dealings with government administrative agencies.[55] White's definition is particularly appealing because it recognizes the importance of legal literacy given the increasing juridification of institutions, and emphasizes the need for literacy as a vehicle for meaningful participation in the legal system. The authors of the American Bar Association's 1989 *Legal Literacy Summary* took a similar participatory approach, defining legal literacy as "the ability to make critical judgments about the substance of the law, the legal process, and available legal resources, and to effectively utilize the legal system and articulate strategies to improve it."[56]

To the extent that these definitions have shortcomings, it is because they approach legal literacy as an *end state* that individuals arrive at, rather than as a continuum. Put differently, much like language literacy, individuals cross a threshold at which they are "legally literate," but perhaps not yet capable of taking charge of their own legal affairs. Mary Sarah Bilder's contribution in 1999 offers a more helpful reading, describing legal literacy as "the reading, writing, speaking, and thinking practices that relate to the conduct of litigation."[57] To Bilder, legal literacy is a "spectrum of functional skills," with lawyers at one end and individuals with complete ignorance of the law at another.

---

54 James Boyd White, "The Invisible Discourse of the Law: Reflections on Legal Literacy and General Education" (1983) U Colo L Rev 54 at 144, online: University of Michigan Law School Scholarship Repository <https://repository.law.umich.edu/cgi/viewcontent.cgi?article=3115&context=articles>.
55 *Ibid.*
56 Quoted in Archie Zariski, *Legal Literacy: An Introduction to Legal Studies* (Athabasca: Athabasca University Press, 2014) at 22.
57 Mary Sarah Bilder, "The Lost Lawyers: Early American Legal Literates and Transatlantic Legal Culture" (1999) 11:47 Yale JL & Human 47 at 51, online: https://digitalcommons.law.yale.edu/cgi/viewcontent.cgi?article=1207&context=yjlh [https://hdl.handle.net/20.500.13051/7276].

Importantly, whether one is a lawyer is not necessarily an indicator of where one exists along the spectrum; though many lawyers will have "high levels of legal literacy," individuals without legal training might, as well.[58]

Here, we build on the definitions of White, the American Bar Association, and Bilder, but suggest a framework that better tracks how we think of language literacy. The foundational literature on language literacy conceives of literacy as having three "levels": (1) basic literacy; (2) comprehension; and (3) functional or practical literacy.[59] As Lawrence L. Smith explains, basic literacy means the ability to translate written material into oral language. A basically literate individual knows, for instance, that the collection of lines and shapes on pages of text are referring to something that can be expressed verbally. The second level, comprehension, means that individuals can "understand the meaning of verbal materials."[60] Functional or practical literacy is the ability to use readable materials to perform tasks.

Universal legal literacy has similar building blocks, as demonstrated in figure 7.1. The first stage of legal literacy is basic legal literacy. Where Smith's basic language literacy is the capacity to recognize shapes and lines as having expressible verbal equivalents, basic *legal* literacy is the capacity to recognize certain information as being legal in character. For instance, an individual with basic legal literacy will recognize a website's Terms of Use and "click if you agree" prompt as suggestive of a contract. If that individual understands what that information means, they are at the next stage: legal comprehension. Like reading comprehension, it is about capacity and not knowledge; just as literate people need not read every book to demonstrate their ability to do so, legal comprehension simply demands that individuals be capable of understanding the law, not necessarily that they have substantive knowledge of most legal provisions. The next stage, practical legal literacy, means that a person understands the information well enough to do something with it – for instance, to dispute some of the terms, initiate a legal process contemplated by the terms, negotiate the terms, or, alternatively, provide informed acceptance. On this continuum, lawyers have what we term "legal professional literacy," which sees functional literacy as minimum competence.

---

58 *Ibid* at 51.
59 See, e.g., Lawrence L. Smith, "Literacy: Definitions and Implications" (1977) 54:2 Language Arts 135.
60 *Ibid* at 135.

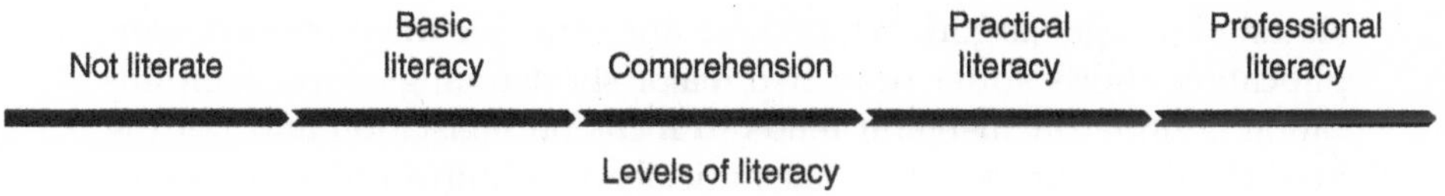

Not literate	Basic literacy	Comprehension	Practical literacy	Professional literacy

Levels of literacy

Figure 7.1. Range of legal literacy

Consider how universal legal literacy disrupts the credence-good problem in the lawyer-client relationship. An individual with basic legal literacy has the capacity to understand actions that give rise to legal needs. This means, at minimum, an informed sense of when to engage a lawyer's services. As an illustrative example, imagine an individual who receives a letter from the Canada Revenue Agency (CRA) alleging that he falsely reported his income for the past three tax years. The letter demands that the taxpayer respond within thirty days with documentation to indicate that he did not underreport his taxable income. If he has basic legal literacy, the taxpayer might recognize that he is in some legal jeopardy and could retain a lawyer to assist with his response. If he has legal comprehension, he might review the letter and understand that no legal process has been initiated. Recognizing this, he could respond with the documentation in his possession and wait to see if the CRA wishes to pursue its allegations further before he decides to engage a lawyer. This example also demonstrates how different degrees of legal jeopardy will demand appropriate levels of legal literacy. Imagine that our taxpayer submits a timely response to the CRA's request, but nevertheless receives a follow-up letter indicating that his documentation is deficient, and that the CRA has assessed him to have a higher taxable income and therefore a sudden tax debt. If our taxpayer disputes the CRA's charges, he would be relying on practical legal literacy.

b. Universal Legal Literacy in the Legal Singularity

Our analysis thus far raises the ultimate question, how can universal legal literacy best be developed and achieved? One strategy for improving legal literacy is to look at simplifying the information so that it is more easily digestible to a wider range of people. Importantly, though, universal legal literacy differs from mere simplification or clarification of the law. Simplification of the law is an age-old concept. In fact, some of the early efforts to codify the law were positioned by proponents as simplification efforts. Modern simplification efforts are usually part and parcel of broader law reform efforts that include redrafting legislation, making adjudication procedures easier to navigate, and eliminating legal jargon. While these are attractive interventions, simplification efforts suffer from two major shortcomings. First, simplification is under-inclusive: it tends to focus on legislation and not the myriad other sources of law, like judicial and administrative decisions. To be fair, simplifying written law is an important start, and perhaps proponents theorize that adjudicated decision-making will be less difficult to parse if the law is clear in the first instance. This may be true generally, but courts have a demonstrated capacity to complicate simply stated laws, in part because the facts established in litigation might demand that the law be stretched to accommodate a new situation. To merely simplify codified laws, then, will not necessarily lead to easier-to-follow legal outcomes.

A second problem with simplification as an objective is that it treats complexity as inherently undesirable. Keen readers may wonder whether we are being inconsistent, given our protestations about legal complexity throughout this book. Our view, however, is that legal complexity is a problem only to the extent that it puts legal information out of the reach of those most affected by it. Some degree of complexity will generally be helpful and will support a given law achieving its normative objectives. Complete law will have to contend with the complexity of life, human relationships, institutions, and so on, and, for that reason, must be fundamentally capable of dealing with subtlety, nuance, and complexity. For instance, given the sophistication of international business transactions, it makes sense to devise sophisticated tax laws for identifying taxable income and protecting the government's tax base. If even the most complex tax laws are well calibrated, they will contemplate and generate the optimal tax treatment for even the most convoluted transactions. Even if such laws are stripped of any legal jargon and written with maximum clarity, their substantive complexity alone would probably demand specialized knowledge. At worst, oversimplification undermines the law's regulative function.

An analogy here might be helpful. At the outset of the personal computer revolution, now often traced to 1977 and the launch of three new PCs – the Commodore PET 2001, the Apple II, and the Tandy/Radio Shack TRS-80 – personal computing attracted users who were comfortable with interacting with command-line interfaces and computer source code, and found delight in tinkering with the new technology. If we may overgeneralize, personal computing in the late 1970s and early 1980s attracted users who were sophisticated, curious, relatively well educated, and, well, nerdy. To get practical work done with computers required significant experience and expertise. And yet the machines themselves and the source code used were orders of magnitudes simpler than the computing devices that we use today and the software that powers our hardware. From the perspective of the user, however, a smartphone in 2023 is vastly more accessible than an Apple II or a TRS-80 to an average person. One does not have to be a nerd to take a selfie, send a text message, or find just the right purchase through an online retailer.

We imagine a future in which the underlying complexity of the law can simultaneously be vastly denser and more technical, and have greater safeguards to ensure fair outcomes – as it must be if we are to approach the realization of complete law through the legal singularity – but in which the users of the law experience it as intuitive, fair, trustworthy, and reliable to use as today's smartphones. We do not take this to be at all implausible. In fact, it is already on its way.

Chapter Eight

Implications for Government

I. Introduction

In the last two chapters, we described how predictive technologies can allow individuals to have a real-time sense of their legal rights and obligations through universal legal literacy, such that the costliness and inefficiencies of the legal services market are no longer as crippling for people with legal needs. The same computational legal technologies have tremendous potential for use in lawmaking and the delivery of government services. With a clearer understanding of causes and consequences, governments can do a better job of governing, with better adjudication, better regulatory decisions, better distributive calls, and better policymaking. Considering that lawyers are already harnessing artificial intelligence to better advise their clients to use legal loopholes, the defensive value for the government in being an adopter of such technology becomes readily apparent. Perhaps most interestingly, government use of AI will not be limited to factual determinations or objective truths. It will cover those, of course, but it will contribute to improving normative, value-laden judgments. AI will also be used to deal with some of the most intractable problems, from predicting consequences of specific legislative rules to proposing new legislative text. We also discuss some of the possible pitfalls and adoption issues that this technology will entail.

In this chapter, we explain how to advance the interests for the populace at large by considering how predictive technology could improve the administration of democratic government. There are a few aspects to this. First is the delivery of services that the government offers, in the broadest sense. That includes decision-making in everything from tax law audits to immigration law decisions. AI can help to make those decisions more consistent, fair, and transparent. AI-based systems can help government agencies better determine need, leading to the potential for improved targeting of social-assistance programs. Second is the making and revising of the law itself: i.e., legislation. This is how the government regulates activity that it does not itself engage in. AI will allow legislators to make better laws that both better reflect their subjective intentions, thereby enhancing democratic control over the executive and the judiciary, and also normatively fit with the rest of the law and our fundamental values through a process of reflective equilibrium.

Finally, the governments will need to adopt this technology to keep up with the private sector. Private actors will adopt AI to help advance their interests and achieve the legal outcomes they want. If AI can find loopholes in the law faster than they can be closed up by human legislators, the private sector will continue to have a permanent advantage over the public sector. Government use of AI will level that playing field and allow the government to regulate in the public interest more effectively. We note that although there may be various issues at first ("growing pains"), governments' use of AI should provide for more consistent law in the long run, not to mention the benefits of more consistency in decision-making as well as better distribution of resources among the populace.

II. Governments and Technology

Generations of political scientists and philosophers have devoted careers to studying the workings of the government and theorizing what an ideal government should look like. Pondering such questions is not limited to the domain of political theorists, however. Anyone who has spent tiresome hours filling out seemingly never-ending forms for government program applications or standing in crowded lines for basic government services has questioned government efficiency. Many may have wondered why they are required, time and time again, to laboriously provide information that the government already has. Why are our interactions with government agencies – from filing taxes and renewing our licences to applying for benefits and updating our addresses on government-issued cards – so frequently wasteful and frustrating?

There is no reason to spend much time presenting evidence for government inefficiency – the reader has probably experienced it in one way or another. The experience is so universal that, in a comical moment that elicits chuckles from both children and adults, Disney portrayed workers at the Department of Motor Vehicles – or the "DMV," a US state-level government agency – as sloths in the animated film *Zootopia*.[1] The

---

1 Michael Cavna, "How Record-Setting 'Zootopia' Is the Perfect Film for This Politically Divisive Campaign Season," *Washington Post* (8 March 2016), online: <https://www. washingtonpost.com/news/comic-riffs/wp/2016/03/07/how-record-setting -zootopia-is-the-perfect-film-for-this-politically-divisive-campaign-season/>.

joke resonates with viewers as representative of their experience receiving services from certain government agencies, the DMV being just one of the most common examples.

The reasons for the suboptimality of government services are manifold, but at least some of the inefficiency is attributable to a failure to integrate cutting-edge technologies at the right time. In *Modern Public Information Technology Systems: Issues and Challenges*, Shannon Howle Schelin reports that

> the [American] government was one of the final sectors to adopt the telephone, approximately 10 to 15 years after its distribution to the public at large. The lag associated with governmental adoption of new technologies continues today. In fact, research decades ago ... indicated that local government, in general, has had about a 10-year lag time between the introduction of new technology and its adoption and use in localities.[2]

As recently as 2016, for example, the US Defense Department was still using floppy disks on some of its legacy systems.[3] The consequences of archaic systems are two-fold. First, and most obviously, outdated technologies slow down operations. Second, the perception of governments as being outdated affects public trust and eventually adversely affects perceived legitimacy. Extensive literature points to the savings that governments could realize through technology. A 2010 report by the Technology CEO Council – a group of chief executive officers from leading American information technology companies – claimed that the US federal government could save over $1 trillion by 2020 with technology-driven solutions to common operation costs. The report, titled "One Trillion Reasons" offers seven recommendations, such as consolidating information technology infrastructure and streamlining government supply chains.[4]

---

2 Shannon Howle Schelin, "E-Government: An Overview" in G David Garson, ed, *Modern Public Information Technology Systems: Issues and Challenges* (Hershey, PA: Idea Group, 2007).

3 "US Nuclear Force Still Uses Floppy Disks," *BBC News* (26 May 2016), online: <https://www.bbc.com/news/world-us-canada-36385839>.

4 Technology CEO Council, "One Trillion Reasons: How Commercial Best Practices to Maximize Productivity Can Save Taxpayer Money and Enhance Government Services," (online): <http://www.techceocouncil.org/clientuploads/reports/TCC _One_Trillion_Reasons_FINAL.pdf>.

Beyond financial savings, technology offers the government another colossal advantage: public trust. Christopher Reddick explains:

> Research shows that e-government is worth pursuing as a means of enhancing a trusting relationship between citizen and government ... Research shows that e-government satisfaction is positively associated with trust in government ... In the offline world, an individual who is frustrated and disappointed with government services is likely to report lower levels of confidence in government services and less trust; research indicates the same finding for the online world.[5]

The connection between improved government efficiency and public trust is intuitive: taxpayers who receive prompt and effective service are more likely to trust their government than are those who experience frustrating delays, confusing instructions, and wrongful penalization. Maintaining and building a trusting relationship between government and citizens is important for several reasons. Consider the findings of the Taxpayer Advocate Service (TAS), which works closely with the American Internal Revenue Service (IRS). TAS reports that "[i]mproved customer service resulting from funding the IRS's modernization plans is likely to improve taxpayer trust of the IRS and, in turn, increase voluntary compliance, increasing overall revenue for the federal government."[6] In summary, technology can help the government improve the trust and compliance of its citizens, and increase its revenue.

In the following sections, we will show how computational methods will improve government services and the workings of the legislature. We will also show that the benefits of computational methods reach farther than simply optimizing existing systems and procedures.

III. Artificially Intelligent Governments

Artificial intelligence, being one of the most advanced developments of technology, stands to benefit government services and its users in myriad ways. Compared to human workers, machines process huge data sets with vastly superior speed and accuracy, work diligently without any breaks and distractions, scale work up or down quickly,

---

5 Christopher Reddick, *Public Administration and Information Technology* (Burlington, MA: Jones & Bartlett Learning, 2012), 23.
6 Taxpayer Advocate Service, *2019 Annual Report*, online: <https://www.taxpayeradvocate .irs.gov/wp-content/uploads/2020/08/ARC19_Volume1_MSP_02_INFORMATION TECHNOLOGYMODERNIZATION.pdf>.

and are better at performing routine and repetitive work, which is an essential part of many government services. Although it is difficult to assign a precise dollar value to the potential savings that will result from government adoption of AI, some speculate that the number will be in the billions. Deloitte reports that AI could free up 30 per cent of the US government workforce's time within five to seven years through automation.[7] There is more to the employment story, however. While some jobs will disappear because of automation, new jobs will emerge. The computational methods that governments will use in the future will require someone to make, research, integrate, supervise, maintain, and fix them. New tasks related to the integration of AI-based tools into government work will be created, which we may not even be able to conceive of from our current perspective. If this prediction does not sound convincing, think back to job seekers twenty years ago. Would they have been able to imagine that, in just two decades, software architects, data scientists, and artificial intelligence specialists would be in high demand?

AI is particularly well suited for government use. Governments function, in part, due to their exclusive ability to collect and maintain vast amounts of data. Thousands of government workers spend their workdays collecting, recording, organizing, analysing, and processing various types of data. Data play significant roles in both the internal operation of government agencies and institutions as well as the external services that governments provide to their citizens. AI lends itself particularly well to these roles. As William D. Eggers and Thomas Beyer observe, "One reason AI can work well for government is that it needs volumes of data – and governments have plenty of volume."[8]

Artificial intelligence researchers and experts observe that the governments with greater data will have an advantage in leading the development of AI-driven services. In his book *AI Superpowers: China, Silicon Valley, and the New World Order*, chairman and CEO of Sinovation Ventures Kai-Fu Lee argues that China has this advantage in the modern world. Lee explains that harnessing the power of AI to its full potential

---

7 Peter Viechniki & William D Eggers, "How Much Time and Money Can AI Save Government?" *Deloitte Insights* (26 April 2017), online: <https://www2.deloitte.com/us/en/insights/focus/cognitive-technologies/artificial-intelligence-government-analysis.html>.

8 William D Eggers & Thomas Beyer, "AI-Augmented Government: Climbing the AI Maturity Curve" *Deloitte Insights* (24 June 2019) at 9, online (PDF): https://www2.deloitte.com/us/en/insights/industry/public-sector/government-trends/2020/ai-augmented-government.html.

requires four inputs: abundant data, hungry entrepreneurs, AI scientists, and an AI-friendly policy environment. China's advantage stems from the fact that it has an "unparalleled trove of real-world data."[9] In fact, according to Lee, "China has already surpassed the United States in terms of sheer volume as the number one producer of data. That data is not just impressive in quantity, but thanks to China's unique technology ecosystem – an alternate universe of products and functions not seen anywhere else – that data is tailor-made for building profitable AI companies."[10]

As AI rapidly advances its capabilities and proliferates in the private sector, its place in the government is shifting from a mere advantage to a significant necessity. The need for governments to respond efficiently to technological developments within the private sector is nothing new; in the United States, for instance, the federal government recognized the value of radio technology and facilitated its proliferation with the passage of the *Radio Act of 1927*, which also created the Federal Radio Commission.[11] Now, as private businesses and individuals harness the powers of AI for their own purposes, governments will have no choice but to adopt these technologies themselves in order to preserve effective regulation and prevent the exploitation of regulatory and administrative loopholes. Consider, for example, the interplay between the government and private entity advisors in the context of tax law. As one of us has written:

> Advisors working with machine learning systems will be able to devise ever more complex and ingenious tax avoidance plans that strain the capacity of the tax administration to respond effectively. For this reason, governments (including the courts, the tax authorities, and policymakers) will use the machines as well. The result will be a legal arms race, with the machines playing a central role in the escalation of tensions.[12]

The need for governments to adopt artificially intelligent tools and improve their AI literacy more generally is urgent, as there are individuals and groups seeking to exploit AI for nefarious purposes. Consider the phenomenon of "adversarial AI": the subversion of AI systems to

---

9 Kai-Fu Lee, *AI Superpowers: China, Silicon Valley, and the New World Order* (New York: Houghton Mifflin Harcourt, 2018) at 17.
10 *Ibid* at 16.
11 See generally W Jefferson Davis, "The Radio Act of 1927" (1927) 13 Va L Rev 8.
12 Benjamin Alarie, "The Path of the Law: Towards Legal Singularity" (2016) 66 UTLJ 443 at 451.

evade detection and manipulate users.[13] Examples of adversarial AI include "deepfakes": artificial video and audio creations that realistically portray an individual or a group of people saying or doing something that never actually happened.[14] Forbes reported an incident whereby a deepfake was used "to trick an executive at a U.K. energy company into wiring money to a supplier. The victim, in this case, received a phone call that he thought was his boss instructing him to initiate the transfer. The call and email that follows replicated the mannerisms, accent, and diction of his boss."[15] Adversarial AI can also be used to exploit common AI-based aid systems, such as embedding voice commands within a piece of music that are inaudible to the human ear and yet can be picked up by Google assistant on an Android phone. These examples portray a clear need for the government to, at least, maintain close supervision on the latest developments in AI and employ knowledgeable AI cybersecurity specialists. The government must be prepared to defend itself and the public from future adversarial AI attacks but is not well positioned to do so without meaningfully embracing the technology for its own purposes.

IV. Current Government Applications of AI

Governments across the world have already shown strong interest in developing and strengthening their AI systems in both the public and private sectors. France has announced plans to invest more than €1.5 billion into AI-related research, with an emphasis on four specific areas: health, transportation, the environment, and security.[16] Similarly, South Korea announced plans to spend US$2 billion by 2022 on strengthening its AI research and development and funding large-scale AI projects related to medicine, national defence, and public

---

13 Kyle Wiggers, "Adversarial Attacks in Machine Learning: What They Are and How to Stop Them," *Venture Beat* (29 May 2021), online: <https://venturebeat .com/2021/05/29/adversarial-attacks-in-machine-learning-what-they-are-and-how -to-stop-them/>.

14 Danielle K Citron & Robert Chesney, "Deep Fakes: A Looming Challenge for Privacy, Democracy and National Security," (2019) 107 Cal L Rev 1753.

15 Rahul Kashyap, "Are You Ready for the Age of Adversarial AI? Attackers Can Leverage Artificial Intelligence Too," *Forbes* (9 January 2020), online: <https://www .forbes.com/sites/forbestechcouncil/2020/01/09/are-you-ready-for-the-age-of -adversarial-ai-attackers-can-leverage-artificial-intelligence-too/?sh=794147cd4703>.

16 Mathieu Rosemain & Michel Rose, "France to Spend 1.8 Billion in AI to Compete with U.S., China," *Reuters* (29 March 2018), online: <https://www.reuters.com /article/us-france-tech-idUSKBN1H51XP>.

safety.[17] In 2018, the United States issued an executive order from the president, naming AI "the second highest R&D priority after the security of the American people for the fiscal year 2020,"[18] while the US Department of Defense announced plans to invest up to US$2 billion over five years towards the advancement of AI.[19] China also invests billions in funding for AI development and takes proactive steps to digitize government administration, much of which was outlined in a comprehensive Artificial Intelligence Development Plan in 2017.[20]

One country that stands out for its integration of technology and artificially intelligent systems into its public sector is Estonia, a small Baltic nation in northern Europe. Hailed as the world's most advanced digital society, Estonia has built an impressive technological statecraft project called e-Estonia. As Nathan Heller explains in the *New Yorker*:

> E-Estonia is the most ambitious project in technological statecraft today, for it includes all members of the government, and alters citizens' daily lives. The normal services that government is involved with – legislation, voting, education, justice, health care, banking, taxes, policing, and so on – have been digitally linked across one platform, wiring up the nation.[21]

On its official website, e-Estonia claims that Estonia "is probably the only country in the world where 99 percent of the public services are available online 24/7" and that the project saves the country "844 years of working time annually."[22] The platform lists several key features,

---

17 David Schwartz, "South Korea Investing $2 Billion in Bid to Compete for Artificial Intelligence Market," *Tech Transfer Central* (16 October 2018), online: <https://techtransfercentral.com/2018/10/16/south-korea-investing-2-billion-in-bid-to-become-to-compete-for-artificial-intelligence-market/>.

18 Kathleen Walch, "Why The Race for AI Dominance Is More Global Than You Think," *Forbes* (9 February 2020), online: <https://www.forbes.com/sites/cognitiveworld/2020/02/09/why-the-race-for-ai-dominance-is-more-global-than-you-think/?sh=49cd1ece121f>.

19 Drew Harwell, "Defense Department Pledges Billions toward Artificial Intelligence Research," *Washington Post* (7 September 2018), online: <https://www.washingtonpost.com/technology/2018/09/07/defense-department-pledges-billions-toward-artificial-intelligence-research/>.

20 Huw Roberts et al, "The Chinese Approach to Artificial Intelligence: An Analysis of Policy, Ethics, and Regulation" (2021) 36 AI & Society 59, online: <https://doi.org/10.1007/s00146-020-00992-2>.

21 Nathan Heller, "Estonia, the Digital Republic," *New Yorker* (11 December 2017), online: <https://www.newyorker.com/magazine/2017/12/18/estonia-the-digital-republic>.

22 "Government Cloud," online: *e-Estonia* <https://e-estonia.com/solutions/e-governance/>.

such as e-governance (e.g., i-Voting and e-Cabinet) and business and finance (e-Tax, e-Banking, e-Business Register). These features have transformed the everyday lives of Estonians, enabling faster and more efficient government service and administration. Citizens' data – ranging from education history and medical records to pet vaccinations and taxes – are tied to a chip-ID card that stores everything in one accessible place. Most bureaucratic processes can be done online, and data are shared with approved bodies, which reduces the need for tedious paperwork and form-filling.

Estonia's digitization also makes it borderless. For example, you can become a resident of Estonia in the next ten minutes through its e-residency program, without stepping foot on Estonian land. Heller explains: "The application cost a hundred euros, and the hardest part was finding a passport photograph to upload, for my card. After approval, I would pick up my credentials in person, like a passport, at the Estonian Consulate in New York."[23] Countries are taking active steps to integrate technology and artificial intelligence into their services and administration, and we are likely going to see many others joining Estonia in the quest for developing a fully digitized nation.

V. Applications of AI in Service Provision and Regulation

Regulation of human behaviour is one of the most important functions of any government. We foresee two broad applications of computational methods in the regulation of human behaviour. First, AI-based tools will help the government streamline the administration of law in different areas. In this section, we discuss how this will affect three areas: tax regulation, government benefits, and immigration. Second, the algorithms will eventually *become* the law, such that AI-based tools will be used to not only reflect the law but also to refine and improve it on a continuous basis.

a. Taxation

In the United States, the IRS deals with over 200 million tax returns every year. To require auditors to check the veracity of each one would be virtually impossible; in fact, tax officials cannot regularly review every filed tax return, to the point that there is a backlog of roughly

---

23 Heller, *supra* note 21.

35 million tax returns for 2021.[24] Thus, for a long time, auditors have picked which returns to audit based on various factors that data, experience, and policy suggest correlate with inaccurate reporting. With the use of AI-powered computational methods, time will no longer be a constraint.

As another scenario, imagine that you are on vacation, far from home. You take out your credit card to pay for a meal at a restaurant, but the card is declined. Although you may not be aware of it, an AI-powered process has just occurred before your eyes. It is likely that the transaction was blocked by your bank because the AI system that the bank employs to check transactions for suspicious activity has picked up on the fact that the card was used in an unusual location, and, therefore, may have been stolen. You may not be surprised to learn that banks use such technological safeguards, but not many people know that they are also commonly employed by tax regulators.

Identity theft is an important issue in tax-regulation services. How can the government catch it on returns? Here, computational methods can be tremendously helpful. In fact, AI-based technologies are already being used by the IRS to combat identity theft and other common issues that tax regulators aim to resolve. Jeff Butler, associate director of data management, at IRS Research, Analysis, and Statistics, reports that the IRS uses various subfields of AI-like machine learning, recommender systems, and natural language processing to optimize various tasks and combat a multitude of problems. He describes how the IRS employs natural language processing:

> Text classification is increasingly being used to analyze tax forms, attachments, internal decision documents, case notes, and third party information. Entity extraction has been applied to Bank Secrecy Act reports, Department of Justice documents, and reportable transactions. Topic modeling is used to analyze corporate change of accounting statements and IRS Appeals decisions. Fuzzy matching has been used as first-stage input to models of tax preparer networks. Word embeddings have recently been introduced to model case notes from customer service interactions.[25]

---

24 Carmen Reinicke, "Still Waiting on Your 2020 Tax Refund? You Aren't Alone" *CNBC* (30 June 2021), online: <https://www.cnbc.com/2021/06/30/the-irs-has-35-million-unprocessed-tax-returns-from-2021.html>.

25 Jeff Butler, "Analytical Challenges in Modern Tax Administration: A Brief History of Analytics at the IRS" (2020) 16 Ohio State Tech LJ 258 at 264.

As Butler's quote shows, computational methods in tax administration do not stop at enforcement. They are offered by the government to individuals to help them with answers to their questions. This will not only increase people's satisfaction with government services, but also lead to an increase in compliance. AI is also used in classification – i.e., the legal characterization of facts. Rather than leaving this task up to the intuition of the auditor, AI-produced classification can predict how courts would rule on any given issue. Such predictions will save the IRS time and will be more accurate, leading to fewer disputes between taxpayers and the government.

The government could agree not to contest an AI-based tool's predictions for classifications, providing certainty to both the government and taxpayers. AI would provide a simple, fair rule for taxpayers that could allow them to structure their affairs to avoid unnecessary tax, but also would allow the government to prevent the needless expenses of time-consuming audits and court battles. The tools could also be pro-taxpayer. For example, they could detect deductions that the taxpayer is eligible for on the basis of the taxpayer's data, and automatically apply them to the taxpayer's generated tax return.

b. Government Benefits Programs

Computational methods will also improve government benefits distribution. Predictive technology can tell governments who is most in need and what might best help them. It could calculate need with dramatically improved algorithms drawing on disparate data sources. Technological needs-testing could compare all the applications for government benefits and determine who should get how much, and potentially do away entirely with the need for applications. Government benefits could become a push system, rather than a pull system. Policy evaluations could also leverage real-time information on the target efficiency of benefit programs and assess possible changes.

In addition to determining who should get how much and when, computational tools can help figure out who is cheating the system. The United Kingdom is an early adopter of such tools. In 2018, the Department for Work and Pensions, responsible for handing out benefits, started using an AI-based system to catch fraud.[26] The system looks

---

26 Lis Evenstad, "Department for Work and Pensions Uses Artificial Intelligence to Crack Down on Benefits Fraud," *Computer Weekly* (2 July 2018), online: <https://www.computerweekly.com/news/252444049/Department-for-Work-and-Pensions-uses-artificial-intelligence-to-crack-down-on-benefits-fraud>.

for patterns in benefits applications. Unlike a human, it is not limited in how many applications it reads, so it can more easily detect patterns that a person might miss, such as one created by a criminal organization applying from different parts of the country. The system also searches social media for inconsistencies with claims, such as a picture of someone at work while that person is claiming unemployment benefits. Similar systems could perform many services and roles that government benefits staff perform daily.

c. Immigration

The decision of whether to grant or refuse permission to enter a country is one of the most high-stakes decisions that governments can make, both because of the dire consequences that such decisions can have for inadmissible individuals and because of the blowback frequently associated with having an ineffective immigration process. For those fleeing violent retribution and political persecution, a decision may equate to a death sentence. Currently, many countries have legions of bureaucrats deciding such applications, generally in accordance with a government department policy on the interpretation of statute law. But decisions can be discretionary and fact specific. Governments have an opportunity to use computational methods to provide more certainty, predictability, and consistency in immigration decision-making.

Yet many are concerned about the use of such methods in this area. In Canada, where such technology has been tested since 2014, the University of Toronto Faculty of Law's International Human Rights Program and the Citizen Lab published an eighty-eight-page study about the problems that could arise. They include lack of procedural fairness, unreasonableness of decisions, and various fundamental rights violations, including those related to equality, association, religion, expression, movement, privacy, life, liberty, and personal security.[27]

Nevertheless, as we discussed in our defence of computational law in chapter 5, the question is not whether AI is perfect, but whether it is better than what we currently have. As the Canadian study shows, there is a great amount of variance in traditional legal decisions, including those dealing with similar facts: "Immigration and refugee decisions

---

27 Peter Molnar & Lex Gill, *Bots at the Gate: A Human Rights Analysis of Automated Decision-Making in Canada's Immigration and Refugee System* (International Human Rights Program, University of Toronto Faculty of Law and Citizen Lab, 2018), online: <https://ihrp.law.utoronto.ca/sites/default/files/media/IHRP-Automated-Systems-Report-Web.pdf>.

are highly discretionary: two immigration officers looking at the same application, the same set of facts, and the same evidence may routinely arrive at entirely different outcomes."[28] The study goes on to note that, "when coupled with weak oversight or limited safeguards at this initial decision-making stage, the highly deferential standard applied by courts can become problematic from a human rights perspective."[29] In his article "Measuring Inconsistency, Indeterminacy, and Error in Adjudication," Joshua B. Fischman makes a similar finding in the context of US immigration. Fischman analysed data from cases involving asylum-seekers in the New York Immigration Court, and found that "a randomly selected pair of judges would disagree about the disposition of a randomly selected case at least one-quarter of the time, and perhaps as often as one-half of the time."[30] How can we say that a system that shows such troubling flaws does not need fixing?

Adopting computational methods for immigration law decisions could be a fruitful path if sufficient safeguards and opportunities for appeal are also provided. For example, authorities can ensure transparency by making data available to the public, as well as by conducting audits to ensure that there are no malicious or negligent errors in the programming and maintenance of computational tools.

Furthermore, it is strange to criticize the AI-based method of decision-making on the basis that it is grounded in statistics. Of course, the careless use of statistics should be avoided. However, the claim that algorithms cannot provide good, reasoned answers simply because they do not "think" the way that we do is mistaken. Models can provide reasonable guidance, and, as computational methods advance, the quality of this guidance will improve. Additionally, given that AI tools would provide guidance based on statistical relationships, we would at least have an explicit reason for AI-informed judgments. As things stand today, with human judges having wide discretionary powers and "black box" minds, decisions are often rendered with few to no explicit accompanying reasons. The troubling truth is that many of these decisions stem from cognitive biases and heuristics. Surely a method of deciding similar cases similarly, in an objective, unbiased manner (with human supervision and intervention) is better than a

---

28 *Ibid* at 53–4.
29 *Ibid* at 54.
30 Joshua B Fischman, "Measuring Inconsistency, Indeterminacy, and Error in Adjudication" (2014) 16 Am L & Econ Rev 40.

completely discretionary decision made by a single human being. Thus, although we do not expect immigration law to be taken over by artificially intelligent robot-judges, we do foresee a future in which humans and machines will work together to reach just, equitable, and consistent rulings.

As computational technologies advance, we will likely see AI-based algorithms eventually *becoming* the law. Machine learning, coupled with other subfields of artificial intelligence, will grow to reflect and refine the law, and reduce errors in it. As the computational powers of legal algorithms grow and accumulate more and more data, these algorithms will provide instantaneous and accurate rulings on any given legal or regulatory matter. Once this occurs, we can no longer say that the algorithms are simply providing predictions of how courts might decide. When we reach this point in technological advancement, the algorithmic rulings will simply be the most accurate and superior reflections of the law as determined by the legislatures – that is the law itself.

VI. Applications of AI in Legislation

a. Drafting Legislation

The effects of legal uncertainty are not limited to the public, lawyers, and judges. Legislatures are also affected by the incompleteness of the law. Our discussion of computational law in chapter 3 invoked a rich law and economics literature to explain that legislators can adopt either a rule or a standard to govern behaviour, after considering the various benefits and drawbacks of each option. But whichever approach is taken, legislators need to predict how the law will be interpreted by its enforcers and the judiciary. To do this, legislators must imagine various factual scenarios and think about how, in the context of those scenarios, a suggested set of words would be interpreted. Generally, a legislative drafter has a purpose in mind when crafting a law, so the drafter must decide how that law ought to describe the circumstances in which it should apply and how to describe what should happen in those circumstances. Once those initial decisions are made, the words used to convey the purpose must increase the likelihood that law enforcement and judges will agree that the words convey that intended outcome. But, of course, every change to the wording of the draft entails possible changes to how the law would apply to other situations, necessitating further analysis and further revision. The cycle could, in theory, go on forever. Indeed, if one includes new bills amending old laws, the cycle really does appear endless. A good example is taxing statutes, which have been on the books for decades and are amended constantly as legislators disagree with judicial interpretations of laws and plug the gaps that such interpretations created. (One needn't look too far into the law reports to encounter the sentiment that, "if that's what members of the legislature actually intended, then that's what they would have said.")

The problem of interpretation is related to another problem: that of legislative intent. Legislative intent is sometimes considered the golden rule of statutory interpretation, as it involves finding out what is meant by what is said. But often, as many have pointed out, there is no such thing as legislative intent. What does it actually mean for the legislature to have a single, unified "intent"? Each legislator has different reasons for voting for any given legislation, and probably has not even turned their mind to the question of how the law should apply in some postulated case. Furthermore, individual legislators are not the legislature; the collective intent of the legislature may well be different from the individual intent of legislators. This all assumes that individual members have specific intent – yet many members of legislatures do not even read the laws they vote on. Finally, even if every member has the exact same opinion on how the law ought to be applied, judges and law enforcement are not obligated to abide by that intent unless it is explicitly conveyed in the wording of the legislation. And if the statute is ever amended by a later legislature, which is not uncommon, to whose intent should we look to understand the legislation – the original group, or the one that came after?

Computational methods can help solve this combined problem of interpretation and legislative intent. They could eventually allow us to transform the legislative process, superseding systems whereby an entire legislature votes "yes" or "no" on a text that may (or may not) become law. Instead, imagine something like the following. The legislature wants to deal with harmful obscene material by banning it, but without interfering too much with freedom of expression. Under the current system, proposed legislative language might be put forward that makes it an offence to publish something "obscene," leaving it up to the courts to decide upon further details. Or the proposed law might provide a menu of specifically identified types of obscene material to be banned.

Under a possible new system, AI-powered tools could generate scenarios involving possible obscenity. For instance, a system might come up with examples of hardcore pornography, softcore pornography, child pornography, sexual literature, sexual health magazines, anatomy text-books, pictures of naked babies having bubble baths posted by proud parents on social media, artistic erotic photographs, iconic photographs like that of the "Napalm Girl," and thousands – or millions, or billions – of other examples that might be relevant and provide information. Next, the computational tools could have the legislators vote on a series of candidate photographs to prohibit as obscene, or not. The more examples, the better. These votes, especially if done in an adaptive way to maximize their informational content, could provide arbitrarily fine-grained ground truth data from which to assemble a machine learning model. From this, the system could generate a draft text for the law, which would have all the specificity of a rule with all the accuracy of a standard. The legislators could then vote on that text and amend it as needed for it to become the law. Alternatively, the legislators could vote on the data and let other experts (perhaps also aided by computational tools) determine the best way to navigate future examples – the results of the votes themselves, as data, could become the law, not unlike how the facts of cases and the results of those cases become legal authority in common law systems.

It is important to understand just what the preceding example represents. Essentially, the suggested process would turn legislators into judges, who are always dealing with a case *ex post*. The difference is that the legislators are anticipating, with the help of a newly designed process of eliciting information, each one of those *ex post* cases and deciding in advance how the law should be applied to them. And just as computational tools can draw out a pattern in decided cases to predict how a judge will decide a new case, they can draw out the legislative intent from the individual legislators' "deciding cases" (i.e., their vote on the various scenarios).

This would revolutionize the legislative process. Legislative intent, rather than being a fiction and postulated – often many years after the fact – by lawyers and judges, would become reality and the guiding principle in the law. This could be a boon to democracy, given that legislators are elected to make laws, while judges are often not elected, and, when they are, are not elected to make laws. The expressed text of the laws would match the intent of the majority of legislators regarding how the law should apply in each case.

There are some legitimate objections to this process, of course. One might say that it is important that legislators draft legislation themselves, rather than relying on machine assistance. Having AI-drafted legislation or machine learning–curated examples, even if human legislators are still doing the voting, may be alarming. Another objection is that such an approach would leave judges with less work. If cases are all "decided" beforehand, then judges are too constrained; they would be simply applying the law to the facts of each case. There would be less room for creativity to deal with exceptional cases. Another criticism is that AI might not be able to predict every possible scenario, and so there would still be gaps to be filled using the traditional techniques, except that these techniques would be applied to machine-made law. Finally, there is the problem of inconsistent legislative intentions discussed previously, and possibly magnified. If every legislator votes on every scenario, odd outcomes could result. We know that politics involves horse-trading. If Senator A votes for outcome X in relation to scenario 1, but then for a seemingly inconsistent outcome, Y, in related scenario 2, the computational tool processing these votes could craft an absurd law in response. To use the above example of obscenity, what if, as a result of political negotiations and inconsistent assessments of examples, a majority was in favour of allowing hardcore pornography but banning softcore pornography? The sketch of the system proposed assumes good faith and well-formed preferences on the part of the legislators. Even stranger outcomes are possible. According to the Condorcet paradox, well known since the 1700s, there can be a majority for A over B, B over C, and then C over A, because the majorities are made up of different groups in each case.

These criticisms can be met. Proposed legislation today in many, perhaps most, jurisdictions is not, in fact, usually drafted by legislators in the stylized sense; our politicians are not picking up the proverbial pen and leading the preparation of our laws for submission. Proposed legislation tends to be drafted by policymakers, interest groups, legislative counsel, or others within government. Modern law is frequently too complex for non-expert legislators to be expected to develop coherent statutory language on their own. Computational methods allow the most unbiased expert with the widest view of the law to do the drafting, without the possibility of unnecessary or even harmful components being shuffled in through the backdoor by special interests. Regarding judicial activity, judges of all stripes tend to support the core principle that policy is made by the legislature. If unconstitutional laws are struck down by judges, the courts expect that legislatures will be the ones to try again to find a legislative solution that would survive constitutional scrutiny. It is possible to imagine AI-based tools that would deftly navigate judicial review jurisprudence to avoid drafting legislation that would run afoul of constitutional law guarantees.

In the matter of prediction incompleteness, consider, first, that this kind of AI-informed approach to legislation would certainly be *less* incomplete than what we currently accept. Second, there is no reason to think that the law drafted by the AI-powered tools is incapable of extrapolation of the pattern shown in the voted-on scenarios to be applied to a new one in a sensible way.

The problem of inconsistent legislative intent is also less damning than it appears. For one thing, it already arises in case law, and yet lawyers and legal-prediction tools have been able to make some sense of the law. Courts routinely make decisions on legal issues within cases, and on case outcomes more generally. Notice that these are two different decision-making processes. To see how inconsistency plays out in the courts, consider Lewis Kornhauser:

> First, since most appellate courts are collegial, the resolution of every dispute depends on the views of more than one judge. Second, each judge on a collegial court decides cases within a doctrinal structure. These two features of adjudicatory practice give rise to a doctrinal paradox. Case-by-case and issue-by-issue adjudication may, in some circumstances, produce two different resolutions of a case. These decision procedures may also influence differently both the evolution of rights and duties that the law ascribes and the development of doctrine.[31]

Even in statutory law, the inconsistency problem is usually just punted off to the judiciary by intentionally ambiguous statutes. The Condorcet paradox presents a genuine issue, but it is rather unlikely to arise. Legislatures vote "yea" or "nay" on legislation – they do not rank it. Thus, the problem could arise only in relation to a legislated preference list. A possible example might be something like bankruptcy priority legislation, creating something like: worker claims > tax claims, tax claims > secured creditors, and secured creditors > worker claims. But even here, computational methods have an advantage: they can logically spot these issues and require the legislature to resolve them. Currently, if such issues arise (and they certainly have, such as in secured transactions), they are left to the judiciary to resolve.

b. Normative Contributions and Second-Order Modelling

Governments' use of AI will not necessarily be limited to discovering what the law is. AI can also be used to suggest – or determine – what

---

31 Lewis A Kornhauser, "Modeling Collegial Courts II Legal Doctrine" (1992) 8 JL Econ & Org 3 at 467.

the law *should* be, based on inferred collective values. This is going one step beyond what we just considered about how the legislative process could be changed by AI. There, we only have AI finding a pattern in expressed preferences of legislators with reference to a particular question. What if AI could figure out our values and construct laws based on the commonalities and overlaps that arise in them? Consider Sam – a player of moderate strength – playing a game of chess. An algorithm trained on Sam's playing could predict Sam's next move based on his observed capabilities, track record, and expressed behaviours. This would be a descriptive suggestion. However, AI could also suggest what Sam's move *should* be – i.e., the most optimal move he could make to maximize the strength of his position with a view to winning the game. This move may or may not be the same move that Sam would have taken in any given position; in this case, the AI would be making a prescriptive suggestion. This scenario recalls the distinction discussed earlier between AI aspiring to humanlike performance and to rationally optimal performance. In the legal singularity, we expect that our collective aspirations for the legal system would be to rationally optimal performance, based on a deeply wise assessment of what matters – and what ought to matter – to us.

The hope, then, is that AI can forge something akin to the Rawlsian reflective equilibrium in law.[32] The idea goes something like this. All our collective beliefs should form a coherent whole. Thus, our specific judgments should follow from our general beliefs: for example, it's wrong for Jimmy not to have free speech, because free speech is a human right, and people have human rights. Rawls has a method for achieving a stronger equilibrium. We start with our moral judgments and then go through many scenarios and search for inconsistencies between those judgments and how we would deal with various scenarios. In doing this, we must decide between one or the other, which allows us to iron out the hidden conflicts in our beliefs. After we keep doing this for quite a while, we get something that is consistent, or at least significantly more consistent than before.

How does this method apply to law? One way might be to do something like the following. Have legislators (or some other group of experts, or the populace) decide several concrete moral issues. Better yet, start with the constraints of current law. With enough data points, an AI-based software could then identify conflicting or unresolved issues.

---

32 See, e.g., Margaret Holmgren, "The Wide and Narrow of Reflective Equilibrium" (1989) 19:1 Can J of Philosophy 43.

A participant could then work through the new scenarios and revise the original positions they had taken. After this is done, the software could work out a pattern in the way that people vote to resolve the issues. Note that this would not necessarily require coincidence of reasons for decision; it would only require commonality in the subject of the decisions. For instance, if a social democrat, a liberal, a conservative, and a libertarian all vote in favour of recognizing certain property rights, it would not matter that their reasons for doing so vary among the utilitarian, deontological, traditional, or religious. The approach would also allow the system to identify the most radical opinions: a communist who is entirely against any recognition of private property, for example, might have their opinion discarded as an outlier perspective that cannot be accommodated based on other widely shared values and commitments. However, even those with outlier views may have a reason to prefer this sort of approach to current systems, since their views will be given equal consideration and will be weighed on an issue-by-issue basis. Thus, a communist's position on workers' rights could make a difference, even if their position on private property does not.

Alternatively, this could be construed as a law reform project. Have legislators come together, as if for legislating. Have some of them come to a few original considered positions in the law at whatever level of specificity they feel comfortable with, and go through the process of reflective equilibrium between these positions and laws that could conflict with them. AI-based tools would be especially good at finding possible conflicts in unlikely places and establishing the right questions to ask to resolve those conflicts. Have the legislators decide between the two positions suggested in each conflict. Continue the process until something coherent emerges.

The process need not transpire in the ways that we have sketched out above, nor do the processes have to end there. The motivation behind advancing these thought experiments is to provide some cognizable means of eliciting enough information through familiar lawmaking mechanisms to adjust laws to resolve inconsistencies, fill gaps, and secure better coverage of the law. The ambition is to conceive of ways to overcome law's current and persistent incompleteness problem. Assuming that means of doing this can be accomplished, there is, again, no reason to consider the complete law to be "done." Instead, the law would have simply achieved complete and consistent coverage. From there, the legal singularity project would be open to – and indeed, require – ongoing change, adjustment, and evolution to respond to changes in society, new learnings, and new developments.

Chapter Nine

Towards Ethical and Equitable Legal Prediction

I. Introduction

On 23 May 2016, the Pulitzer Prize–winning news outlet ProPublica published a tour de force investigation called "Machine Bias" about the use of algorithmic risk assessments in criminal sentencing.[1] The article analysed the "risk scores" assigned to some 7,000 arrestees in Broward County, Florida, in 2013 and 2014.[2] These risk scores – generated by a program called Correctional Offender Management Profiling for Alternative Sanctions (COMPAS) – were meant to forecast the likelihood that an individual would reoffend.[3] Predictably, the data were rife with suggestions of racial bias.[4] One of the article's enduring examples involved two arrestees in Florida – an eighteen-year-old black woman and a forty-one-year-old white man – who were accused of the theft of items valued at a total of roughly eighty dollars.[5] Broward County's risk-assessment system rated the young black woman as having a high risk of reoffending (score: 8) and the middle-aged white man as low-risk (score: 3), despite the white arrestee's considerably more extensive criminal history, which included a five-year prison sentence for armed robbery.[6] The prediction

---

1 Julia Angwin et al, "Machine Bias," *ProPublica* (23 May 2016), online: <https://perma.cc/MJ9U-Z5FH>.
2 *Ibid.*
3 See generally T Brennan & W Dieterich, "Correctional Offender Management Profiles for Alternative Sanctions (COMPAS)," JP Singh et al, Handbook of Recidivism Risk/Needs Assessment Tools (Wiley Online Library, 2018), online: <https://doi.org/10.1002/9781119184256.ch3>.
4 Angwin, *supra* note 1.
5 *Ibid.*
6 *Ibid.*

was widely viewed as unfair,[7] and also proved to be inconsistent with what happened subsequently: the eighteen-year-old black woman successfully completed her probation and had not since reoffended, whereas the forty-one-year-old white man had been, by 2019, charged with thirty additional felonies and is currently serving an eight-year prison sentence for theft-related crimes.[8]

Predictably, ProPublica's investigation ignited much debate. Since its publication in 2016, the article has been cited in hundreds of academic works.[9] For their part, Northpointe – the company that developed COMPAS, now called Equivant[10] – defended themselves vociferously against charges of algorithmic bias on methodological grounds, leading ProPublica to issue its own response that reiterated the article's initial conclusions.[11] The debate and its resulting scholarship have been fruitful; where earlier discussions about the propriety of predictive algorithms used obscure examples or were somewhat abstract, the ProPublica investigation and the sheer amount of information shared about COMPAS methodology equipped researchers with a much-needed focal point. In other words, the debate was finally happening on a common terrain. And though the investigation itself was focused on the problems associated with predicting recidivism, it represents just one popular example in a fast-growing universe of policy and academic literature that is highly critical of the disparate racial, gender, and class outcomes of machine learning applications.[12]

---

7   See, e.g., T Mbadiwe, "Algorithmic Injustice," (2018) 54 New Atlantis 3. https://www.jstor.org/stable/90021005; Megan Garcia "Racist in the Machine: The Disturbing Implications of Algorithmic Bias" (2016) 33(4) World Policy Journal 111, online: <https://www.jstor.org/stable/26781452>; Anupam Chander "The Racist Algorithm?," Book Review of *The Black Box Society: The Secret Algorithms That Control Money and Information* by Frank Pasquale" (2017) 115:6 Mich L Rev 1023, online: <https://www.jstor.org/stable/44984908>; A Fabris et al, "Algorithmic Fairness Datasets: The Story so Far" (2022) 36 Data Min Knowl Disc 2074, online: <https://doi.org/10.1007/s10618-022-00854-z>.

8   Clinton Castro, "What's Wrong with Machine Bias" (2019–20) 6:15 *Ergo*, online: <https://doi.org/10.3998/ergo.12405314.0006.015>.

9   Authors' search of Google Scholar (December 2022).

10 Sophie Bushwick, "Will Past Criminals Reoffend? Human Are Terrible At Guessing, and Computers Aren't Much Better," *Scientific American* (14 February 2020), online: <https://www.scientificamerican.com/article/will-past-criminals-reoffend-humans-are-terrible-at-guessing-and-computers-arent-much-better/>.

11 Jeff Larson and Julie Angwin, "Technical Response to Northpointe," *ProPublica* (29 July 2016), online: <https://www.propublica.org/article/technical-response-to-northpointe>.

12 See, e.g., Deborah Hellman, "Measuring Algorithmic Fairness" (2020) 106 Va L Rev 811.

Public sentiment has taken a similar turn. In 2019, the Los Angeles Police Department discontinued the use of an algorithmic system meant to predict gun violence "hot spots,"[13] largely in response to sustained criticism from civil rights organizations, privacy groups, and the department's own civilian oversight panel, but also after an internal report found that the efforts lacked sufficient oversight.[14] A similar project was aborted in Chicago,[15] and the city of Santa Cruz in California altogether *banned* any "predictive policing" tools.[16] Public resistance is perhaps most pronounced in the context of technologies like facial recognition software, which have been likened in popular media to dystopian control mechanisms.[17] Pressure has mounted to the point that Brad Smith, the president of Microsoft, called for governments to begin regulating the very sort of facial recognition software that Microsoft itself produces.[18]

The high-stakes nature of criminal justice might present the problems of algorithmic decision-making (ADM) most acutely, but it is hardly the only area to generate sustained public outrage. Algorithms are being considered or used for such vital government decisions as tax collection[19] and welfare benefits administration all over the world,

13 David Uberti, "After Backlash, Predictive Policing Adapts to a Changed World," *Wall Street Journal* (8 July 2021), online: <https://www.wsj.com/articles/after-backlash-predictive-policing-adapts-to-a-changed-world-11625752931>.

14 Mark Puente, "LAPD Data Programs Need Better Oversight to Protect Public," *Los Angeles Times* (12 March 2019), online: <https://www.latimes.com/local/lanow/la-me-ln-lapd-data-20190312-story.html>.

15 Kathleen Foody, "Chicago Police End Effort to Predict Gun Offenders, Victims" *Associated Press* (23 January 2020), online: <https://apnews.com/article/41f75b783d796b80815609e737211cc6>.

16 Kristi Sturgill, "Santa Cruz Becomes the First U.S. City to Ban Predictive Policing," *Los Angeles Times* (26 June 2020), online: <https://www.latimes.com/california/story/2020-06-26/santa-cruz-becomes-first-u-s-city-to-ban-predictive-policing>.

17 See, e.g., James Gant, "UK Faces 'Dystopian' Future with Facial-Recognition AI Cameras Turning Public Spaces Into 'Open Air Prisons', Warn Privacy Campaigners Over New CCTV Guidance Given to Police and Councils," *Daily Mail* (17 August 2021), online: <https://www.dailymail.co.uk/news/article-9900501/UK-faces-dystopian-future-facial-recognition-AI-cameras-turning-public-spaces-prisons.html>; see also Kashmir Hill, "The Secretive Company That Might End Privacy as We Know It," *New York Times* (18 January 2020), online: <https://www.nytimes.com/2020/01/18/technology/clearview-privacy-facial-recognition.html>.

18 Brad Smith, "Facial Recognition Technology: The Need for Public Regulation and Corporate Responsibility," *Microsoft on the Issues* (Blog) (13 July 2018), online: <https://blogs.microsoft.com/on-the-issues/2018/07/13/facial-recognition-technology-the-need-for-public-regulation-and-corporate-responsibility/>.

19 T Rinta-Kahila et al, "Algorithmic Decision-Making and System Destructiveness: A Case of Automatic Debt Recovery" (2012) 31:3 European Journal of Information Systems 313.

just to name a few.[20] Some of these decisions have culminated in high-profile lawsuits: in one particularly distressing example, the state of Arkansas replaced its human-led process for determining whether disabled individuals should have access to a home caregiver with an algorithmic system developed by the non-profit consortium InterRAI. The result was that the funds allocated for home caretakers "dropped precipitously for many people, by as much as 42 percent."[21] In the Netherlands, an algorithmic program with a familiar sounding name – SyRI, or system risk indication – was used to identify public benefits fraud until human rights activists demonstrated that the program led to unduly aggressive monitoring of low-income neighbourhoods.[22] These examples not only demonstrate that algorithmic decision-making can be deployed in ways that provably violate substantive rights, they also lend credence to charges from critics that algorithmic decision-making tools are veiled efforts at instituting austerity measures.[23]

At the same time as these ADM tools were entering public debate, scholars were explaining the critical biases. Safiya Umoja Noble's excellent and influential book *Algorithms of Oppression*, for instance, focuses on how racism is amplified on search engines.[24] Ruha Benjamin's equally stellar *Race after Technology* demonstrates the way algorithms reproduce disparate racial outcomes in everything from mapping applications and beauty contests to gang databases.[25] Taken together, these and other texts call advocates of algorithmic decision-making on the carpet for being irresponsible in failing to consider and actively combat the ways in which machine learning can encode and amplify social ills as devastating as racism, sexism, and economic inequality.

---

20 Dario Sansone & Anna Zhu, "Using Machine Learning to Create an Early Warning System for Welfare Recipients," IZA Institute of Labor Economics Discussion Paper Series, IZA DP No. 14377, online: <https://docs.iza.org/dp14377.pdf>; see also M van Bekkum & FZ Borgesius, "Digital Welfare Fraud Detection and the Dutch SyRI Judgment" (2021) 23:4 European Journal of Social Security 323, online: <https://doi.org/10.1177/13882627211031257>.

21 Colin Lecher, "What Happens When an Algorithm Cuts Your Health Care?" *The Verge* (21 March 2018), online: <https://www.theverge.com/2018/3/21/17144260/healthcare-medicaid-algorithm-arkansas-cerebral-palsy>.

22 Van Bekkum & Borgesius, *supra* note 20.

23 Alexander Babuta & Marion Oswald, "Machine Learning Predictive Algorithms and the Policing of Future Crimes," in J McDaniel & K Pearse, eds, *Predictive Policing and Artificial Intelligence* (London: Routledge, 2021) 214.

24 Safiya Umoja Noble, *Algorithms of Oppression* (New York: NYU Press, 2018).

25 Ruha Benjamin, *Race after Technology: Abolitionist Tools for the New Jim Code* (Cambridge, UK: Polity, 2019).

We agree. Artificial intelligence – for all its promise – can be deployed in ways that reproduce social, political, and economic disparities. Worse yet, the use of such tools is so widespread that their growth is far outpacing public understanding of their mechanisms and consequences. As Sandra G. Mayson explains, "algorithmic prediction has the potential to perpetuate or amplify social inequality, all while maintaining the veneer of high-tech objectivity."[26] But there is no sign that the development and use of these applications will decelerate. Given their decreasing costs, algorithmic decision-making tools will likely increase both in availability and sophistication.[27] On one end of the debate, advocates of ADM make the mistake of ignoring the empirical truth of race, gender, and class biases. At the other end, critics of ADM make the mistake of assuming that the technology's trajectory can be slowed. As the outcomes of certain litigation – such as the case against Arkansas's home-care decision-making – suggest, ADM projects are more likely to be revisited and reformed than abandoned, even after sustained outrage.[28] We take stock of these and other issues associated with ADM and consider how the damage might be averted. The main point is that ADM is fraught with problems that the computer science, law, and public policy communities ought to be mitigating. However, to take the blanket position that the use of ADM tools is *per se* worse than the status quo risks not only missing out on some of the promise of these tools, but also ensures that ADM design will continue without the healthy scepticism that critics have to offer. Responsibly developed algorithmic decision-making tools have the potential to add significant value and provide traction for desperately needed improvement where our cognitive biases make it difficult for us to achieve the fairness and equity we aspire to.

In this chapter, we offer a new framework for evaluating social problems attributed to AI and specifically algorithmic decision-making. We suggest two categories of issues that demand distinct legal, regulatory and policy responses: (1) reflection and amplification problems, and

---

26 Sandra G Mayson, "Bias In, Bias Out" (2019) 128 Yale L J 2218 at 2221.

27 Since 2018, the cost to train an image classification system has decreased by 63.6 per cent, while training times have improved by 94.4 per cent. See Daniel Zhang, Nestor Maslej, et al, "The AI Index 2022 Annual Report," AI Index Steering Committee, Stanford Institute for Human-Centered AI, Stanford University, March 2022, online: <https://aiindex.stanford.edu/wp-content/uploads/2022/03/2022-AI-Index -Report_Master.pdf> at 3.

28 Lecher, *supra* note 21.

(2) techno-epistemic problems. Reflection and amplification problems are those involving AI-informed prediction projecting current or historical social issues into the future. Put differently, reflection and amplification problems exist where technology is not necessarily responsible for an issue – like racial bias – in the first place, but plays a vital role in reifying or accelerating it. A core component of this is the decontextualization process, wherein the use of historical and contemporaneous data as inputs for prediction reduces said data to two-dimensional representations of complex social problems. At their worst, reflection and amplification problems can lead to the reproduction of harmful, oppressive hierarchies. Techno-epistemic problems, by contrast, are those that are essentially *unique* to AI-enabled prediction or are new problems introduced to the legal landscape specifically by the technology. These tended not to exist before the proliferation of AI in legal settings. For instance, algorithmic prediction is resistant to traditional modes of legal reasoning.

The benefit of the new framework is twofold. First, a better categorization of the problems associated with algorithmic decision-making makes effective policy prescriptions more likely. Critics of algorithmic decision-making that are focused on ADM's capacity to reproduce discrimination, for instance, may be thoroughly disappointed that more algorithmic *transparency* – an intervention that is frequently called for – will likely do little to mitigate ultimate social harm. As Anupam Chander observes in his review of Frank Pasquale's formidable book *The Black Box Society*, "transparent, facially-neutral algorithms can still produce discriminatory results."[29] Recognizing the problem as one of reflection and amplification, instead, locates the source of the social harm at its correct site. A second benefit of the framework is that it understands technology in its proper context. As this book makes clear, we recognize that technology has a certain kind of totalizing power; however, there is a pronounced risk that, if we interpret problems as chiefly technological, we prematurely absolve ourselves of responsibility for problems like racism and gender discrimination that have predated our new technologies and will likely survive them without the concerted – and often analogue – effort required to forge a more just and equitable society.

After offering a framework for understanding algorithmic decision-making's *problems*, we evaluate some of the proposed solutions. We conclude by suggesting some interventions.

---

29 Chander, *supra* note 7 at 1024.

II. The Problem Framework

Criticism of algorithmic prediction has come from all corners of law and technology's epistemic community. As different times, the conversation has been led by scholars, non-academic policy observers, civil society groups focused on privacy and civil rights, and even aggrieved consumers. When considered in isolation, many of these critiques are levied effectively against the further proliferation of AI: for instance, concerns from scholars about the opacity of AI algorithms creating space for bad actors to engage in nefarious discrimination is a serious critique, but deserves a focused discussion that is separate and apart from, for instance, other well-founded concerns about AI leading to intolerable labour market disruption. Public debate has reached the stage where trepidation about AI is in the mainstream, and thus the cacophony of voices demands more coherence than is thus far observable.

To that end, we attempt to disentangle the morass of concerns by suggesting that algorithmic prediction presents two sorts of problems: (1) reflection and amplification problems, and (2) techno-epistemic problems. We elaborate on each of these below.

a. Reflection and Amplification Problems

In chapter 3's discussion of the computational era of legal information, we explained that AI-enabled prediction involves processing and inputting historical data to generate "predictions on what is likely to happen in the future."[30] Put differently, data are used to inform the construction of mathematical models that are then applied to current or real-time data to make predictions about what will likely occur next.

As an illustration, consider figure 9.1, which is a stylized example of a machine learning process. The historical data that inform future predictions are represented at the top of the diagram in the node labelled "training data." These data are real, of course; an event that happened in the past is represented as digital information, to be ultimately submitted as inputs for prediction.

Yet, in the process of representing real-world events, some context is invariably lost. This process of decontextualization happens in at least two ways. First, the factual circumstances giving rise to the data are obscured. As an example, imagine an algorithmic decision-making system that determines who qualifies for federal mortgage assistance

---

30 Dipti Parmar, "What Is Predictive Algorithmic Forecasting and How Is It Used?" *The Forecast* (5 April 2022), online: <https://www.nutanix.com/theforecastbynutanix /business/what-is-predictive-algorithmic-forecasting-and-why-should-you-care>.

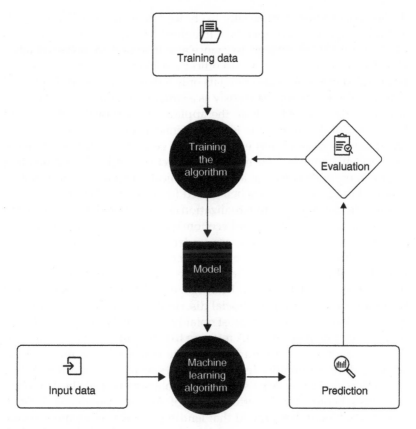

Figure 9.1. Stylized Example of a Machine Learning Process

from the US Federal Housing Administration (FHA). Such an algorithm would likely be informed by years of loan applications, perhaps making reasonably accurate predictions only after absorbing tens of thousands of mortgage applications as training data. To the new ADM system, those data are valuable in large numbers. To individual loan-seekers, however, the application represents their efforts to purchase a home and contains personal stories that go beyond the narrow question of whether the application was successful. These stories – call them "narrative information" – are not legible, structured data for machine learning purposes. In fact, training data are not limited merely to categorizable data, but incorporate data that the drafters of the loan-application forms considered to be important. If data such as race, gender, or bankruptcy history were not solicited by the loan-application forms in the past, this information is unlikely to be represented in training data for future ADM systems. This form of decontextualization is especially likely for historical data that was collected through analogue methods. Imagine, for instance, that the process for securing FHA mortgage assistance also involved an in-person interview for applicants. Here, a loan officer's subjective impressions would be included in the ultimate loan data only if these impressions happened to be recorded contemporaneously as a structured input. More likely, the surviving data would include the application, approval decision, and little else. Put differently, the intangible information that generations of social science research has established as germane to decision-making in interview contexts – for example, subjective considerations like first impressions, agreeableness, and communication styles – would not be captured in the training data being used for future predictions.

A second form of decontextualization occurs when data are extracted from their social, political, and economic context. In this frame, events that are represented in data are understood without any reference to other information. As an example, consider once more the FHA's hypothetical ADM system. An expansive social science literature has demonstrated that US federal mortgage assistance has been marred by a pattern and practice of racial discrimination (just as have private mortgage lending markets), most notably through a practice of "redlining," which involved the FHA refusing to insure mortgages in and near African-American neighbourhoods.[31] The policy of redlining and the associated discriminatory lending practices were so rampant that they are understood by a large subset of scholars as one of the key driving forces behind the "ghettoization" of African Americans. Indeed, recent scholarship has argued that lending bias was even more severe than what is commonly understood. As historian Louis Lee Woods II explains, FHA-led policies and practices helped create a situation where African Americans were being limited to "the worst dwellings in the nation" despite their average income per annum roughly tripling during the same period.[32] Any algorithm that does not take this reality into account – or ignores the parallel histories of practices such as redlining and banking discrimination – risks projecting those inequalities into the future. Mitigating this form of decontextualization demands that historical data be considered against the environment that produces them.

---

31 For an extended discussion of the practice of redlining, see Richard Rothstein, *The Color of Law: A Forgotten History of How Our Government Segregated America* (New York: Norton, 2017).
32 Louis Lee Woods, "The Federal Home Loan Bank Board, Redlining, and the National Proliferation of Racial Lending Discrimination, 1921–1950" (2012) 38:6 J of Urban History 1036 at 1039, online: <https://doi.org/10.1177/0096144211435126>.

On one level, it is widely accepted that data abstracted from their context may result in poor decision-making. As a simple, stylized example, consider that an algorithm designed to predict and set wages based only on simple inputs like experience and career seniority will likely reproduce the gender pay gap, because it fails to account for the well-established historical factors that lead to broad wage inequity (e.g., women experience a motherhood wage penalty where the compensation gap between males and females tends to expand as women work reduced hours, take on part-time work, or take leaves of absence following the birth of a child).[33] An ADM system of this sort has little chance of meaningful acceptance, given the broad social consensus that pay should not vary based on gender. In this sense, public opinion serves its necessary regulative function. Yet similarly simple models could proliferate and reproduce social bias in contexts where there is less agreement about what the normatively desirable outcomes are. "Preemptive policing" algorithms purport to equip governments with predictions to inform law enforcement, including IBM's i2 Enterprise Insight Analysis, which company officials said could assist with identifying ISIS fighters among asylum-seekers in Europe.[34] The idea suggests significant *reflection* risk: to the extent the algorithms depend on data about the demographic profile and travel history of ISIS members, they have significant potential to cast aspersion on already vulnerable and frequently maligned asylum seekers. Yet unlike the gender wage gap, which persists *despite* an emerging social consensus about its unfairness, there are divergent views in the mainstream about how refugees ought to be treated, and perhaps even more disagreement about counterintelligence methods and national security enforcement. The relative absence of a social consensus here creates broad latitude for irresponsible use without a bulwark against abuse.

Thus far, our discussion of decontextualization of algorithmic data has suggested that social harms can be reflected in predictive results. Just as importantly, social harms can be *amplified*. Here, we conceive

---

33 See Claudia Goldin, "A Grand Gender Convergence: Its Last Chapter" (2014) 104:4 Am Econ Rev 1091, online: <https://doi.org/10.1257/aer.104.4.1091>.

34 On "pre-emptive policing," see Andrew Guthrie Ferguson, *The Rise of Big Data Policing* (New York: NYU Press, 2017). See also, Patrick Tucker, "Refugee or Terrorist? IBM Thinks Its Software Has the Answer," *Defense One* (27 January 2016), online: <https://www.defenseone.com/technology/2016/01/refugee-or-terrorist -ibm-thinks-its-software-has-answer/125484/>; and Rachel Levinson-Waldman, "IBM's Terrorist-Hunting Software Raises Troubling Questions," *Just Security* (3 February 2016), online: <https://www.justsecurity.org/29131/ibms-terrorist -hunting-software-raises-troubling-questions/>.

of amplification in two ways: expansion and entrenchment. "Expansion" evokes the colloquial understanding of amplification as something akin to *signal boosting* – that is, extending the reach of harmful bias. "Entrenchment" is a related concept but refers to how algorithmic prediction can fortify harmful bias by embedding it in an institutional context and cloaking it in technology's "neutral" imprimatur. For a simple explanation, return once more to the example of the FHA's hypothetical ADM system determining who gets mortgage assistance. A model based on problematic training data that is decontextualized may, absent any interventions, disproportionately exclude Black applicants. The process is not complete, however. In addition to reflecting the harm back, the algorithm risks not only amplifying the harm by manufacturing yet more harmful data (which is fed back in to prediction processes), but also, and perhaps more importantly, contributing to real-world disparate home ownership and access-to-credit experiences. Further, misapprehensions about technology's purported neutrality help insulate the bias against public critique. Perhaps as importantly, the bases for critique are more remote than ordinary, analogue decision-making. Simply put, identifying and demonstrating algorithmic bias requires a level of computational and scientific know-how that – although simple to some – is in its technical details somewhat beyond mainstream reach. This, coupled with the fact of algorithmic prediction outpacing legislative and regulatory responses, suggests that the harmful outcomes of biased algorithmic predictions can take up long-term residence in our society and its institutions. The risk of amplification is especially acute in contexts where the discourse around bias in general has focused inexorably on personal or unconscious bias.

It also bears emphasis that this form of bias may persist even where algorithm designers have neutral (or even laudable) objectives. Recall the COMPAS controversy discussed at the beginning of this chapter. As the authors of the ProPublica article explain:

> We ... turned up significant racial disparities ... In forecasting who would re-offend, the algorithm made mistakes with black and white defendants at roughly the same rate but in very different ways. The formula was particularly likely to falsely flag black defendants as future criminals, wrongly labeling them this way at almost twice the rate as white defendants. White defendants were mislabeled as low risk more often than black defendants.[35]

---

35 Angwin et al, *supra* note 1.

These claims were highly contested by Northpointe and some recent academic observers.[36] The COMPAS researchers claimed that ProPublica's investigators were judging the quality of the predictions by an incorrect metric, and they argued that black and white defendants with the same recidivism risk scores "were equally likely to recidivate."[37] ProPublica did not disagree with that point, but took a different measure of equality, arguing that, among the population of arrestees who did not commit future crimes, black arrestees were assigned higher risk scores. Deborah Hellman describes the divergent approaches most clearly: where Northpointe's "measure begins with the score and asks about its ability to predict reality," ProPublica's "begins with reality and asks about its likelihood of being captured by the score."[38]

b. Techno-Epistemic Problems

While reflection and amplification problems refer to algorithmic technologies' capacity to project social harm forward and embed it in our institutions, the second category of problems with algorithmic decision-making – techno-epistemic problems – refers to harm that is a distinct or unique result of algorithmic prediction. In other words, where reflection and amplification problems originate in our broader society and are projected forward by technology, techno-epistemic problems are peculiar to the medium. For instance, the data complexity inherent in algorithms is a new problem for the legal profession, in that the traditional building blocks of legal argument are familiar, text-based materials and not mathematical representations of information. The occasional disjuncture between the legal process and algorithmic construction and reasoning is another; for instance, how should we absorb machine output into our traditional notions of evidence, particularly our standards of admissibility in adjudication settings? Of course, as we discuss here and elsewhere in this book, one of the overarching techno-epistemic problems is the neutral valence that technology often lends to fraught issues, creating the impression of certainty or confidence when the underlying reality is more complicated.

Techno-epistemic problems have similar capacity for social harm as do reflection and amplification problems, but are considerably more amenable to technological interventions because their origins are less

---

36 Jeff Larson & Julia Angwin, "Technical Response to Northpointe," *ProPublica* (29 July 2016), online: <https://www.propublica.org/article/technical-response-to-northpointe>
37 Aziz Z Huq, "Racial Equity in Algorithmic Justice" (2019) 68 Duke LJ 1043.
38 Deborah Hellman, "Measuring Algorithmic Fairness" (2020) 106 Va L Rev 811 at 816.

diffuse. The distinction is crucial; in fact, the costs of misapprehending the nature of the problem are high. A reflection and amplification problem that is treated as a purely technological issue not only risks ineffective intervention, but imports the additional risk of obscuring the empirical truth of the underlying social harm. Recall our earlier example of an algorithm designed to predict and set wages. Assuming that algorithm was designed using historical data alone, it would risk projecting the gender wage gap forward (a reflection and amplification problem). Because the gender wage gap exists, a model trained on historical data should actually produce results that we may deem socially unacceptable. Any manipulation on a technological or data level, then, would be unrepresentative of its context. The larger concern here is that society becomes complacent about the fact of a gender wage gap because these newly proliferating tools obscure its presence in our institutions and relationships.

As an illustrative example of this, consider one of the more compelling proposed interventions of "algorithmic affirmative action." The concept was introduced by Anupam Chander in the article "The Racist Algorithm?" to describe how algorithm designers can develop tools in "race- and gender-conscious ways to account for existing discrimination lurking in the data."[39]

In practice, algorithmic affirmative action refers to interventions to even out underlying data sets, such that algorithms "produce statistical parity, equal false-positive rates, or equal false-negative rates."[40] Sandra Mayson further clarifies algorithmic affirmative action's raison d'être:

> In the context of criminal justice risk assessment, the gravest concern is that racial disparity in overall arrest rates reflects disparate law enforcement, rather than disparate rates of offending. If this is true, and what we assess is the likelihood of arrest, then risk scores will overstate the risk posed by black men relative to the risk of actual crime commission. The goal of algorithmic affirmative action is to adjust the data to cancel out this racial distortion in arrest rates.[41]

There are two main problems with this approach. First, the practice of manipulating underlying data introduces significant opportunity for error. Imagine, for instance, an algorithm used by FHA-approved lenders to issue federally backed mortgages. As we described in the

---

39 Chander, *supra* note 7 at 1027.
40 Mayson, *supra*, note 26 at 2267.
41 *Ibid* at 2268.

preceding section, FHA data used to train such an algorithm would likely be rife with evidence of racial discrimination because of the agency's history of inequitable lending. The historical data might demonstrate, for instance, that African-American mortgage applicants were denied at a rate far exceeding that of white applicants. Out of concern that a future algorithm would project these racial disparities into subsequent decision-making, an algorithmic affirmative action intervention would supplement and artificially counterbalance the information such that the disparities did not exist in the training data. The challenge, of course, is that the full extent of the racial disparities is unknowable; we may suspect that discrimination existed in the loan applications that were denied, but there is little hard evidence to back this up. This is because the data are already decontextualized and are, at best, an imperfect representation of the original encounter. Much like the true crime rate is unknown to us because we can measure it only through arrests, the true extent of racial discrimination in mortgage lending is invisible to us because real-time decision-making is unobservable. As Mayson explains, unless the "scale of the distortion is known,"[42] it makes little sense to try to augment existing data. How *much* to correct and precisely *what* to correct are virtually impossible to determine without having devised an accurate model of the true state of the world.

A second problem with the algorithmic affirmative action approach is that it undermines one value of predictive tools: empirical evaluation of existing practices. To manipulate training data might bring us – directionally and imperfectly – closer to desirable outcomes for decision-making purposes; however, it may also conceal some of the truths, thereby "distorting the predictive mirror" to the point that "it reflects neither the data nor any demonstrable reality."[43] Indeed, one wonders what the purpose of using predictive algorithms is in situations where users hope to engineer a specific result. If a specific result is the goal, then ADM can be bypassed altogether in favour of, say, explicitly ameliorative or reparative programs aimed at increasing black homeownership. If, however, administrative agencies want to improve decision-making systems to root out bias and discrimination, then manipulating the data makes bias and discrimination considerably harder to detect.

This does not mean that proponents of algorithmic decision-making need to be fatalistic, however. There are, of course, middle roads. We worry about taking society "off the hook," so to speak, for issues that

---

42 *Ibid.*
43 *Ibid* at 2225.

predate algorithmic technologies. The path to equitable outcomes along categories like race and gender involves the collective and concerted heavy-lifting of reducing systemic barriers, critically interrogating biases (both conscious and unconscious), and making substantial social, political, and economic investments. If – and only if – these important measures are also being taken, then a concurrent program of techno- logical safeguards and interventions will likely yield more equitable results.

With that established, one relatively low-hanging solution for legal algorithmic designers is to take a more expansive view of inputs (a task that we acknowledge in chapter 2 is made difficult by barriers to accessing meaningful information). Data decontextualization is prone to occur in situations where algorithm designers insist on using nar- row data inputs. In other words, it is a function of poor algorithmic design choices. Take, for instance, an ADM tool designed to determine the appropriate parole conditions for a soon-to-be-released incarcer- ated person. One way to design that algorithm would be to consider all the factors that the law dictates must be considered. In Florida, where COMPAS was used in Broward County, release conditions are guided in part by Florida Statute § 947.18, which advises that parolees should be prohibited from associating with known gang members and, if being released after a drug conviction, must submit to ongoing random test- ing for substance abuse. It follows that judges setting post-release con- ditions will include these requirements as part of the post-release order, where applicable. Judges, however, tend to consider much more than the law requires. And, as humans, judges can, of course, be influenced by non-legal inputs, only some of which ought to be material and ger- mane to parole analyses. A famously controversial 2011 study suggested that there is some evidence that judicial rulings can be influenced by the timing of a judge's most recent meal.[44] Regardless of whether the timing of judicial lunch breaks has a measurable effect on judges' decision- making – a claim that intuitively strains credulity – there can be little

---

44 See, e.g., S Danziger, J Levav & L Avnaim-Pesso, "Extraneous Factors in Judicial Decisions" (2011) 108:17 Proceedings of the National Academy of Sciences 6889, online: <https://doi.org/10.1073/pnas.1018033108>; K Weinshall-Margel & J Shapard, "Overlooked Factors in the Analysis of Parole Decisions" (2011) 108:42 Proceedings of the National Academy of Sciences of the United States of America, E833; and S Danziger, J Levav & L Avnaim-Pesso, "Reply to Weinshall-Margel and Shapard: Extraneous Factors in Judicial Decisions Persist" (2011) 108:42 Proceedings of the National Academy of Sciences of the United States of America E834, online: <https://doi.org/10.1073/pnas.1112190108>.

doubt that, at least some of the time, non-legal factors will include less obviously disfavoured variables, such as the strength of the legal representation, the defendant's attitude and demeanour, the judge's history with counsel, and even evidence that has been procedurally excluded but is – in the real world – known to the judge. Common sense suggests that litigants who "present" to judges well – according to judges' own subjective (read: possibly biased) expectations – will fare better in court, though perhaps not in a manner that is outcome-determinative. These considerations should be legally irrelevant, but, also relying on common sense, we suspect that, if pressed about the influence of such extra-legal considerations, many judges would intuitively justify them as being observable proxy indicators of difficult-to-observe legally cognizable considerations. We take no position on this question, but raise these observations to make the point that what is or is not legally relevant – and what actually affects how a judge decides – is likely to be difficult to isolate reliably.

Any algorithm that aspires to legitimacy among human decision-makers must, then, consider the *appropriate* extra-legal considerations. As Jens Ludwig and Sendhil Mullainathan explain, judges necessarily process far more information than is typically available to algorithms attempting to make the same decision.[45] Why? The reasons are understandable. Data are costly to collect. Most data are being collected for purposes other than building accurate models to guide future ADM. Algorithm designers usually are doing the best that they can with what they have access to: data historically collected for other purposes. These data tend to be decontextualized.

This discussion points in the direction of another way in which better algorithmic design helps solve the decontextualization problem: the insights yielded from leveraging data can be used to discipline and correct algorithms, influencing the way in which data are collected in the future. Take, for example, information gleaned from studies of how judges vary in their decision-making. Imagine data were available about how those judges vary in the relative flexibility or restrictiveness of post-release conditions for incarcerated individuals. The state can set a policy preference of, say, stricter post-release conditions for violent offenders and more relaxed conditions for individuals with drug convictions so long as they submit to random testing. These improvements

45 Jens Ludwig & Sendhil Mullainathan, "Fragile Algorithms and Fallible Decision-Makers: Lessons from the Justice System" (2021) 35:4 J Econ Perspectives 71.

are relatively simple – and, despite their simplicity, can lead to significant improvements in the legal system.

This is not to say that any of this is particularly easy. Improved algorithmic decision-making is unlikely to be simple to design or implement, but it remains the best instrument for securing the most effective and safest path to the legal singularity.

Chapter Ten

Conclusion

It is difficult to overstate the impact that AI is having and will continue to have on the law and its institutions. The legal singularity – which we have described in these pages as the future point at which we settle into a stable and complete legal order – is, understandably, a radical notion to many. For our part, we have not tried to run away from that perception. We have done our best to imagine, speculate about, and document what lies ahead, despite our inevitably limited experiences in contributing to the construction of legal technology and as legal scholars with our inescapably blinkered window onto the world. We hope that you will contribute to the unfolding dialogue.

Our goals for this book were three-fold. The first was to firmly root the idea of the legal singularity in the popular imagination. Today, manifold conversations about AI and the law are taking place among members of the public, policymakers, academics, and practitioners, often without meaningful consideration of the likely future-state of these rapid technological changes. In advancing the notion of a legal singularity, we are not only describing what we think is likely to occur, but also trying to motivate the kind of future-oriented discussion that is necessary for safe and responsible technological development. Scholars will build on our framework, refine it, or reject it and seek to tear it down. Observers will, over time, measure the correctness of our projections of a legal singularity. We welcome this scrutiny.

Our second aim was to press the point that steady and initially gradual (though eventually quite profound) changes to our legal systems are not simply an intellectually curious possibility – the changes are already manifesting, and they are being propelled by powerful creative and economic forces. Even the most cursory glance at the world around us shows that computing power continues to grow exponentially, algorithms continue to make inroads across all private industries, and are being embraced – with different levels of enthusiasm – by governments across the globe. There is no reason to expect law to be immune from these developments.

Our third aim was to signal our intention to join the emerging international movement – comprising academia, government, civil society, and the judiciary and other actors in the legal system – to secure the best path to the legal singularity. By now, readers have sensed our cautious optimism. We are optimistic because, given the experience of humanity over the past several centuries with respect to improved life expectancy, nutrition, education, health care, and so on, we cannot help but believe in the potential of technology – including legal technology – to improve the human condition. As legal scholars and legal technologists, we continue to observe and participate in the early development of the computational era. The advent of accurate legal prediction and the increasing application of sophisticated AI techniques to legal questions give us a vision of a near-term future with little-to-no legal uncertainty. As we have discussed throughout this book, that can mean faster and cheaper legal research, improved professional service delivery, fairer and more accurate judging, better-informed and more robust lawmaking, and – perhaps most important – a deepened public understanding of real-time legal rights and obligations. Our vision of the legal singularity is ultimately a positive one; artificial intelligence can make law radically better.

But our optimism is tempered by some cautiousness. We write not only as legal scholars and legal technologists, but as sons, parents, and engaged citizens who have a stake in the future path of the law. Our view – which we have tried to make plain throughout this book – is that, inevitable as radical legal technological developments are, their trajectory and ultimate endpoint depend on collective effort. We are keenly aware that technology, including legal technology, if not managed well, can exacerbate many of the problems that already plague our legal systems. Early missteps are instructive: algorithms have, in multiple high-profile examples, reproduced race, class, and gender discrimination. To be able to mount improvements, we must acknowledge systemic deficiencies and failures with respect to these and other social problems and allow ourselves to be informed by those perspectives in building technologies and inventing necessary new future legal institutions.

Which brings us to a sober reality: the legal profession's slow pace of adoption of AI with respect to even the simplest, laborious tasks has not been promising. Recent history has demonstrated that rapid technologization of analogue professional tasks is all but unavoidable. AI *will* be an important part of modern lawyering, judging, and administrative decision-making, and, indeed, a central part of legal analysis of any kind. Denying this truth forestalls some of the active participation that we need from the profession's most sceptical corners. Worried that legal prediction might miss some of the nuances that are not captured in legal texts? Rather than treat this as the end of the conversation, we implore critics to contribute their expertise to build more sensitive and parsimonious models. Worried about the essential fairness of algorithmic decision-making? Help design policies that promote human-in-the-loop systems or better algorithmic design. For legal technology's impact to remain positive, we need an epistemic community that is motivated to do the work of ensuring that our systems operate with essential fairness.

The good news is that we can see this community forming. Practitioners, entrepreneurs, and governments are working hand in hand to co-develop legal technology tools. Scholars – many of whom we respond to in these pages – have turned their attention to the notion of the legal singularity, and, even in their deepest criticisms, have accepted that there is an inexorable trend toward technologization. Policymakers and activists have responded, in turn, by developing legal, regulatory, and ethical frameworks to inform the design and application of AI tools, all while contributing to a growing public conversation about AI and its consequences. The story of the legal singularity so far is not just one of cynical resistance, but also one of an emerging ecosystem of individuals and institutions all grappling with what the future holds. The rest of the story, of course, has yet to be written.

Afterword

The recent meteoric rise of OpenAI's ChatGPT, an interactive text-based chat application leveraging state-of-the-art language models, has captivated the attention of the world, marking it as the fastest computer application to reach 100 million active users. This surge of interest in the power of AI has created a renewed focus on the topics discussed in this book. Consequently, with its publication in mid-2023, *The Legal Singularity* arrives at a most opportune moment.

The primary objective of this volume is to stimulate informed conversation and debate concerning the manner in which AI will shape the future of law and its societal impact. It is our firm belief that such discussions are vital to directing AI development towards a path that benefits all. In light of the rapid advancements we are witnessing, including those of ChatGPT, the necessity for this book is more pressing than when we began writing it four years ago.

Our work on this book commenced in earnest in May 2019. At that time, only those closely monitoring technological developments were aware that the ongoing progress in artificial intelligence research would soon disrupt conventional legal practices and present numerous opportunities for radical improvement in the field of law. Since then, AI advancements, particularly those of OpenAI's ChatGPT, have surpassed even our most optimistic predictions. The transformative potential of AI in the legal field is becoming increasingly evident, and this book serves as an authoritative resource for those seeking to comprehend and navigate this evolving landscape.

The Legal Singularity provides an extensive analysis of the ways in which AI is already revolutionizing the legal profession. By automating routine tasks and expediting complex research, AI is empowering attorneys and legal professionals to work with unprecedented efficiency and effectiveness. Furthermore, AI-driven tools like ChatGPT are democratizing legal services and granting unparalleled access to legal information and resources, enabling individuals to better understand and advocate for their rights.

However, the remarkable benefits of AI are accompanied by equally significant challenges. This book probes the ethical, societal, and regulatory implications of AI-driven legal technology. We explore many critical questions: How can we prevent AI from perpetuating or exacerbating existing biases within the legal system? What are the implications of AI-generated legal advice on the attorney-client relationship? How can we ensure AI-powered tools are utilized responsibly and ethically by legal professionals?

In addition to addressing these urgent concerns, *The Legal Singularity* also examines the potential for AI to redefine our understanding of law itself. As AI systems become increasingly adept at interpreting and analysing intricate legal concepts, we may experience a paradigm shift in legal reasoning and decision-making and in the creation of new laws. This prospect invites an engaging and essential discourse on the potential for a more rational, equitable, and efficient legal system in the future – a legal singularity.

Reflecting upon the four years since we embarked on writing this book, we are astonished by the accelerated progress of AI in the legal domain. *The Legal Singularity* stands as both a testament to AI's incredible potential and a call to action for legal professionals, policymakers, and society at large. It is incumbent upon us to engage in thoughtful discussions, rigorous debates, and collaborative efforts to guarantee that AI's development and deployment in the legal sphere align with our values and contribute to a more just and equitable world.

At this pivotal juncture, *The Legal Singularity* aims to establish a solid foundation for understanding and addressing the myriad challenges and opportunities presented by AI in the legal sphere. Our hope is that this book will ignite meaningful conversations and inspire collective action towards a future where AI-powered legal tools enhance and enrich the pursuit of justice for all.

Acknowledgments

We express our profound gratitude to our employers – Blue J and the University of Toronto – our academic colleagues, our research assistants, the University of Toronto Press, and our friends and family who have supported us throughout the writing of this book.

Our work at Blue J, a Toronto-based legal technology company, has served as the backdrop for much of our research, offering real-time insight into the potential of artificial intelligence to revolutionize the legal field. We extend our deepest appreciation to the Blue J data science team, including Brett Janssen, Jesse Provost, Nicholas Mirotchnick, Anthony Niblett, Fadl Nabbouh, and Albert Yoon, who have been unwavering in providing invaluable feedback and responding to inquiries crucial to the accuracy of the book's more technical discussions.

The University of Toronto has been tremendously supportive. At the Faculty of Law, we have benefited immensely from the exceptional support of our law deans, Edward Iacobucci and Jutta Brunnée, who have firmly believed in the merit of this project. Our work has also been enriched by the vibrant intellectual environment at the university, including engaging conversations with judges, colleagues, visiting academics, and our law students.

Numerous law school colleagues have provided feedback on earlier drafts and have participated in countless discussions about the legal singularity. Among them are Michael Trebilcock, Anthony Niblett, Edward Iacobucci, Andrew Green, Albert Yoon, and Brenda Cossman. Beyond the University of Toronto, we have consulted a broader group of colleagues who have also offered valuable feedback, including Katie Sykes, Ed Morgan, Ori Freiman, Bob Sharpe, Taki Sarantakis, and David Masuhara.

We are deeply indebted to our outstanding research assistants, Stephen Hope, Matthew Marchello, and Bella Soblirova, who were both JD students at the University of Toronto at the time of their involvement.

Their significant contributions to early versions of the manuscript and their assistance in canvassing extensive background material have been invaluable to the final product.

We would also like to extend our deepest gratitude to Rose Duggan and Emily Stewart for their invaluable support in both the writing and marketing of the ideas in this book. Their unwavering commitment, dedication, and expertise have been instrumental in bringing this project to fruition.

The University of Toronto Press enthusiastically supported this project from its inception, demonstrating patience and encouragement throughout the production process. We would like to extend special thanks to Daniel Quinlan, senior acquisitions editor, for his unwavering support and assistance in bringing the manuscript to completion, as well as to Mary Lui and Barbara Tessman for helping to bring this book to the finish line.

Above all, we are grateful to our families for their love and patience. This book would not have been possible without their support.

Ben wishes to express his gratitude to Khrista, Charley, and Frankie for their love, encouragement, and unwavering moral support.

Abdi would like to thank Halah and Yasmine for their daily inspiration, as well as Mohamed, Safia, and Zeinab for their support and friendship. We would like to dedicate this book to the memory of Abdi's mother, Marian, who passed as we were preparing this manuscript. Her memory continues to inspire and guide.

Index

Page numbers in *italics* indicate a figure.

change: as gradual or abrupt, 16–17;
as hard for legal system, 87–8, 140,
142–3, 200–1
Chasse, Ken, 150
checkers-playing program, 62
China, 166–7, 169
Christian, Brian, 19–20
citizens, relationship with state, 85
civil codes, 15, 34–5
civil law systems, 15–16, 65–6, 75
Civil Resolution Tribunal, 139
classification, IRS and, 172
Cobbe, Jennifer, 93, 94
Code of Hammurabi, 34–5
cognitive bias. See bias
cognitive illusions, 121
*Commitment and Cooperation on High
Courts* (Alarie & Green), 124
common law systems, 16, 65–6, 76–7,
78. See also case law
COMPAS. See Correctional Offender
Management Profiling for
Alternative Sanctions
complete law: characteristics of,
78–9; complexity as part of,
160; computation encouraging,
87–91; defined, 92; incomplete
law compared, 76–9; specificity
levels and, 79–85; uncertainty and
incompleteness of law, 74–5
complexity: benefits of, 160–1; cost
of legal services and, 98; issues
with complexity of law, 95–9; legal
profession as purveyors of, 150–6;
quality of lawyers' performance
and, 154–5
compliance cars, 86–7
computational era: artificial
intelligence approaches and, 61–4,
61; benefits of, 58–9, 65–8, 75–6;
earlier eras compared, 44, 58

computational law: accuracy-
efficiency trade-off and, 70–1;
advantages of, 69–72; analogue
law versus, 91, 92; applying AI to
law to get, 64–72; completeness
encouraged by, 87–91; defined, 59;
judicial reasoning shortchanged
by, 95; judiciary benefiting from,
125–35; limits of case law as data
for, 106–7; predictiveness of law
increased by, 58–9, 65–8, 75–6; as
reductionist, 94–108; uncertainty
addressed by, 67–8; unstructured
data as challenge for, 68–9
computer science information as
purposive, 38–9
computer vision, 5n7
Condorcet paradox, 178, 179
confirmatory research, 155–6
conservatism in legal system, 23
continuum of legal literacy, 157–9, 159
contract law, incompleteness of, 77
control problem, 20–1
corporations, 71–2, 144, 146
Correctional Offender Management
Profiling for Alternative Sanctions
(COMPAS), 182–3, 192–3
cost of legal services: complexity
and, 98; credence goods and,
151–6, 159; decreasing computing
costs and, 29–30; unaffordability
problem, 143–50
court design, 124, 140
court filings, 106–7, 127
credence goods. See cost of legal
services
criminal cases, 4n5, 123, 128, 182–3
criticism of legal singularity:
93–4; ideology and social context
and, 102–6; limits of, 106–8;
predictability principle and,

Gans, Joshua, 125
gender pay gap, 191, 194
General Problem Solver (GPS), 61
Goldfarb, Avi, 125
Good, Irving J., 10
government: 162–3; benefits of
    artificial intelligence for, 165–8;
    benefits programs of, 172–3, 185;
    current applications of AI in,
    168–70; inefficiency of due to lack
    of technology integration, 163–5;
    legislation and, 56–7, 86, 163,
    175–81; public trust and, 164–5;
    regulation of human behaviour
    using AI, 170–5
GPS. See General Problem Solver
Green, Andrew, 124
Grotius, Hugo, 15
Grove, William M., 66
Gruber, J., 155
Gusick, Spencer M., 110
Guthrie, Chris, 120–1, 128–9

Hadfield, Gillian, 98, 146, 151, 154–5
Hamilton, Alexander, 118
Harari, Yuval, 14
Harris, Angela, 113
Harvard Caselaw Access Project
    (CAP), 57
HDI. See human development index,
    26–7
headnotes, 45
Heller, Nathan, 169, 170
Hellman, Deborah, 193
Heminway, Joan, 111
Hildebrandt, Mireille, 100–1, 108
Hofstadter, Douglas, 11
Holmes, Oliver Wendell, Jr., 16, 39–40
home caretakers, algorithmic
    decision-making about, 185
Horty, John, 49–50
hourly rates of lawyers, 144
Hovenkamp, Herbert, 41

human development index (HDI),
    26–7
humans: brain-machine interfaces
    for, 136–7; judgment as faulty, 66;
    predictive algorithms compared,
    174; role in court system of, 125–6

i2 Enterprise Insight Analysis, 191
IDB. See Integrated Data Base
identity theft, 171
immigration, government use of AI
    for, 173–5
incomplete law: artificial intelligence
    in legislation and, 181; defined,
    76–9; problems caused by, 79–85;
    relationship between citizen and
    state, 85; uncertainty and, 74–5
Indigenous legal traditions, 37
information as incomplete, impacts
    on judicial system of, 122
information costs, of rules, 80–1
inner morality of law, 18
Integrated Data Base (IDB), 56
Internal Revenue Service (IRS), 165,
    170–2
InterRAI, 185
inverse fallacy, 128–9
ISIS fighter identification, 191
Italy, 27

Jabour, Donald, 148–9
Jacobellis v Otto (1964), 77
job changes due to AI, 166
judicial reasoning, computational
    law shortchanging of, 95
judiciary: bias and, 83, 121–3,
    174–5; challenges to adoption
    of computational methods, 95,
    139–40; computational solutions
    for, 125–35; emphasizing facts
    that support their rulings,
    106–7; future evolution of,
    140–1; identities not linked to